D1561582

When Bosses Ruled
Philadelphia

When Bosses Ruled
Philadelphia

The Emergence of the Republican Machine

1867–1933

Peter McCaffery

The Pennsylvania State University Press

University Park, Pennsylvania

Library of Congress Cataloging-in-Publication Data

McCaffery, Peter.
  When bosses ruled Philadelphia : the emergence of the Republican
machine, 1867–1933 / Peter McCaffery.

      p.   cm.
  Includes bibliographical references and index.
  ISBN 0-271-00923-3
  1. Republican Party (Philadelphia, Pa.)—History.   2. Philadelphia
(Pa.)—Politics and government.   I. Title.
JK2359.P53M33   1993   92–42467
324.2748'1104—dc20   CIP

Published by The Pennsylvania State University Press,
Barbara Building, Suite C, University Park, PA 16802-1003

It is the policy of The Pennsylvania State University Press to use acid-free paper for the first
printing of all clothbound books. Publications on uncoated stock satisfy the minimum require-
ments of American National Standard for Information Sciences—Permanence of Paper for
Printed Library Materials, ANSI Z39.48–1984.

To Carol,
Sean and Kyle

CONTENTS

LIST OF TABLES

LIST OF FIGURES

ACKNOWLEDGMENTS

Many people helped, advised, prodded, and supported me during the years I grappled to understand Philadelphia's politics. It's a real pleasure, therefore, to acknowledge those who rendered me such assistance in the completion of this study.

In the first instance, I owe a special debt of gratitude to Lee Benson of the University of Pennsylvania, who in addition to being a source of much inspiration was particularly helpful in advising and guiding me through the formative stages of this work. Special thanks also go to Bill Issel, who suggested the topic to me in the first place, and to Dennis Clark, President of the Samuel Fels Foundation; Maxwell Whiteman, Archivist of the Union League of Philadelphia; and Henry Williams, Assistant Director of the Philadelphia Social History Project—all of whom freely shared their knowledge of the local source materials that form the basis of this study.

I am grateful to Esmond Wright and the Idlewild Foundation for the financial support that enabled me to conduct a preliminary study visit to the city, and also to Jack Reece and Lynn Lees of the University of Pennsylvania for a fellowship that permitted me to complete the primary research for this work. I also benefited from a term's sabbatical, thanks to my colleagues in the History Department at Thames Valley University, a leave of absence that enabled me to prepare the initial draft of this manuscript.

Thanks are also due to the staffs of the Historical Society of Pennsylvania, the Free Library of Philadelphia, the Van Pelt Library of the University of Pennsylvania, the Urban Archives Center at Temple University, and especially the Department of Records, Philadelphia City Hall, who were so helpful in facilitating my research. City archivist Ward J. Child, in particular, not only kept me in good spirits but also filled the gaps in my knowledge of local corruption, both past and present. I hope that, in return, his understanding of the peculiarities of English politics and society likewise benefited. Other friends who provided intellectual and moral support during my stay included John Tierney, Karl Ittmann, Josh Newberg, Seamus Ross, Valerie Hansen, and Patti Lank, who tragically is no longer with us.

I am additionally grateful to Jim Potter and Mary Morgan of the London School of Economics for successfully guiding me through the doctoral dissertation on which this study is based, and to John A. Thompson and Melvyn Stokes for the valuable suggestions they offered on revising for publication.

I would also like to thank my editors and the readers at Penn State Press, for similar reasons. Contrary to what I was led to believe about academic publishing, this novitiate found the production process relatively painless, thanks to the encouragement and advice offered by Peter Potter, and the careful copyediting provided by Peggy Hoover.

My final and greatest debt I owe to my wife, Carol. This project has been an intruder in our lives for a long time, and throughout this period she not only offered sound advice, but also tolerated the process with patience and understanding, even when its demands competed with those of our two more recent "intruders," Sean and Kyle. My deepest thanks to her and to Sean and Kyle for the final encouragement they gave me to complete this work.

INTRODUCTION

In the summer of 1903, investigative journalist Lincoln Steffens set out for Philadelphia, confident of confirming his theory that the level of corruption in American cities was greater in the nation's older municipalities than in its younger ones. His expectation, he reported, was based on the claims made by those in "other American cities" who, "no matter how bad their own condition," all pointed "with scorn to Philadelphia as worse—the worst governed city in the country."[1] Steffens was not disappointed, for Philadelphia turned out to be "not merely corrupt, but corrupted" beyond redemption.[2] Indeed, it provided him with the ideal model of civic corruption, which he used for the series of articles on municipal government he had been commissioned to write for *McClure's Magazine*. Subsequently published in book form as *The Shame of the Cities*, these articles brought Steffens national fame for the first time, and brought the city of Philadelphia lasting notoriety as "the most corrupt and the most contented" urban center in the nation.[3]

Steffens's text was heralded as a classic muckraking exposé, not so much because there was anything new or surprising about the corrupt practices he chronicled, but because of the scale of corruption he revealed and the explanation he offered for its prevalence. Unlike other contemporary observers, Steffens did not trace the source of urban misgovernment back to the presence of large immigrant populations. Instead, he blamed "the American people" themselves, and in particular the respectable middle classes, who turned a blind eye to corruption while "big businessmen" ("the chief source of corruption") used bribery to debauch city governments for their own selfish ends.[4] Steffens did, however, agree with fellow observers on one aspect of urban politics, a characteristic that was apparently exemplified in Philadelphia: the belief that city governments were invariably dominated by all-powerful and, in Steffens's view (if not that of his contemporaries), beneficent political party "bosses" and their "machines."[5]

In more recent times, Steffens's claims, like those of other "reform" observers, have been shown to be either inaccurate—as in the case of his proposition that a city's age and its degree of corruption were positively correlated—

or too simplistic, in that they were based on analyses that failed to consider the social context in which urban politics operated.[6] His contention concerning the dominance of the omnipotent boss and the political machine is no exception. Recent scholarship now suggests that observers like Steffens deliberately exaggerated the power of bosses in order to heighten the urgency of their critique, a distortion of historical reality that was subsequently reiterated unwittingly by a second "generation" of scholars writing after World War II (principally Robert Merton, Oscar Handlin, and Richard Hofstadter) whose analyses of bossism were based almost solely on Steffens's autobiography. Recent scholarship also contends that urban politics was simply too contested, and urban policymaking too complicated, for cities to sustain the all-powerful political bosses that Steffens portrayed.[7]

Persuasive though these revisionist arguments may seem, they still remain hypotheses in need of close studies of individual cities to demonstrate, in empirical terms, the true nature and extent of boss rule. For example, despite scholarly preoccupation with bossism, we still do not know in most instances the degree to which so-called "bosses" actually bossed. Nor are we any better informed about the actual process by which bosses consolidated power within their party organizations, or about the extent to which such institutions managed to establish themselves as the dominant force in cities where this system of politics prevailed.[8]

These deficiencies in the literature are not surprising. They are a direct consequence of the singular mode of inquiry that has characterized research on machine politics in the past. Until recently, analysts interested in the origins of machine politics focused on mass immigration and the close association between bosses and ethnic groups. These investigations, while affirming that political machines were supported disproportionately by the poor and by voters of immigrant stock, produced differences of opinion about the emergence of this type of organization: Some scholars regarded it as a product of immigrant culture and ethnic conflict, others as a response to "needs" that alternative institutions failed to satisfy, and still others as a political expression of living conditions in the inner city.[9]

The main problem with inquiries of this nature, however, is that they fail to accommodate any sense or element of political change over time.[10] At best, they offer plausible (though not necessarily accurate) reasons for the attachment (or opposition) to the political machine of social groups like the immigrant poor and the native-born middle class. But they do not explain fully when and how control was centralized within the machine or why such institutions managed to stay in power for so long, and they do not help us draw

meaningful distinctions between the successive leaders or "bosses" who allegedly headed these party organizations. Because they have failed to test empiri-
cally the hypotheses advanced to account for the distribution of electoral
support for the political machine, they also do not explain which sections of
urban populations attached themselves to these institutions, or why.[11]

This book addresses these issues using Philadelphia as the model for
inquiry. Philadelphia provides a particularly appropriate setting for such an
inquiry, not just because of the notorious reputation it acquired following
Steffens's damning indictment, or because of its inherent importance as one
of the nation's largest cities, but because it was also a city that, according to
traditional accounts of local politics, was subject to political control by a
succession of party bosses between the 1850s and the 1930s.[12] The sphere of
influence of these "feudal barons," such as "King James" McManes, Israel
Durham, "Sunny Jim" McNichol, and William Vare, if the conventional
narratives are to be believed, were not dissimilar in any way. The city's
Republican machine (or "Organization" as it was popularly known) has
moreover—and somewhat surprisingly—not been subject to critical examination until now.[13]

This inquiry also examines the other unresolved issue in the existing
literature on the political machine: the "functions" of such institutions in the
American city. The conventional wisdom on this subject, based on sociologist Robert Merton's theoretical model of machine politics, is that political
machines performed a beneficent role because they met needs "that were at
the time not adequately fulfilled by other existing patterns and structures."[14]
In the absence of alternative official structures, they functioned as the natural
substitute for government in the constituencies of a variety of subgroups,
notably immigrants and the poor but also businessmen as well. This view of
the machine—as an uncritical respondent to the needs of these particular
groups—prevails in varying degrees in the work of such scholars as Oscar
Handlin, Richard Hofstadter, Eric McKitrick, Elmer Cornwell, Alexander
Callow, Seymour Mandelbaum, Zane L. Miller, and John Allswang.[15] Indeed, the machine's ability to fulfill this role, these theorists maintain,
explains why this particular political institution was so successful and durable. Consequently, the "bosses" who helped machines perform this function
are now considered to have been the "good guys" (and reformers, inciden-
tally, the "bad guys") of urban government—the exact opposite, that is, of
the way these political actors were traditionally portrayed in the literature
before the 1950s.

Plausible though this "functional" explanation may seem in accounting for the role played by the political machine, it is not necessarily accurate. As Terrence McDonald has demonstrated, the "functional" explanation rests on two assumptions, neither of which can be taken for granted. One is the notion that political institutions mechanistically reflect the social configurations that underlie them (in this case, the assumption that the political machine *must* have represented the social needs of the urban immigrant poor, for how else can we explain why this social group supported this political organization), the other is the notion that such organizations that did persist *must* have been serving some useful purpose or they would not have been able to survive.[16] In making these assumptions, however, scholars who subscribe to this "functional" analysis make no allowance for the fact that the machine could have performed another, quite different, role in the American city, one, for instance, that was self-serving and exploitative, or misrepresentative, in nature.

The precise functions the machine was supposed to have fulfilled have rarely been examined.[17] This is because, as McDonald has persuasively argued, most scholars writing after the mid-1950s were prepared to accept and apply uncritically the "functional" theory of the political machine, because they in turn supported the same political goal—that of protecting the New Deal heritage from postwar opponents who sought to roll back its institutional legacy—as that of the liberal pluralists (Handlin, Hofstadter, and Merton) who initially propagated it. Such scholars were also persuaded that the theory was legitimate (without testing it) because it was "scientifically" based—that is, on an amoral premise as opposed to the unreliable "moralism" (or "patrician-elitism," as David Hammack puts it) that underpinned much of the earlier work on machine politics.[18] The question still remains: What functions did the machine really fulfill? How valid is Merton's analysis of the relationship between the machine and its supporters? Were "bosses" really the "good guys" of the urban drama, as the new conventional wisdom suggests that they were?

The purpose of this study, however, is not simply to point out deficiencies in the existing literature. By using Philadelphia as a case study, this investigation tests whether a city with an acknowledged political organization was subject to boss control over the period suggested by conventional wisdom. It also attempts to determine the *true* nature of the power that bosses wielded within their political domain. In specific terms, it identifies the extent to which these party "bosses" managed to exercise control over their followers in party office, the distribution of patronage, the membership and decisions of their party organizations' local units, their party's nominations for public office, the behavior of elected officials nominally affiliated to them, the passage of legislation through the city council, and city government.

The method of inquiry is different from that of conventional theorists of the political machine; it focuses less on the relationship between bosses and their supporters and more on the way machine politics was structured and organized in the city. In enabling us to determine precisely *when* the city's politics came to be dominated by a political machine, this approach also furnishes us with the essential prerequisite for providing either a satisfactory explanation for the emergence of this institution or for drawing meaningful distinctions between the city's various "bosses."

The book begins with local politics in antebellum Philadelphia, the period during which, according to conventional wisdom, the city first experienced "boss rule." Chapter 1 traces the exodus of the city's men of wealth from public office and their replacement by professional politicians (or "bosses"), a familiar theme in the literature on urban politics and one from which Philadelphia was not immune. It also explains why, in spite of this development, it is inaccurate to speak of a full-fledged political machine (and with it genuine boss rule in the literal sense) at this point in the city's political development.

Chapters 2 and 3 focus on the first two decades after the Civil War, a period during which party politics in the city were apparently dominated by an overriding cleavage between well-organized machine and reform forces. Chapter 2 describes how Republican party leaders James McManes and William Stokley established "centers of power" in the city's gas trust and Public Buildings Commission respectively, and assesses the extent to which they can be considered to have been genuine city bosses. Chapter 3 examines their demise and assesses the role the local political reform movement played in bringing it about.

Chapters 4 through 6 offer an explanation for the gradual emergence (or "institutionalization") of the Republican machine as the central force in the government and politics of Philadelphia. Chapter 4 explains how power was (internally) consolidated within the Republican party organization; Chapter 5 identifies the characteristics that distinguish successive party leaders David Martin, Israel Durham, "Sunny Jim" McNichol, and William Vare from their predecessors, McManes and Stokley. Chapter 6 examines how the "Organization" was able to overwhelm its (external) electoral opponents and assesses the extent to which the relationship between the Republican machine and its supporters corresponded to that suggested by Robert Merton's theoretical model.

Those who benefited from and supported the establishment of this centralized party organization, and those who were opposed to it, are the subject of the final two chapters. Chapter 7 focuses on the relationship between consolidation in the urban polity and in the local economy and describes how Republican party leaders helped a clique of plutocrats establish monopoly control over Philadelphia's public utilities industry. Chapter 8 offers an explanation for the emergence (as well as the failure) of the nonpartisan reform movement as the principal opposition to the "Organization's" hegemony in local affairs.

Taken together, these chapters argue that a mature political machine—and with it *genuine* boss rule—did not emerge as the dominant institution in Philadelphia's politics until the turn of the century. The basis for this conclusion is the generally accepted view of what constitutes a political machine. Most scholars now agree that such institutions had two distinguishing characteristics.[19] In terms of *structure* (that is, the degree to which control was reliably centralized), they were well-disciplined and cohesive citywide political institutions, party organizations that functioned as their hierarchical structure suggested they should, with the party leader (or boss) capable of exercising control over subordinates both in party office and in public office. In terms of *style* (that is, the nature of political attachments), they were characterized by what James Scott has called the peculiar "organizational cement" (or linkages, such as the exchange of patronage and favors for votes), which bound machine politicians and their supporters together.[20]

The number and structure of political formations that contended for power in Philadelphia during the second half of the nineteenth century reveal that it was not until after 1887 that a party organization exhibiting these twin characteristics gradually emerged as the central force in the city's politics. Put another way, not until just before the turn of the century did machine politics manage to establish itself in Philadelphia as both a (centralized) political *structure* and a political *style*.

It emerged when it did, this study suggests, not (as Robert Merton contends) as a response to needs and demands that other institutions failed to satisfy, nor as a product of immigrant culture and ethnic conflict. Rather, the establishment of a full-fledged machine was the result of a series of innovations initiated by state and local Republican party leaders, which transformed the way the Republican party organization *functioned* at both the state level and the city level at the turn of the century. These changes originated at the top of the political system, instead of emanating from the masses at its base, and they were in the interests of, and supported by, a major segment of the local business community.

This study further contends that, even though the "Organization" managed to secure the support of the overwhelming majority of the city's new immigrant, poor, and black population in return for the "personal service" it rendered, it exploited these social groups as much as it helped them. Therefore, rather than being the natural functional substitute for government that Merton's theoretical model suggests, the machine's role was if anything of a dysfunctional nature—that is, destructive of functioning government for the vast majority of immigrants and poor people who needed such government the most.

The findings of this inquiry then are both similar to and different from those of Steffens's investigation. They concur with the muckraker that Philadelphia was indeed governed by a powerful political machine and that the relationship between its emergence and that of the influx of "new" immigrants to the city was one of coincidence rather than causal. On the other hand, I argue that, because the political machine emerged independent of and not subservient to business interests, it was the party boss rather than the "big businessman" who was "the chief source of corruption" in Philadelphia.

Philadelphia's bosses did not perform the beneficent role Steffens suggested. Steffens, it now seems, deliberately set out to portray such figures as pragmatic, self-conscious, and essentially humane individuals, in order to prick the conscience of his middle-class readers to reform.[21] While such a revelation should not lead us to conclude that bosses were devoid of any admirable traits, it should also not deter us from acknowledging corruption where corruption did indeed exist. It was Philadelphia's machine leaders, rather than the reformers, who were the "bad guys" of the urban drama. Their omnipotence and not the "sinful contentment" of the middle class made "good city government" such an elusive goal in turn of the century Philadelphia.

1

Local Politics in
Antebellum Philadelphia

Philadelphia's politics prior to the turn of the century was not always synonymous with corruption, nor was it dominated by career politicians. In the wake of the Revolution, and the half-century thereafter, the city's government was the exclusive preserve of members of the local aristocracy, of merchants such as Stephen Girard, Thomas Cope, Robert Wharton, and Roberts Vaux—men of substance, that is, who drew no sharp distinction between their public duties and private interests, and to whom officeholding seemed natural and proper, if not indeed a tribute to the leading role they played in directing the city's economy.[1]

These "generalists in business and politics" reciprocated the trust their fellow citizens had placed in them, by launching a series of initiatives that included establishing, in 1801, America's first municipal waterworks: the Fairmount Water Works on the Schuylkill River, which subsequently provided the basis of what was to become the first large urban park in the nation. They also created a system of free public education in 1836, and with it another first, this time the nation's first high school, Philadelphia Central.[2]

These achievements, however, were not sufficient to arrest the decline in authority this patrician class suffered during the 1830s and 1840s. Unable to rely on deference as a means of maintaining social and political control, these men of substance not only lost the monopoly they exercised over local public offices, but also found their leadership role in the city's politics usurped by career politicians. In fact, by the end of the Civil War, public office in Philadelphia bore the same hallmark of exclusivity it had a half-century earlier, only on this occasion the stamp was that of the professional party specialist rather than that of the "old-style generalist."[3]

The Civil War marked a watershed not just in terms of the type of individuals who were elected to public office in Philadelphia but also in the level of electoral support the Republican party was able to attract throughout the city—from, that is, a mere 1 percent of the total vote in the 1856 mayoral election, to more than half (53 percent) in that of 1865. Indeed, Morton McMichael's successful candidacy in the latter election marked the beginning of almost a century of unbroken Republican rule in Philadelphia, and in the case of the period from the mid-1890s through early 1930s, an almost total hegemony over local affairs as a one-party system of politics emerged in the city.[4] How, though, do we account for these developments— that is, for the emergence of the career politician, on the one hand, and the Republican party's ascendancy, on the other? It is with these two questions that our inquiry into Philadelphia boss politics begins.

The Emergence of the Career Politician

The displacement of men of wealth in local politics by career politicians was not a phenomenon unique to antebellum Philadelphia. This development was part of a national trend that affected most American cities in the 1830s and 1840s; it was the local counterpart to the "revolution" in government and politics that followed Andrew Jackson's election as President in 1828.[5] It follows, therefore, that the explanation for this development probably lies in large-scale forces that were national in scope, rather than with changes that were local or peculiar in character. Indeed, it is now generally accepted that this phenomenon was the consequence of a combination of circumstances whose coincidence was unique to America—the onset of industrialization occurring in a political setting where there was universal white manhood suffrage and where a newly established national two-party system had taken root at the local level.[6]

Antebellum Philadelphia, like many other cities nationwide, exemplified just such an economic and political environment. By the mid-nineteenth century, for example, industrialization had wrought significant changes in Philadelphia, changes that had made a profound impact both on the city and on the life of its citizens. For instance, by this time Philadelphia had almost shed its colonial reputation as a commerical port and distributor of European manufactures and had emerged as an important center of manufacturing in its own right. "A virtual emporium of commodity production" with a thriving commercial and financial sector, the city manufactured everything from silk handkerchiefs to iron rails. Indeed, it had a larger industrial workforce (57,958) and a bigger gross product (6 percent of the national total) than any other city in the nation, with the exception of New York.[7]

This transformation in the local economy had also been accompanied by rapid population growth (a remarkable sixfold increase from 67,811 in 1800 to 408,762 by 1850) and mass immigration. By mid-century, foreign-born immigrants, principally Irish (71,787) and Germans (22,788), made up 29.6 percent (118,343) of Philadelphia's population, the highest proportion in the city's history and again, with the exception of New York, the largest of any city in the nation.[8]

Such changes had transformed the city's economic and social order. The artisan and merchant had given way to the worker, the industrialist, and the financier. Even more profound, the consensus and community ethos that had characterized the eighteenth-century town had been shattered. Residents of the mercantile core of the old city were now separated from those in the adjacent (county) suburbs along social class, ethnic, religious, occupational, and political lines.[9] So acute were these differences that local inhabitants did not hesitate—as the series of antiblack riots in the 1830s and the devastating nativist riots of 1844 testify—to use violence as a means of resolving them. The degree of conflict was so great that by mid-century the city had found it necessary both to professionalize the local police force and to standardize political representation by consolidating the City and County of Philadelphia into one governmental unit (see Figure 1).[10]

This transformation in the city's economic and social order also coincided with important changes in the local political environment, and these innovations, in conjunction with industrialization, had important repercussions on the conduct and style of political competition in the city. On the one hand, the emergence of the (second) national two-party system in the local polity

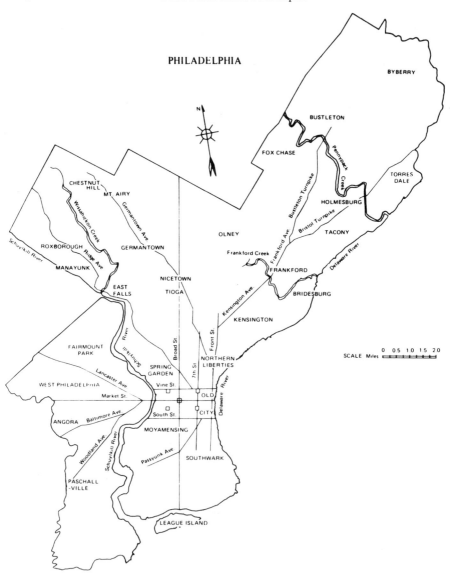

Fig. 1.   Map of the City and County of Philadelphia, 1854 to the present. In 1854 the "old city" was merged with twenty-seven other political subdivisions within Philadelphia County and grew from 2 square miles to 130—the same area it covers today. (From Theodore Hershberg [ed.], *Philadelphia: Work, Space, Family, and Group Experience in the Nineteenth Century* [New York, 1981], 127.)

meant that city elections in Philadelphia from the late 1830s on became more like state and federal elections—that is, a contest between parties rather than rival individuals, and one in which egalitarian appeals, as opposed to claims based on social standing, proliferated. On the other hand, the extension of the franchise (in 1838) beyond that of local taxpayers meant that both the Whig and Democratic parties had to establish grass-root links in order to mobilize this new enlarged electorate at the polls, a task for which the career politician was ideally suited. In sum, these changes fundamentally altered the basis on which local political life was organized. Once based on general social deference to a paternalistic elite, the city's politics came to be based on mass partisan loyalty and career politicians.[11]

This political transformation, though, contrary to received wisdom, was not an immediate one.[12] The city's merchant class continued to provide leadership in local affairs well beyond the "Age of Jackson." Drug manufacturer John P. Wetherill, woollen trader George Morrison Coates, and Theodore Cuyler, general counsel for the Pennsylvania Railroad, for example, each served as president of the City (or Select and Common) Council in the 1850s and 1860s.[13] Nor can the transformation be said to have been one over which men of substance exercised a freedom of choice. On the contrary, the evidence—the complaints of "men of character" that they were being "driven away" from the council, and their subsequent attempts to organize reform groups to clean up City Hall by securing the election of men "whom office seeks rather than those who seek office"[14]—suggests quite the opposite conclusion: that men of substance were indeed *forced* to "abandon the city's politics" as much as they chose to leave of their own accord.[15]

By the end of the Civil War the transformation was complete. Men of substance had all but been displaced by career politicians both in the City Council—which as the *Inquirer* put it had been inundated with an influx of "fourth rate political ward jobbers who go [there] not for the honor but for the plunder"[16]—and in local party organizations, a political takeover that English Liberal peer James Bryce attributed to the fact that

> during the Civil War, the [city's] best citizens [had been] busily absorbed in its great issues and both then and for some time after, welcomed all the help that could be given to their party by any man who knew how to organize the voters and bring them up to the polls; while at the same time their keen interest in national questions made them inattentive to municipal affairs. Accordingly the local control and management of the party fell into hands of obscure citizens, men

who had their own ends to serve, their own fortunes to make but who were valuable to their party because they kept it in power through their assiduous work among the lower class of voters.[17]

Another contemporary observer, reform publicist George Vickers, described this process in more colorful and dramatic fashion:

> During the war years there came to the front of the party organization, a baser element . . . the rag-tag and bob-tail in politics. They were the moths of humanity drawn from the four quarters of the earth to the staid Quaker City by the glare of opportunity. One party to them was as good as another so far as principles were concerned. The main consideration that influenced their actions was opportunity for self-advancement. With the Democratic party laboring under reverses, and the Republican party successful in city and state their lot was, of course, cast with the latter. These political Ishmaelites worked darkly and noiselessly. . . . At a time when every vote in the Republican party was needed, they were accepted without question. They at once made themselves useful, showed a practical disposition to look after the welfare of the party in the city, and thus in a measure relieve the real leaders of the party, some of whom were at the front. . . . Carefully and with great system did they lay their plans and push their fortunes.

So successful was the "baser element" that, according to Vickers, the Republican party no longer qualified as a "political party. . . . Public freebooters was a more appropriate title."[18]

"Public freebooters" or not, the Republican party organization was, as Vickers correctly identifies, dominated by those who owed their livelihood to politics. Professional politicians constituted a majority of the party's executive committee in 1869 (see Table 1). The ascendancy of the professional politician within the Republican party was also matched, as Vickers observed, by that party's progress in the city's electoral arena. Incapable of polling more than a few hundred votes in the first city election it contested in 1856, the party moved, within a few years, into a position where it could command a majority of the electorate; it continued to achieve this level of support—to a varying degree—in local elections over the next century. On what basis, though, were Philadelphians drawn to the Republican party? Why did the city become so fervently attached to Republicanism?

Table 1.   Union Republican City Executive Committee, 1869–1870

Officers & Members	Name	Ward	Public Office/ Occupation
President	John L. Hill	9	Collector of delinquent taxes
Vice-presidents	John W. Donnelly	5	
	John H. Seltzer	13	Lawyer
Secretaries	John McCullough	10	Assessor
	Robert T. Gill	2	Customs clerk
Treasurer	George Boyer	19	Liquor dealer
Members	Samuel Lutz	1	Alderman
	William Kelly	3	
	Richard Butler	4	Inspector
	Charles W. Ridgway	6	Customs clerk
	John V. Creely	7	Lawyer/congressman
	Charles A. Porter	8	County clerk
	Jacob Albright	11	Albright & Sheeler
	William Andress	12	
	William H. Johnson	14	Clerk
	Henry Huhn	15	Fowler & Huhn
	Joseph Ash	16	Highways inspector
	George W. Painter	17	County registrar
	Joseph S. Allen	18	Allen & Stites
	Gideon Clark	20	Register of wills
	John F. Preston	21	
	Thomas Dutton	22	Customs inspector
	A.L. Dungan	23	
	James Newell	24	Federal assessor
	John C. Sees	25	Deputy coroner
	Morton A. Everly	26	Collector
	Harry Hancock	27	Bricklayer
	Hiram Miller	28	Lumber dealer

SOURCES: *Union Republican City Executive Committee, 1869–1870* (Philadelphia, 1869); *Gopsill's Philadelphia City Directory for 1870* (Philadelphia, 1870).

The Foundations of Philadelphia Republicanism

The Republican party's success in Philadelphia was not based on any widespread sympathy in the city for the antislavery principles on which the new national party had been organized in 1854. Indeed, in view of the city's well-established commercial links with the South (reflected in the dominant pro-Southern sympathies among Philadelphia's ruling elite) and the local strength of antiblack feelings (exhibited in the remarkable deterioration in the socioeconomic condition of the city's antebellum black community), it would have been surprising if the Republican party's first local campaign had ended in anything other than ignominious failure.[19]

That the party managed to overcome this initial setback and subsequently prosper was attributable not so much to any change in attitude on the part of Philadelphians (most of whom remained steadfastly indifferent if not downright hostile to antislaveryism) as to the calculated decision made by the city's Republican leaders, in the wake of the Panic of 1857, to join with local (nativist) Know-Nothings in a new (People's Party) coalition, the linchpin of which was a program advocating high protective tariffs, popular sovereignty, and the "Protection of American Labor against the Pauper Labor of Europe."[20]

This electoral pact benefited the Republicans in a number of ways. In committing themselves to a broader program, it enabled them to dispel their earlier image of single-minded devotion to antislaveryism, but it also allowed them to tap the groundswell of nativist sympathy that flourished in the city. In promoting protectionism, it also made Republicans appear both more conservative and united, a condition that eluded local Democrats who, already hopelessly split over slavery, had been divided still further over how to combat the depression. The degree of popular support the program attracted was such that the Republicans managed to elect (and subsequently reelect in 1860, 1862, and 1864) one of their own leaders, abolitionist Alexander Henry, as mayor in 1858.[21]

The electoral coalition the Republicans made with local Know-Nothings was crucial to the party's emergence as a major force in the city's electoral arena. But short-term concessions to nativists cannot by themselves explain the Republican party's enduring appeal to the local electorate. In the postwar era, the party came to rely almost solely on its commitment to a high tariff (in addition to its record of wartime loyalty) as a means of attracting support, a strategy that paid handsome dividends. But why was tariff protection so successful as a rallying cry? What was the basis of the tariff's appeal?

Most Philadelphians, both workers and employers, were apparently attracted to the tariff because they regarded it as the best means of advancing their individual interests as well as those of the city as a whole. That is, they subscribed to and accepted the view of party propagandists that the tariff not only protected the worker as much as the manufacturer, but also provided the basis on which the economy—and with it the local community—prospered.[22] This acceptance on the part of Philadelphians that the interests of labor and capital were alike rather than fundamentally antagonistic did not suddenly spring into being when the Republicans emerged onto the local scene. It was the product of an antebellum society in which class ideologies had failed to take root, in which the division between masters and "men" was neither great nor fixed[23]—in other words, a society whose members were prepared, on occasion, to place the interests of the wider community before those of their own.[24]

The Republicans were not the first political party to have appealed to such sentiment in the city. Mutual dependence and class collaboration had indeed formed the basis by which the Whigs, through their "American System," had succeeded in establishing themselves as the majority party in the city from the mid-1830s through mid-1850s. In this respect, when the Republicans advocated a program similar to that of their political predecessors—a program based on government taking a positive role in promoting the welfare of the people, a role which in their view was itself dependent on high tariffs generating the necessary economic expansion and requisite tax base—they became the beneficiaries of and heirs to the "Whig tradition" in the city.[25] As the party not only of protection but also of internal improvements and local services, the Republicans proved irresistible to the bulk of (native-born if not foreign-born) Philadelphians.[26] Since their program was to be kept within the bounds of fiscal integrity, they also attracted the support of the new business and industrial elite that had displaced the city's old upper class (the Biddles, the Ingersolls, and the Whartons, who had been identified disproportionately with the discredited Constitutional—or Peace—Democratic faction) during the war years. By the end of the Civil War, then, Philadelphia's Republicans had managed, as a result of embracing the public-service ethic of the national party and acquiring the support of local self-made men, such as locomotive manufacturer Matthew Baird and ironmaster Charles Wheeler, to establish themselves as *the* party of progress and respectability in the city. This new-found reputation was enhanced even more by the selection of newspaper publisher, protectionist, and Union loyalist Morton McMichael as the party's mayoral candidate in 1865.[27]

McMichael's election, while it confirmed the ascendancy of the Republican party in Philadelphia, proved to be a short-lived triumph for respectability. Much to their chagrin, the city's "best men" were forced to witness the takeover, by career politicians, of the new party to which they had recently become attached and of the city council they had been used to controlling. This development brought both institutions into disrepute, and men of substance were determined to resist it. By the late 1860s, the struggle between reformers (respectability) and "bosses" (corruption) had begun in earnest and was to dominate local politics over much of the next century. Career politicians would, more often than not, prevail.

The Style and Structure of Boss Politics

Career politicians, while different in almost every respect from the men of substance they displaced, had, however, a style of leadership that was similar to that of their political predecessors. For example, in seeking to attract the support of the electorate, they, like the patricians before them, boasted about their personal generosity and the benefits they had secured for their constituents. They also, like the patricians, demonstrated their courage and fitness for public office by providing leadership in the city's volunteer fire department.[28]

The leadership style of the career politicians differed from that of their political predecessors in the means they used to secure electoral success and the way they rewarded their followers. Unlike men of substance, career politicians could not rely on deference (or personality) for political victory, nor could they draw on their own capital resources to provide for their supporters, because their personal wealth was invariably meager. Therefore, if they were to realize their personal ambitions, they were compelled to tap other resources in the antebellum political environment. This they did by soliciting votes on the basis of party sentiment rather than social standing, and by using public revenues, rather than private funds, to reward loyal supporters. In so doing, however, career politicians did not just modify the patricians' style to suit their own personal ends; they also established a system of politics that has been characterized ever since as bossism, one in which the prospect of material gain is the overriding factor binding politicians and their supporters together—put another way, one in which politicians and their supporters are linked together through a web of parochial loyalties and individual payoffs, such as, for example, in the exchange of patronage and favors for votes.[29]

Although the "organizational cement" (or character of political bonds) peculiar to machine politics emerged as a prominent feature of political life in antebellum Philadelphia, it does not necessarily follow that a well-disciplined and cohesive citywide political machine also appeared at this point in the city's political development. And simply because bossism flourished as a political *style* in antebellum Philadelphia, we should not therefore assume that genuine boss rule also emerged at this time. Nevertheless, Philadelphia in the mid-nineteenth century closely resembled, more than at any other time in its history, the "structural context" Robert Merton identified as being a necessary prerequisite for the establishment of a political machine.[30] There was, for instance, considerable diffusion and fragmentation of local political power and responsibility. For example, executive duties once concentrated in a Board of

City Commissioners appointed by the mayor were by the 1850s dissipated among thirty-two separate boards and departments that all actively competed for their share of city revenues.[31] And by the mid-nineteenth century, representation once based on the city at large had not only become centered on the ward and division (or precinct) but was also increasingly elective rather than appointive. School directors, tax collectors and assessors, guardians of the poor, aldermen, and representatives on the Board of Health, as well as city councilmen, were all elected ward officials.[32]

Ward representation, electoral democracy, and government fragmentation, however, far from providing the basis of the general setting or environment that gave rise to a political machine, actually militated against the creation of such a centralized political structure, not in favor of one. They hindered rather than encouraged the development of a well-disciplined political machine, because power within the local political party organizations was also as fragmented and diffuse as it was in the city's governmental system.

In short, political parties at this time were loosely structured, poorly organized, ill-disciplined, and not subject to legal controls.[33] Accordingly, they could be treated as just what they were: private organizations designed to operate openly on the basis of personal favors and rewards—in the spirit of Plunkitt, who "seen his financial opportunities and took 'em."[34] In these circumstances, party leaders could not control the behavior of local party officers or party workers in public office. The party apparatus was so weak that career politicians relied on, and were often products of, organizations whose primary purpose was *not* to deliver the vote. Consequently, it was such groups as the volunteer fire companies, street gangs, social clubs, coteries of saloon frequenters, and other structures of status and prestige within neighborhoods that dominated the electoral process, and not party organizations.

Philadelphia fire companies were apparently the most significant group. Frank Willing Leach, secretary to the state Republican party leader Matt Quay, recalled in 1905:

> In those days [1856] local political battles at the polls were not fought by Executive Committeemen, by division workers and the like, as is the case nowadays. The chief factor then and for many years afterward were the active members of the volunteer fire company.[35]

Philadelphia was considered to have an excess of fire companies in 1856; seventy of them functioned within the city. These provided an arena in which a man who wanted to be a political leader could demonstrate his courage and leadership capacity; the colorful uniforms, exciting dashes to fires, and competition for community recognition made these fire companies very attractive to young men in the city. Those who wanted to exercise political leadership attempted to gain executive office by demonstrating their ability to the satisfaction of their peers. Directors were elected from and by the members and bestowed with the considerable honor of supervising the fighting of fires.[36] Company members created each company's distinct identity. Some company names, such as Franklin, Washington, Lafayette, and Americus, suggested patriotism; some, Schuylkill, Southwark, and Moyamensing, were named after the neighborhood; some, Harmony and Good Will, reflected a sense of duty; and others, such as Shiffler and Hibernia, indicated nativism or national origin.[37]

The circumstances surrounding fire-fighting (such as the race to arrive first at a fire, and the honor of extinguishing it), community loyalties, and political and religious differences provided the basis for trouble between these rival companies. Indeed, "the conflicts between these rival associations became the major source of organized violence before the Civil War."[38] For example, in Moyamensing the Irish Protestants of the Franklin Hose Company fought savage contests against the Irish Catholics of the Moyamensing Hose Company, while in Southwark arson and fighting accompanied the uncompromising hostility between the Weccacoe Engine Company (a temperance, nativist outfit) and the Weccacoe Hose Company (an Irish and nontemperance organization).[39] It was in the bitter competition with rival companies that men were able to prove loyalty, courage, and leadership capacity to the satisfaction of their fellows, thereby proving themselves worthy of support and loyalty. Such local city politicians as Mayor William Stokley (Harmony Engine Company), Sheriff William R. Leeds (Goodwill Engine Company), Councilmen William E. Rowan (Columbia Engine Company) and William McMullen (Moyamensing Hose Company), Congressman Charles O'Neill (Franklin Hose Company), State Representative Lewis Cassidy (Hibernia Hose Company), Chief of Police Samuel Ruggles (Columbia Hose Company), and future "bosses" of the city in the 1890s, Dave Martin (Taylor Hose Company) and Charles Porter (Schuylkill Hose Company), all began their political careers in the ranks of the volunteer fire companies.[40]

Street gangs were another significant source of support for the career politician. Although we do not know how many of these bands existed, one survey uncovered fifty-two street gangs in the city during the period 1836 to 1878.[41] They tended to be concentrated in poorer working-class districts, such as Southwark, Moyamensing, Northern Liberties, and Spring Garden, on the edge of the old city (see Figure 1.1). The vast majority of these groups had very short lives of three years or less, though some, such as the Snakers (seven years), the Buffers (ten years), and the Schuylkill Rangers (twenty-six years), persisted for much longer periods. Headquartered at a saloon, clubhouse, abandoned building, or simply a street corner, these gangs had distinctive dress, fashioning clothing styles that became their hallmark. Their names were also assertions of their distinct identity. The Schuylkill Rangers and the Kensington Black Hawks were named for their turf; the Killers, Rats, Bouncers, Spitfires, Tormentors, Smashers, and Flayers drew on slang, while the Shifflers, American Guards, Orangemen, and Kerryonians expressed ethnicity or nativism.[42] Sometimes the turf and neighborhood loyalties of the gangs coincided with those of the fire companies. For example, the Weccacoe Hose Company ran to and from fires escorted by the Bouncers, while the Killers and Moyamensing Hose Company, and the Shifflers and Shiffler Hose Company, had established alliances. Often there was little distinction between the two institutions.

Gangs complemented the role of fire companies in the electoral process by promoting the political fortunes of those whom they supported. They were particularly useful in guarding ballot boxes and keeping opponents away from the polls. In return, they were courted with donations, patronage, and freedom from arrest.[43] Gangs, fire companies, and the like thus provided the bases for grass-roots political organization in antebellum Philadelphia. This development had important consequences for political parties and the nature of political competition. From the partisan and party leaders' point of view, as these groups were not primarily political, they were a poor substitute for ward organization or for a permanent presence in the wards. Collectively they served to give the parties popular ties and a popular base, but individually most of them were unreliable, for they were tied more to individuals than to parties and therefore capable of changing partisan affiliation. Even when they remained faithful to their partisan allegiance, however, these organizations maintained their own self-direction and autonomy. There was thus no compelling incentive for them to accept centralized control or to follow the wishes of the party leadership.

The independence of these groups had significant implications for political competition. Their size and strength (often literally their physical strength) were regarded as a measure of the influence of the individual politicians they promoted, for the latter relied on them to secure party nominations and subsequent election. The electoral arena, then, became increasingly violent and corrupt, as brawlers, cash payments, and patronage were variously used to achieve victory.[44]

Government fragmentation and an absence of centralized control within political parties provided the basis of an environment that gave rise not to a political machine but to a political setting in which multiple political formations and individual actors, in contending for position and power in the city, mobilized whatever resources were available to them. It was a "structural context" in which enterprising politicians became ward "bosses"—"statesmen," as Plunkitt put it—by building up personal followings and exploiting opportunities for financial and personal gain.[45]

William "Squire" McMullen's career as Democratic "boss" of the fourth ward throughout the second half of the nineteenth century provides an excellent illustration of this political style.[46] Born in Moyamensing in 1824, the son of an Irish Catholic grocer, McMullen held a variety of jobs before he settled into politics. He served as an apprentice printer and carpenter, worked in his father's store, and finally decided to join the navy. On his return to Philadelphia in the mid-1840s, after his enlistment expired, he established his reputation as a street fighter with the Moyamensing Hose Company, earning the epithet "Bull" because of his brute strength. When the Mexican War broke out, the company enlisted, and McMullen the loyal Democrat went with them. He was ultimately placed in command of the "Moya" troops and returned to the city a genuine war hero.

McMullen was a conspicuous leader of the Moyamensing Hose Company and considered a protector of the local Irish Catholic community against the attacks of nativists, Protestants, and a police force drawn exclusively from the native-born population. In 1850, he was elected president of the Keystone Club, an association of Democratic party workers, and established an alliance with the "Killers" street gang. A few years later he became a saloonkeeper. He was elected alderman in 1856 and simultaneously became a prison inspector in the wake of the Democratic victory in the mayoralty election. He ruled paternalistically over his "subjects" and earned the title "Squire" for the way he helped his neighbors gain parole and other considerations from the legal system.[47]

Because he controlled votes in this poor section of the city "through favors, patronage and outright cash payments to voters,"[48] McMullen enjoyed a successful political career. His "political style was based on rowdyism," as his biographer puts it. "His reputation as a street-fighter, a scoundrel and a lawless thug marked McMullen's youth. Later these same traits would characterize his election day behavior."[49] Indeed, in the local election of October 1871, Octavius V. Catto, president of the fourth ward black political club, was shot dead by one of McMullen's associates. McMullen managed to survive the public outcry following this incident. He also survived the abolition of the volunteer fire department in 1871 and that of the position of alderman in 1873, as well as the demise of the local Democratic party. He was able to do this because he had been a loyal Democrat, made deals with Republicans like James McManes and William Stokley whenever politically expedient, and increasingly relied on his saloon as a focus for his supporters. McMullen's strategy was so successful that he was able to serve an uninterrupted tenure as select councilman for the fourth ward from 1874 until his death in 1901.[50]

Ward "bosses" like McMullen yielded little strength beyond their respective ward boundaries, but they were crucial to those who sought election to city or county office. Because these positions were elected at large, those who aspired to such an office had to draw up alliances with career politicians at the grass-roots level. For example, in 1856 "gentleman-Democrat" Richard Vaux was elected mayor largely through his alliance with local "bosses" and firehouse gangs, notably Irish Catholic politicians Lewis C. Cassidy and William McMullen.[51] A lawyer, Quaker, and son of merchant and philanthropist Roberts Vaux, Richard connected himself with working-class interests and organizations, such as the Columbia Hose Company, and posed as the champion of the common man. The price for the latter's support was evident after Vaux's victory, when "lines of his supporters seeking jobs with the city filled the Chestnut Street sidewalks."[52] McMullen, for example, rejected a lieutenancy in the police force in favor of a position on the Board of Prison Inspectors, but he did secure the appointment of at least six volunteer firemen from Moyamensing Hose Company to the police force.[53]

The most successful aspirant for city office at this time was William B. Mann, who was elected district attorney in 1856 and served until 1874 with just one interruption, the three-year term 1868–71. Born in 1816 the son of a clergyman and teacher, Mann practiced as a lawyer in the Northern Liberties district. He stood as the Whig, Know-Nothing, and Republican candidate in 1856 and defeated Democrat Lewis Cassidy. Like Vaux and Cassidy, Mann courted the support of local "bosses" and fire companies and was himself a member of the Pennsylvania Hose Company. The election result was contested in the courts by both candidates, and it seems that Mann prevailed as victor because the ballot frauds perpetrated in the "uptown" district of Northern Liberties were of less magnitude than those carried out by McMullen in the "downtown" areas of Moyamensing and Southwark.[54]

As a county (or "Row") officer, Mann enjoyed "a princely revenue" of between $75,000 and $100,000 a year in fees, which he used to cement a personal following with various local "bosses" and fire companies throughout the city.[55] Consequently, Mann was a major influence within the local Republican party and depicted as its first great leader and "Boss" by his enemies.[56] Mann's position within the Republican party was soon contested, however, by two career politicians who, unlike Mann, did not have to suffer the insecurities that went with constant public reelection; they owed their influence to the unusual positions they occupied in Philadelphia city government. These were James McManes and William S. Stokley.

2

Ring Rule

While the power of city and county officeholders, such as William Mann, rested on a shaky organizational base, and ward "bosses" like William McMullen rarely exercised influence beyond ward level, James McManes and William Stokley were able to establish citywide organizations as a consequence of their respective power bases in the gas trust and the Public Buildings Commission, which occupied unique positions in Philadelphia city government.

James McManes and the "Gas Ring"

An Irish immigrant of Ulster Presbyterian stock, McManes was only eight years old when his family emigrated to Philadelphia in 1830. After a brief education, he went to work as a bobbin-boy in a Southwark cotton mill and later became an apprentice weaver. At twenty-six years of age, McManes had saved sufficient money to set up his own modest spinning business, but this was destroyed by fire, so he reverted to being a supervisory foreman for Thomas Harkness, a manufacturer of cotton goods. In 1855, he joined with Edward C. Quinn, a conveyancer, in settting up a real-estate business that allowed him to pay off his old creditors, lay the foundations of his future fortune, and boost his political career, which had begun halfheartedly twelve years earlier.

Naturalized in 1844, McManes joined the Whigs and was a prominent campaigner for Winfield Scott, their presidential candidate in 1852. After Scott's defeat, McManes switched parties and organized a People's Republican Club in the seventeenth ward. He also joined forces with other individual political operators, such as William H. Kern, William Kemble, Henry Bumm, Alfred C. Hormer, and H. C. Howell, in a "log-rolling" venture in which they all agreed to help one another achieve political success. As a result, McManes was elected school director in 1858, a position he held until 1866, when he joined the city Board of Education. In 1860, McManes helped nominate Andrew G. Curtin for governor at the state Republican convention, and he supported Abraham Lincoln when he was a delegate to the Republican National Convention. As a reward for loyalty, Curtin appointed him bank inspector of Philadelphia.[1]

In 1865, McManes was elected to the board of gas trustees by Common Council and remained a member, except for one break in 1883 to 1884, until the trust was abolished in 1887. He quickly emerged as the dominant figure on the board because, by the admission of his enemies, he possessed "the personal qualities—courage, resolution, foresight, personal capacity [and] the judicious preference of the substance of power to its display" needed for political leadership.[2] With his "center of power" in the gas trust, he became all-powerful in the city's politics, because, according to James Bryce, McManes, "by his superior activity and intelligence, secured the command of the whole [Republican] party machinery and reached the high position of recognized Boss of Philadelphia."[3]

Why, and how, did the gas trust become the "center of power" with McManes as the "Boss of Philadelphia"? In 1835, City Council passed an ordinance that provided for the establishment of a gas works with a capital outlay of $100,000 to be secured by an issue of stock. The city reserved the right to purchase the plant at any time by converting the stock into a twenty-year loan. In addition, the administration of the plant was placed in the hands of a board of twelve members elected by the Councils, who were trustees of the loans issued for the construction and enlargement of the gas works. By an ordinance of June 17, 1841, the city exercised its right to become the owner of the gas works. The ordinance also provided that the trustee system be continued until the loans on the gas works account had been paid off. Because thirty-year loans under these conditions were issued until 1855 (after 1855, subsequent loans required by the gas trustees were made payable by the city treasurer) the board of trustees had an assured lease of life until 1885.[4]

It was soon apparent that the gas trust had been unwittingly invested with autocratic power. Local publisher, historian, and civic reformer Henry C. Lea pointed out:

> When the Gas Trust was organized in a shape that rendered it impervious to political influences, it seems to have been the fond belief that it would always be kept in the hands of such men as Alexander Dallas Bache, Samuel V. Merrick, Frederick Brown, Joseph S. Lovering, M. W. Baldwin and others of similar high character whose names figure in the early lists of Trustees. With the gradual deterioration of our municipal administration, such names as these disappear and are replaced by working politicians whose earnest efforts to obtain admission to unsalaried position, entailing no little labor, can scarcely be expected to arise from disinterested self-sacrifice. The inevitable result is that the Gas Trust becomes a vast political machine, wielding the influence derivable from hundreds of appointments and millions of expenditure.[5]

As Dr. Frederick W. Spiers of the Municipal League later recalled:

> The unique opportunities for spoliation offered by this irresponsible administrative board were speedily recognized, and during the Civil War period a body of political bandits succeeded in capturing the Trust. From this vantage ground, they proceeded to corrupt the whole municipal administration, and the Philadelphia Gas Ring speedily created a political machine which rivalled that of its contemporary—the Tweed Ring—in the neatness and dispatch with which it transferred the money of the people from the public treasury to the pockets of the politicians.[6]

The trust was able to achieve this because, although Select Council and Common Council each elected six trustees who served for a period of three years, they did not control the board. Henry C. Lea explained to Bryce:

It might be thought that the power of election vested in the councils would enable the latter to control the trustees, but when "politics" invaded the trust, a vicious circle speedily established itself and the trust controlled the councils. Its enormous pay-roll enabled it to employ numerous "workers" in each of the 600 or 700 election divisions [precincts] of the city, and aspirants for seats in the councils found it almost impossible to obtain either nomination or election without the favor of the trust. Thus the councils became filled with its henchmen or "heelers," submissive to its bidding, not only in the selection of trustees to fill the four yearly vacancies, but in every detail of city government with which the leaders of the trust desired to interfere. It is easy to understand the enormous possibilities of power created by such a position.[7]

McManes's clout depended on the resources of the gas trust, which were considerable. The board spent more than $4 million a year, half of which took the form of large contracts for purchasing supplies. It also employed a workforce that fluctuated from 800 to 2,000.[8] Henry C. Lea, in his report for the Citizens' Municipal Reform Association, claimed that the gas works was grossly overmanned, produced gas of an inferior quality, had excess leakage, and made too little profit for the city.[9] One reason for the low profit was that the trustees paid approximately one dollar a ton over the current market price for coal. This "drawback" amounted to a total "wastage" of $1 million a year, much of which the gas trustees probably received back, it was alleged, in the form of a rebate or "kickback."[10]

Reformers and the Councils made several attempts to improve the accountability of the gas trust, but all these efforts in 1854, 1858, and 1868 failed in the courts, which ruled that the trustees had a secure lease on life until the final loan matured in 1885. Henry C. Lea pointed out the "anomalous position" occupied by the gas trust as a result of these judgments:

Its property is in reality the property of the city, which holds the title to all its real estate: if ably managed, its profits would enure to the benefit of the public; if recklessly or corruptly conducted, the loss falls upon the city. The city is liable for the loans which are administered by the Trust. The Trustees are elected by Councils, and yet when once elected, they are practically independent of the power creating them, which is responsible for their acts, and for whose profit or loss they are acting. . . .

. . . The Gas Trust is thus a close corporation, permitting no intru-
sion or investigation, holding its sessions in secret, giving out contracts at its pleasure, without public competition, submitting its
accounts to no auditor, presenting to the public such information, and
no more, of its acts and doings as it pleases, spending annually more
than four million of public money and practically admitting no accountability to anyone. That it should become a political engine of vast
influence was inevitable and that its management should share in the
general degradation of municipal politics is a necessary consequence.[11]

Thus, the gas trust became "the center of power," as the *Public Ledger* put it.
Its authority "became absolute. Political caucuses were held in the Board
Room. Appointments to the local, state and national offices emanated from
its walls and aspiring young politicians looked to its sacred precincts for
inspiration."[12] Bryce explained that this was not so remarkable:

When a number of small factions combine to rule a party, that faction
which is a little larger or better organized, or better provided with
funds than the others, obtains the first place among them and may
keep it so long as it gives to the rest a fair share of the booty, and
directs the policy of the confederates with firmness and skill. . . .
     The merit of the system was that it perpetuated itself, and in fact
grew stronger the longer it stood. Whenever an election was in
prospect, the ward primaries of the Republican party were thronged
by the officers and workpeople of the Gas Trust and other city departments who secured the choice of such delegates as the Ring had
previously selected in secret conclave.[13]

The influence of McManes was particularly strong in the Tax Department, for
example, which he controlled between 1873 and 1882, as the Office of
Receiver of Taxes was occupied successively by his close associates and fellow
gas trustees, Thomas J. Smith (1873–76) and Albert C. Roberts (1876–81).
Indeed, Independent Republican, Joseph Caven, called the Tax Office "a
graduating place for gas trustees."[14] The position was attractive in the 1870s
because a new office, the Office of Collector of Delinquent Taxes, had been
created to recover the $10 million of outstanding tax arrears that had accumu-
lated in the city. The collector, appointed by the receiver of taxes, was paid a
5 percent commission on the taxes he recovered. This office yielded fees of

between $150,000 and $200,000 a year between 1873 and 1881, making it "one of the richest prizes of the political spoilsman."[15]

The material benefits McManes gained from the gas trust and the Tax Office meant that "his power in city politics equalled and ordinarily exceeded that of any other person." According to Harold Zink, McManes "had become sufficiently powerful to deserve the appellation 'King.'"[16] Similarly, one obituary on McManes suggested he was "one of the most powerful dictators who ever ruled this city. His rule was absolute, as that of a Czar, and his word was law."[17]

William Stokley and the "Buildings Ring"

William S. Stokley was the other leading politician who emerged in the immediate postwar years. He was to challenge McManes for the title of "city boss" from his center of power on the Public Buildings Commission and as mayor of the city from 1871 to 1881. Stokley epitomized the self-made man. Born in Philadelphia in 1823, the eldest child of three, he was only in his youth when his father died, leaving him with the responsibility of caring for the family. He established a successful confectionery business and entered politics through the Franklin Hose Company. An active fireman for sixteen years, he served as the hose company's treasurer and its representative on the city's Fire Association. In 1860 Stokley was elected as a Republican to Common Council from the ninth ward and, after being successively reelected for four terms, gained the council presidency in 1865. By 1867, Stokley had moved on to the upper chamber, and in 1868 he was elected president of Select Council.[18]

While president of Select Council, Stokley established a modest reputation as a "law and order man" and "reformer" based on two controversial ordinances he introduced, one calling for the abolition of the volunteer fire companies in favor of a professional fire department, the other advocating the transfer of the gas works from the gas trust to a Department of Gas. Both ordinances successfully passed both Councils, though the gas works remained under the trust after McManes's appeal to the state supreme court was upheld.

The 1867 measure advocating establishment of a paid fire department by 1871 seems to have been successful for a number of reasons. First, public opinion had become increasingly hostile toward the volunteer system, as fire companies had a long record of street-fighting, arson, shootings, and murder. Second, new technology in the form of the steam-powered fire engine drove a wedge into the volunteers' ranks. The new engines were both costly and heavy, requiring horses rather than men to pull them. Consequently, the city argued, it was now opportune to modernize operations. Finally, professional politicians, who like Stokley himself were often former firemen, believed there was a need for change. They recognized that the volunteer fire companies were too unruly and unpredictable and too much inclined to adopt independent lines of action to fit comfortably into the Republican party organization's efforts to unify political control of the city. Stokley's reform of the fire service, and his efforts to transfer the gas works to the city, won general support throughout the city and formed the basis of his successful bid for the mayoralty in 1871.[19]

As president of Select Council, Stokley was also involved in the dispute over the erection of new public buildings. The controversy about their location and who was to build them and control the expenditures left Stokley in an unprecedented position of power in Philadelphia. What was not disputed was that Philadelphia desperately needed public buildings to house its growing government and court systems. As early as 1838, rapid population growth, commercial developments, and the expansion of government services and bureaucracy led civic leaders to advocate concentrating these services in a single forum. The failure to agree on how this should be done meant that the problem had intensified considerably when the Councils again revived the issue after the Civil War. In February 1867 an ordinance was drafted authorizing building commissioners of the Councils' Committee on City Property and suggesting that the new buildings be erected on Penn Square in the ninth ward. A special joint committee of the Councils set up to consider the issue reported back with two amendments designed to satisfy the city's commercial interests. It suggested that a number of prominent businessmen replace the Committee on City Property as building commissioners and proposed that the site be changed to Independence Square in the fifth ward commercial area. Stokley, as select councilman for the ninth ward, opposed the change of site and—along with A. Wilson Henszey (tenth ward), his ally in Common Council—successfully led the effort to reject the ordinance and postpone the issue indefinitely.[20]

In 1868, William Bumm, an associate of McManes and chairman of the City Property Committee, introduced a new bill for public buildings that retained the Independence Square site but replaced the businessmen commissioners with men who were more politically oriented, such as the chief engineer and surveyor, the highways commissioner, and members of the Committee on City Property, all of whom were appointed by the Councils, plus some other councilmen, and contractors who could sell their services to the city. The bill passed both Councils and was approved by the mayor in January 1869. The Public Buildings Commission brought together jobbers and contractors belonging to the Mann wing of the Republican party. As a sop to Stokley, who joined the commission by right of his position as president of Select Council, the commissioners elected him president of the body.[21]

Unable to gain support for the Penn Square site, Stokley turned to newly elected State Senator Wilson Henszey for help. He supported Henszey's successful efforts in guiding bills through the state legislature that made Independence Square "a public green forever," submitted the issue of the site for the buildings to a popular vote, and established a new commission. The new Buildings Commission set up on August 5, 1870, did not include any members of the original commission established the previous year. Instead, it was composed of the mayor, the Council presidents, and Councilmen John Rice, Henry Phillips, and Stokley—as well as Theodore Cuyler and John P. Wetherill, two former councilmen with close ties to the business community. This development represented a considerable coup on the part of Stokley and Henszey, for they had entirely changed the complexion of the Buildings Commission.[22] However, the new commission "aroused general indignation" because of its unlimited power. The Councils were denied supervisory powers and were directed to accept any contracts the commission entered into and to raise money through an annual tax on property.[23] As lawyer and reformer Horace Binney put it, the state legislature "have appointed for us a Building Commission, empowered to tax us without limit, and to spend our money without supervision, to hold office without restriction of time and to fill all vacancies in their own body, . . . inflicting on us all the evils of taxation without representation."[24] Although the commission "was so subversive of the principles of self-government," reform efforts to abolish it failed, and it remained intact until 1901, when the task of building a new city hall was complete.[25]

The referendum on the site of the city hall gave a narrow majority in favor of Penn Square over Washington Square, even though many business leaders argued that the former was too isolated from the city's commercial district.[26] The Buildings Commission then entered a new controversy by proposing to build a single mammoth city hall at the intersection of the city's major thoroughfares, Broad and Market Streets, instead of having separate offices on each of the four blocks constituting Penn Square. The intersection scheme was vehemently opposed by the city's business community, and Stokley voted against the proposal when it was presented in June 1871. Stokley also suggested that all the contracts awarded by the commission should be subject to the approval of City Council. These actions enabled Stokley to deflect public criticism against himself in the crucial period prior to his nomination and election as mayor in November 1871.

Stokley's behavior, however, subsequent to his proposal advocating Council supervision, "reveals calculated deceit," because far from seeking to dilute the commission's powers, he worked hard to fill it with allies.[27] For example, when Henry Phillips, Theodore Cuyler, John P. Wetherill, and John Rice resigned from the commission over a six-month period between October 1871 and April 1872, Stokley secured the election of such associates as Mahlon Dickenson, Former Receiver of Taxes Richard Peltz, and the latter's brother-in-law, marble-cutter John Hill, all of whom had known him since his days as a fireman.[28] Moreover, except for Hill who served until 1894, they all remained commissioners for thirty years, until the body was abolished in 1901.[29] In the process, they spent $24 million, well over double the original $10 million estimate for the construction of City Hall. More than 20 percent of this amount was attributable to a single contract, the largest ever awarded in the city's history. In October 1872, without advertising for bids, the commission gave a $5,300,000 contract to William Struthers & Son to provide marble as the foundation material for the new building. Critics were quick to point out that Struthers would provide marble from the Lee Quarry in Massachusetts, which was owned by Former Commissioner John Rice and was where John Hill had served his apprenticeship. Soon afterward, both Stokley and Hill moved into $20,000 brownstone houses on Filbert Street, provided, the press alleged, by city building contractors.[30]

Stokley's position on the Buildings Commission paved the way for further political alliances. District Attorney William Mann, for example, was made one of the sureties for the Struther's contract. In addition, as the intersection scheme disrupted street railway traffic, Stokley used his influence to help the Union Railway Company break the West Philadelphia Railway Company's exclusive privilege of laying tracks on Market Street. Stokley bestowed a number of favors on Union directors and major stockholders. For example, in 1873 Stokley's friends in the Councils secured authorization to deposit city money in Union directors' William Kemble and James McManes's People's Bank. The commission also named City Treasurer and Union Railway stockholder Peter Widener as its own treasurer. Another Union stockholder, Sheriff William Leeds, secured from the commission brick contracts worth more than $50,000 in 1873 alone. Another contract, worth more than $200,000 over five years from 1874 to 1879, was awarded to the Excelsior Brick Company, which listed among its directors Widener's business colleague William Elkins.[31]

The links between these individuals were cemented still further through the practice of what George Washington Plunkitt has termed "honest graft."[32] Under Mayor Stokley and Highways Commissioner John Hill, highway expenditures mushroomed into a $1 million a year business. The bulk of this money was appropriated for city improvements in Philadelphia's growing suburban districts (see Table 2).[33] Hill, along with close associates, such as Leeds, Henszey, Dickenson, Widener, and Elkins, as well as Councilman George Dorlon, Prothonotary John Loughridge, Registrar of Water James Wark, and contractor Charles Porter, bought land in west and north central Philadelphia and then made sure the city provided the improvements necessary to enhance the value of the property.[34] The "highway ring's" success was guaranteed because Stokley had secured Henszey's election as president of Common Council (1873–76), and Henszey in turn had appointed William Ellwood Rowan (twenty-seventh ward) as chairman of the Committee on Highways and John Bardsley (twenty-eighth ward) as head of the Finance Committee. Both councilmen were keen to provide municipal services for their own districts and approved every highway appropriation requested.[35]

The *Philadelphia Times* in March 1875 suggested that the control of city services allowed Stokley, Hill, and Leeds to rule the city:

> The secret of the great influence exercised by the triumvirate is that they usually work together and being the dispenser of almost unlimited patronage, and to the extent of millions of dollars annually, they wield immense power in local politics and whenever they undertake a thing, they are bound to put it through.[36]

Stokley's new politics found social expression in the Society of Mysterious Pilgrims, established in 1872. In addition to prominent Republicans, such as the mayor and his chief supporters, Hill, Leeds, and Peltz, it included such Democrats as Public Buildings Commissioners Lewis Cassidy and Thomas Barger, as well as the city's most active ward politicians, who made their living through a variety of elective and appointive offices (see Table 3).[37] In 1875 a watchdog subcommittee of the Union League (a social club composed of members of the local business elite) publicly condemned the

Table 2. Population Distribution in Philadelphia, 1850, 1880

	Old City	Districts[a] Adjacent to Old City	Outlying Districts	Total
1850	121,376	218,669	68,717	408,762
	(29.7)[b]	(53.5)	(16.8)	
1880	112,846	361,024	373,300	847,170
	(−7.0%)	(+65.1%)	(+443.0%)	(+207.3%)
	(13.3)	(42.6)	(44.1)	

SOURCE: John Daly and Allen Weinberg, *Genealogy of Philadelphia County Subdivisions*, 2nd ed. (Philadelphia, 1966), 92–100.

[a]Spring Garden, Northern Liberties, Kensington, Moyamensing, and Southwark districts.

[b]Figures in parentheses represent the proportion of the total population in Philadelphia County.

Pilgrims as "that dictatorial band of men, nominally of both parties, but without true allegiance to either, which now rules and oppresses our city and is disgracing and destroying the Republican organization."[38] At the head of this "dictatorial band" were Stokley, Hill, and Leeds, whom journalists likened to Rome's first triumvirate of Caesar, Pompey, and Crassus.[39]

The Limits of Boss Power

McManes and Stokley have been depicted as "bosses" who wielded enormous power and influence citywide. McManes has been described variously as "James I," "King James," and "Boss of Philadelphia." With Stokley "as a powerful auxiliary," he became "one of the most powerful dictators who ever ruled this city."[40] To what extent are these characterizations accurate? How far do McManes and Stokley qualify as genuine "city bosses"? That is, to what extent did they control their followers in party office, the distribution of patronage, the membership and decisions of the party organization's local units, the party's nominations for public office, the behavior of elected officials nominally affiliated with them, and city government? Did they head a well-disciplined and centralized party organization that was capable not only of routinely centralizing power in the city as well as distributing patronage?

The observations of contemporaries and later historians suggest they did. As we saw earlier, Henry C. Lea explained to James Bryce that although the

Table 3. The Society of Mysterious Pilgrims, 1872–1875

Name	Public Office	Affiliation
John E. Addicks	Health officer	Stokley
James B. Alexander	State senator	
Joseph R. Ash	State representative	
William Baldwin	Councilman	
Thomas J. Barger	Buildings commissioner	Democrat
David Beitler[1]	Alderman	
Henry H. Bingham	Clerk of quarter sessions	Cameron
Joseph A. Bonham	Solicitor, register of wills	
James Brearly	Chief clerk, register of Wills	
William M. Bunn	Guardian of the poor	
William C. Calhoun	Sealer of weights & measures	
Lewis C. Cassidy	Buildings commissioner	Democrat
Gideon Clark[1]	Register of wills	
Charles C. Cochrane	Cashier, city treasurer	Democrat
John Cochrane	Councilman	
C.H.T. Collis	City solicitor	Stokley
Harry Coward	Highways contractor	Stokley
E.W. Davis	State senator	
Jacob B. De Haven[1]	Tax collector	
William A. Delaney[1]	Bookkeeper	
Hamilton Disston[1]	Fire commissioner	Indep.
George Dorlan	Councilman	Stokley
Joseph H. Edwards[1]	Deputy sheriff	
William L. Elkins	Councilman	Cameron
William Elliott[O]	Sheriff	Cameron
N.F. English	Flour inspector	
George D. Glenn[1]	Caterer, Clerk of Quarter Sessions	McManes
E.W.C. Greene[O]	Pension agent	
A. Wilson Henszey	Pres., Common Council	Stokley
John L. Hill[1]	Highways commissioner	Stokley
Marshall C. Hong[1]	Deputy sheriff	Stokley
Harry Hunter	State representative	
Hiram Hunter	State senator	
Samuel P. Jones[1]	Clerk	
Samuel Josephs[1]	State senator	Democrat
James N. Kerns	U.S. marshall	Cameron
William King	Chief clerk, city controller	
John Lamon	State senator	McManes
David H. Lane	Deputy recorder of deeds	Cameron
Peter Lane	Clerk, city treasurer	
William R. Leeds[1]	Former sheriff	Stokley
Robert Loughlin	Councilman	

Table 3. *(cont'd)*

Name	Public Office	Affiliation
John Loughridge	Former prothonotary	Stokley
John McCall	Councilman	
Alexander McCuen[I]	Fire commissioner	
John McCullough	Councilman	McManes
Robert Mackey	State treasurer	Cameron
William Mann	Prothonotary	Cameron
George H. Moore[I]	Alderman	
Robert Morris	Mercantile appraiser	
Richard Peltz[I]	Buildings commissioner	Stokley
Charles A. Porter[I]	Highways contractor	Stokley
William A. Porter	Fire commissioner	
Erastus Poulson	Solicitor, receiver of taxes	
William E. Rowan	Councilman	McManes
Harry C. Selby	Registrar of water	Stokley
William Siner	Councilman	
William L. Smith	City commissioner	
William S. Stokley[O]	Mayor	Stokley
William H. Taggart[I]	Coal inspector	
William A. Thorpe[I]	Police magistrate	
Joseph Tittermary[I]	Mercantile appraiser	
R.C. Tittermary[I]	Mercantile appraiser	
Isaac W. Van Houten[I]	Superintendent	
Frederick J. Walter[I]	Clerk	
John Welsh[I]	Port warden	Democrat
Peter A. B. Widener[I]	City treasurer	Cameron

SOURCES: Public Law 934 (April 5, 1872), *Laws of Pennsylvania, 1872,* 979–80; *Gopsill's Philadelphia City Directory for 1872* (Philadelphia, 1872); *Manual of Councils, 1872–1873* (Philadelphia, 1872); *Times,* June 19, 1875.

NOTES: "Cameron" indicates members whose chief loyalty was to the state Republican party leader, Simon Cameron; I = Original incorporator; O = Officer.

Councils elected gas trustees, it was the gas trust that controlled the Councils.[41] This was because the trust had secured control of Republican party nominations due to the judicious distribution of patronage at its disposal, which allowed it to employ numerous party "workers" in the city's seven hundred divisions. Bryce reiterates: "Nearly all the municipal offices were held by their nominees. They commanded a majority in the Select and Common Councils."[42] Lea's biographer, Edward S. Bradley, confirms that McManes "secured command of the whole party machinery."[43]

Other contemporaries agreed with Lea's assessment. For example, Quaker reformer and manufacturer Philip C. Garrett noted how "Seventh Street," where the office of the gas trust was situated, had become a "synonym" for "the Ring" in Republican party circles.[44] More dramatic was the claim of reform publicist George Vickers:

> James McManes held sway as an imperious and exacting taskmaster. Artful in politics as a Machiavelli, his name was synonymous with all that an autocratic and unscrupulous control of political machinery and methods could imply. . . . Entrenched in a political position which he had converted into a veritable fortress for purposes, offensive and defensive, he had gathered about him as his aides and lieutenants, men who were apt and skillful in executing his orders and prompt in sharing his spoils. . . .
>
> To enter public service, whether as a Councilman, a member of the legislature or as an officer of a public department, was to first give satisfactory proof of allegiance to these men, to their claims and methods, with no reference whatever to personal scruples or to convictions of personal duty. The ease with which these combined spoilsmen made and unmade public offices . . . was performed with the facility of a simple wave of the hand. Under their rule, although elections still went on with their accustomed regularity, . . . every material outcome of such elections was in the interest of the self-constituted dictators and against the interests of the people. To the cause of the former, Stokley with his twelve hundred police officers was a powerful auxiliary.[45]

The *Public Ledger* and the *North American* repeated these claims in their obituaries of McManes, as did historian Harold Zink, writing in the 1930s, who suggested: "Republican nomination conventions followed 'King' James' orders because he controlled the organization or machine which sent the delegates to the conventions." McManes was able to control the Councils, in turn, because "in Republican Philadelphia, nomination as a rule carried with it election to office."[46] More recently, Howard Gillette has argued that Stokley built a new political machine by turning the "machinery of government into a vast patronage system" and that Philadelphia's city hall now stands as a "monument" to it.[47] These characterizations of the power wielded by McManes and Stokley do not, however, stand up in a closer examination of political competition in the city in the immediate postbellum period (even after making allowance for dramatic license on the part of these chroniclers of political affairs in Philadelphia). In the first place, there is the nature of the relationship between the two party leaders to consider. Stokley was not always McManes's "powerful auxiliary," as Vickers claimed; he contended for power in his own right, and not as an adjunct to McManes. Their relationship oscillated between mutual cooperation and outright hostility. In brief, McManes resented Stokley's periodic interference in the running of the gas works. In 1868 it was Stokley who introduced the ordinance that attempted to abolish the trust and transfer the works to a Department of Gas. Again in 1875, Stokley attempted to bring the gas works with all its patronage under his control as mayor, but this effort also failed.[48] Nevertheless, Stokley's hostility toward the gas trust did not prevent McManes from endorsing him for the mayoralty in 1874 and again in 1877, because Stokley had secured a number of favors for the Union Railway Company, of which McManes was a major stockholder, and in 1877 had agreed to support Albert C. Roberts, McManes's candidate for receiver of taxes (thereby guaranteeing McManes control of the Collectorship of Delinquent Taxes).[49]

Thereafter, however, a serious rift developed between the two as they fought bitterly to gain the upper hand within the Republican party. In May 1878, at the state gubernatorial convention, the division of the city's delegates into factions was apparent when McManes's supporters donned "Black Hats" and Stokley's supporters put on "White Hats."[50] Relations worsened in 1880 after Rufus Shapley, one of Stokley's closest allies and friends, published an anonymous political satire entitled *Solid for Mulhooly,* which gave an unflattering account of McManes's career. It traced Michael Mulhooly's (McManes's) rise to fame from his ancestral roots or "Paddy-Gree," "among the bogs of County Tyrone" to "Boss of the Ring," by way of the saloon, "in which his first lessons of life were learned," to his "apprenticeship as a repeater at the polls" following his fraudulent naturalization, and then as "a corrupt and perjured member of the municipal Legislature, always to be hired or bought by the highest bidder, and always an uneducated, vulgar, flashily-dressed, obscene creature of the Ring which made him what he is, and of which he is a worthy representative."[51] Mulhooly is portrayed as a bull-necked, beefy thug chomping on a cigar, decked out in a gaudy vest and patterned pantaloons, complete with derby hat and cane—the familiar image the public has associated with the boss for generations (see Figure 2). Though published anonymously, the authorship of the satire was speedily traced to Shapley, and in the subsequent mayoral election in February 1881 Stokley lost his bid for a fourth term of office partly as a result of McManes's supporters cutting the Republican ticket in a number of key wards.[52]

HIS PORTRAIT.

Fig. 2. The following three frames depict "Michael Mulhooly (James McManes): His Ancestry, Education, and Portrait." Illustrations by Thomas Nast. (From *Solid for Mulhooly: A Political Satire by Rufus E. Shapley,* 2nd ed. [Philadelphia, 1889], 1, 16, 20.)

Second, contemporary observers and later historians have ignored the fact that neither Stokley or McManes satisfactorily controlled City Council. The Council presidency, for example, was a very important position because the occupant appointed councilmen to the Council committees that considered and discussed prospective legislation and appropriations and made recommendations to the legislature. Because the Council president was elected each year at the start of each session, the office provides us with a gauge of the factional superiority of the various groups contending for power. The affilia-

HIS BIRTHPLACE.

tions of the various Council presidents between the Civil War and 1884 suggest that McManes and Stokley exercised, at best, only intermittent control over the Councils (see Table 4). Stokley was at the height of his power between 1873 and 1876 when his close associate, A. Wilson Henszey, was president of Common Council. In January 1876, Henszey was defeated by Independent Republican Joseph L. Caven, from the fifteenth ward (a district renowned for its "independence" in politics), and he held the office for five years before retiring to private life.[53] McManes's strength rested largely in Select Council, but his control was so insecure that he himself was defeated as a candidate for reelection to the gas trust in 1882.[54]

McManes and Stokley failed to control City Council because they did not control the Republican party either. Let us take, for example, the Republican party's nominations for public office. The Republican party rules provided

HIS FIRST SCHOOL.

for a party organization and a nominating system. The organization of the Republican party paralleled the city's governmental structure. It included bodies representing the electoral division, the ward, and the city at large. Division associations organized annually and were designed to be popular assemblies of the resident Republican voters. At the regular annual primary, Republican citizens met at their respective club rooms to elect three (or, from 1877, two) members from each division to the ward executive committee. In turn, each of the ward committees elected a member to the City Executive Committee.[55]

The candidates for all offices were nominated by either a ward or city convention. Initially, all public offices at large were nominated at one city convention, but the opportunities this created for log-rolling led to a "growing indignation [among] the people," and by 1868 separate conventions for

Table 4. Presidents of the Philadelphia City Councils and Their Political Affiliation,
1865–1884

	Ward	Years of Office	Affiliation
Common Council			
William S. Stokley	9	1865–67	Stokley
Joseph F. Marcer	20	1867–69	IR
Louis Wagner	22	1869–71	IR
Henry Huhn	15	1871–72	IR
Louis Wagner	22	1872–73	IR
A. Wilson Henszey	10	1873–76	Stokley
Joseph L. Caven	15	1876–81	IR
William H. Lex	8	1881–84	IR
Select Council			
William S. Stokley	9	1868–70	Stokley
S.W. Cattell	24	1870–72	Stokley
W.E. Littleton	12	1872–74	IR
R.W. Downing	14	1874–75	Stokley
W.W. Burnell	15	1875–76	Democrat
George A. Smith	28	1876–78	IR
George W. Bumm	18	1878–81	McManes
William B. Smith	28	1882–84	IR

SOURCES: *Manual of Councils, 1889–1890* (Philadelphia, 1889), 124–25; George Vickers, *The Fall of Bossism: A History of the Committee of One Hundred and the Reform Movement in Philadelphia and Pennsylvania,* vol. 1 (Philadelphia, 1883); Frank W. Leach, "Twenty Years with Quay," *North American,* February 12, March 12, and April 23, 1905; Howard F. Gillette Jr., "Corrupt and Contented, Philadelphia's Political Machine, 1865–1887" (Ph.D. diss., Yale University, 1970), chaps. 2, 5, 7, 8.

NOTE: IR = Independent Republican.

each public office had been instituted, "in order to render less easy the purchase or dictation of nominations by the managers of rings," as local reformers put it.[56] Each division elected one delegate to each city convention and two representatives to the ward convention. Before the direct primary was introduced in 1906, the only alteration in these arrangements occurred between 1877 and 1881, when the number of delegates each ward was entitled to send to a city convention became dependent on the number of Republican votes polled in the particular ward in the preceding general election—that is, each ward was entitled to one representative for every 500 Republican votes, or majority thereof, although every ward was to be represented by at least three delegates.[57] This meant that, before 1887, the average size of city conventions was 688 delegates, though only 160 between 1877 and 1881.

With such large numbers of delegates at city conventions held at the same time on the same day, it would have been extremely difficult to exercise central control even under circumstances of party harmony. As it was, however, the Republican party was rent by factionalism, particularly during the period 1877–81. As well as the triumvirate of Stokley, Hill, and Leeds, and the supporters of McManes, such as Councilman William E. Rowan and City Committeeman Christian Kneass, it is possible to distinguish a third faction that contended for power within the Republican party. This faction was led by Hamilton Disston and included State Treasurer Robert Mackey and the leader of the nineteenth ward, David Martin. Disston was a man of considerable independent wealth. In 1878, at the age of thirty-four, he inherited his father's saw-manufacturing works, which employed more than 2,000 and was reputedly the largest of its kind in the nation. Disston, like Mackey and Martin, was interested in the state political arena as well as the local one.[58]

Consequently, there was no single "boss" dictating party nominations; rather, the various factions fought it out (sometimes, literally) in the convention hall. A successful nomination depended on factions securing the largest number of delegates, so conventions occasionally became rowdy and violent as disputes arose, particularly over the admission of delegates when seats were contested by rival factions.[59] Sometimes the factions were able to compromise on a slate, but when such negotiations failed, and if the differences were strong enough, the struggles between them spilled over into the electoral arena. For example, in November 1876, William E. Rowan, McManes's candidate for sheriff, was defeated by almost 7,000 votes, while other city-wide Republican candidates gained a majority of between 14,000 and 15,000 votes. Rowan's defeat was attributed to the refusal of Disston and Stokley supporters to vote for Rowan.[60] A similar explanation was offered a year later when Democrat Robert E. Pattison defeated James Sayre, another McManes candidate, to become city controller. Finally, as noted earlier, Stokley himself was defeated for the mayoralty in 1881, when McManes's supporters cut the Republican ticket.[61]

Furthermore, these three broad factions did not exercise a monopoly on the candidate-selection process, for it was still possible, given the number and size of city conventions, for an individual politician to secure a nomination by making an independent and direct appeal to party workers. Success in such a venture usually depended on how well their campaign was organized, the personal popularity of the individual concerned, and their record of party service.[62] Frank W. Leach, a Republican party worker in the eighth ward in the 1870s, recalled in 1905:

> The methods resorted to thirty years ago to secure a nomination for an important city or county office were so unlike those employed nowadays that the lack of resemblance almost suggests another nationality and a different form of city government. Then the ward and precinct workers who possessed minds, souls, individualities much as they were of their own were duly sought after and consulted. Candidates went from ward to ward and almost from house to house.[63]

By 1905, division representation had become an "abstract principle," according to Leach, but a quarter of a century earlier it "meant division representation pure and simple."[64]

In these circumstances, John O'Donnell was able to secure the nomination for recorder of deeds in 1881, and George de B. Keim got the nomination for sheriff in 1882, entirely independent of the various party factions. Moreover, William B. Smith secured the mayoralty nomination in January 1884 despite a position of open defiance toward McManes.[65] Thus, contrary to the claims of reformers and later historians, Republican nominating conventions apparently did not follow orders from McManes, or anyone else. As Leach put it wistfully:

> In these days [1905] of enormous majorities, when Philadelphia's wonderful "Organization" glides upon the even tenor of its way, seemingly unmoved and undisturbed by criticism or opposition, it is difficult to comprehend the conditions as they existed a quarter of a century ago. Whereas placidity prevails today in the inner councils of the party managers, then all was turbulence and strife. First the factions fought among themselves. Then the people combined to overthrow the factions. Encounter succeeded encounter, as the night the day; charge followed charge along the entire line of battle. The militant host slept upon their guns, or slept not at all.
>
> Surely these were strident, stringent, strenuous days![66]

It is not surprising, then, that since these factions struggled to gain control over party nominations for city offices they exercised even less influence over ward public offices. The party appeared to be somewhat centralized, because it was governed by the City Committee, but this appearance was illusory.

The party organization did not function as its centralized and hierarchical structure suggested. So, even if McManes was the sole boss and party factionalism was absent, he would still have had no formal control over the membership and decisions of the party's local units because the wards were the prime units of the organizational structure. For example, representatives on the party's City Committee were selected at the ward level and could be removed from office only by a two-thirds vote of the ward committee.[67] Moreover, as we have seen, each ward elected candidates to the Councils, and as City Council became increasingly involved in the decisions that allocated the city's tangible resources, the ward caucuses acquired even greater political importance. In practice, what evolved was a bottom-heavy structure in which candidate selection and voter mobilization depended on action at the ward level. The City Committee did not function as a centralized and powerful institution capable of extinguishing dissent and controlling the candidate-selection process. It had no institutionalized means to control the selection process for the increasingly important seats on the Councils, and it could not slate or de-slate nominees for public office nominated at Republican ward conventions. In sum, it had no monopoly over the recruitment of candidates to public office.

Consequently, neither McManes or Stokley was able to ensure that followers nominally affiliated with them would be renominated, or that those who opposed them would not be renominated. For example, when Stokley's ally Wilson Henszey was defeated for the presidency of Common Council by Joseph Caven in January 1876, the terms of seventeen of the twenty-eight councilmen who voted for the former were about to expire. Only six of these sixteen faithful Stokley supporters who sought renomination were successful, and just four were reelected in February 1876. By contrast, ten out of eleven of the thirty-two councilmen who voted for the Independent Republican were successfully renominated and elected, including Caven himself, despite "organized hostility on the part of a considerable number of office-holders" in the fifteenth ward.[68] Stokley and McManes also failed to prevent Caven's reelection in 1879 and were similarly unsuccessful in their efforts to dislodge the committee chairmen, appointed by Caven, either at the ward nominating conventions or in subsequent elections.[69]

Furthermore, they could not prevent Republican politicians not endorsed by the party organization from being elected. For example, John Hunter, Caven's finance committee chairman, was successfully elected as an Independent Republican from the twenty-fourth ward in 1877 and reelected in 1880, even though he was denied the Republican party's nomination on both occasions.[70] Even more damaging for McManes, his closest associates were vulnerable to electoral defeat. For instance, in February 1881 Nathan Spering was defeated in his bid for reelection to Select Council when dissident Republican "regulars," organized by Samuel Houseman and Israel W. Durham, split the party vote in the seventh ward when they opted to support the Democratic candidate, George R. Snowden.[71] Again, in February 1882, in the elections to Select Council in the eighth, thirteenth, twenty-eighth, and thirty-first wards, four Independent Republicans (A. Haller Gross, J. P. Woolverton, William B. Smith, and James Whitaker) defeated four McManes stalwarts (Don Blair, James Miles, James Dobson, and Frances Martin), even though they failed to secure the Republican party nomination in their respective wards.[72]

The methods of patronage distribution and the nature of party organization enhanced the "independence" of wards and weakened prospective centralized control still further. As noted earlier, the mayor had been gradually shorn of his powers as executive, and the responsibility for city services had become fragmented among more than thirty separate boards and departments. As the bulk of these departments reported to the Councils and not to the mayor, the patronage associated with the new city services fell to the councilmen (see Table 5). Because each ward nominated and elected its own representative, the ward leaders had direct control over the increasing number of municipal jobs. Excluding the gas works and the police department, as well as the "Row" offices, there were more than 4,000 municipal jobs available in 1879, worth more than $2.5 million.[73] An examination of the patronage appointment books for the Water Department reveals that the party that was successful in the Councils in electing its nominee as head of the department secured the spoils. In this case, the Republicans successfully elected William H. McFadden as chief engineer of the Water Department (1873–82), and patronage appointments were distributed among Republican councilmen regardless of the faction with which they were affiliated.[74] The City Committee did not control the distribution of patronage, and neither did any single individual. McManes's chief source of power lay in the gas trust, while Stokley's power, as mayor, lay in the 1,200 privates and 98 officers of the police department.[75]

So Stokley did not build a new political machine by turning the "machinery of government into a vast patronage system." Indeed, the Republican party organization at this time seems to have resembled a feudal hierarchy, because local officials, in return for their partisan support, exercised control over a significant proportion of the material rewards available to the party.

Table 5. The Jurisdiction of Political Appointments, Philadelphia, 1854–1887

Mayor	Councils	City Officers	County ("Row") Offices
Chief of police[a]	Clerks & messengers of Councils	City controller	City treasurer
Chief boiler inspector	Highways commissioner	City coroner	District attorney
Positions held by virtue	Commissioner of markets & city property	City solicitor[a]	Recorder of deeds
of mayoral office:	Chief engineer, Water Dept.	Receiver of taxes[a]	Register of wills
Sinking Fund commissioner	Chief surveyor		Sheriff
Parks commissioner	Fire commission		
Director, Board of City Trusts	Chief of Electrical Dept.		
Managers, House of Refuge	Managers, House of Correction		
Trustee, Penn Museum	Board of Guardians, Phila. Alms House		
	Trustees of the gas works		
	Board of Port Wardens		
	Trustees of city ice boats		
	Board of Health		
	Trustees, N. Liberties Gas Co.		
	Sinking Fund commissioners		
	Buildings inspector		
	Directors of Girard College		
	Directors of railroad cos.[b]		

SOURCES: *The Republican Manual Containing Information in Relation to the Government of the Republican Party in the City of Philadelphia* (Philadelphia, 1857), 81–82; *Manual of Councils, 1885–1886*, 55–99.

[a]Appointments subject to confirmation by Select Council.

[b]The Pennsylvania Railroad and Philadelphia & Erie Railroad companies.

This control not only enhanced their influence within their petty domains but also increased their bargaining power against those who wanted to centralize power within the party organization.

Furthermore, although the abolition of the volunteer fire department in 1871 paved the way for a more disciplined party organization, the Republican party apparatus still remained weak in the 1870s. For example, more than two-thirds of the divisions (twenty-three out of thirty-three) in the nineteenth ward had no year-round organization as late as October 1877, even though this had been mandatory rather than merely permissible in the party rules since 1871.[76]

The absence of an effective party apparatus and the lack of control over the distribution of rewards combined with a set of party practices (ward-level nominations and elections) that effectively precluded the City Committee or any individual "boss" from exerting firm discipline over party workers. Consequently, party leaders such as McManes and Stokley also had difficulty controlling the behavior of their nominal followers in public office. For example, when Stokley received the news that Caven had been elected president of Common Council against both his and McManes's wishes, the *Sunday Times* reported: "His fat cheeks became flushed with excitement and rage." At once, he announced his intention to suspend and revoke the police appointments previously made for the nineteen Republicans who voted for Caven.[77] This incident underscores the weakness of Stokley's position—namely that patronage by itself, without a strong party organization, was not a sufficient guarantee that subordinates would always follow orders.[78]

In sum, then, neither Stokley or McManes was a genuine city boss, though they have been portrayed as such largely because of contemporary assessments of their powers by such observers as Lea, Bryce, and Vickers. Lea and Bryce accurately describe the Republican party structure and organization, but not how it functioned. In their defense, they are not the only ones to have overlooked this crucial distinction. Historians and social scientists, such as Robert Merton, have also subsequently mistaken the hierarchical structure of party organizations for their actual functioning. However, Lea and Bryce also assumed that all officeholders were beholden to McManes, and they failed to distinguish the various factions and contenders for power within the party. One is left with the colorful picture, drawn by Vickers, that depicts a Republican political machine as a monolithic mob with McManes as the supreme nabob, dictating every act and every crime (see Figure 3). Historians like Zink perpetuated the traditional myth of the dictatorial sway of the boss because their research was based on the reform-inspired apocrypha of the times.[79]

"THE GREAT SUPREME."

Fig. 3. Above and facing page: "Michael Mulhooly (James McManes): The Supreme Nabob." Illustrations by Thomas Nast. (From *Solid for Mulhooly: A Political Satire by Rufus E. Shapley*, 2nd ed. [Philadelphia, 1889], 70, 185.)

This is no longer adequate. It is perhaps more accurate to describe McManes and Stokley as leaders of "Rings," an intragovernmental operation that tied a loose coalition of politicians together in the quest for specific material benefits. Unlike ward "bosses," McManes and Stokley were able to exercise power and influence citywide because of the public rather than party offices they *personally* occupied.[80] Ironically, their respective power bases, although unusual features of Philadelphia city government in the second half of the nineteenth century, actually resembled the closed corporation of the eighteenth-century colonial town. The Public Buildings Commission and the gas trust were secret bodies,

THE GENIUS OF THE RING.
The Boss's 'I Will' is the Leaders' 'We Must.'"

not accountable to the Council—the former created by the state legislature, the latter unwittingly invested with autocratic power. The claim that City Hall now stands as a "monument to a new political machine" is misleading, because it was the Republican political machine that emerged in the late nineteenth century that actually canvassed for the abolition of the Buildings Commission. Indeed, when the commission was finally abolished in 1901, U.S. Senator Boies Penrose, Quay's heir as state Republican party leader, telegraphed his congratulations from Washington to his faithful lieutenant in Harrisburg, State Senator James P. McNichol, who along with Israel Durham controlled the new Republican machine in Philadelphia.[81]

A final limitation on "boss" power at this time (and indeed right up until 1951, when Philadelphia finally achieved home rule) was the fact that the city was not a self-contained arena of political activity. The city government was a

creature of the state legislature, and the boundaries of the urban polity were
highly permeable. The dependence and permeability of the urban polity meant
that things happened not only in Philadelphia but also to Philadelphia. For
example, in the absence of a general incorporation law before 1874, the state
legislature exercised its constitutional right to enact special and local legislation. Street railway companies, for instance, were granted access to the streets
of Philadelphia on such terms as the legislature saw fit. In 1868 the legislative
jurisdiction of the city was bypassed completely when the state legislature
passed the so-called "Railway Boss Act," which prohibited the city from
regulating street railroads without specific authorization from the state assembly.[82] The creation of the Public Buildings Commission in 1870 was another
example of the legislature undermining the principle of self-government.[83]

Henry C. Lea blamed the lack of self-government for the failure of Philadelphia's municipal administration, as he explained to fellow reformer John P.
Wetherill in October 1872:

> The source of much of the evil which we suffer is to be found in the
> exaggerated powers exercized by our legislature. We boast that we are
> a free people, and yet there is not a municipality in the state that is
> not subject to a despotism as arbitrary and as irresponsible as that
> which vexes the inhabitants of Moscow or Constantinople. . . . The
> theory of absolute and indefeasible sovereignty residing in the State,
> supreme in all things not specially reserved to the Federal authority,
> places every fragment of the people under a domination as autocratic
> and irresponsible as that of an Eastern despot.
>   . . . Every detail of municipal government . . . is regulated for us
> by those who cannot possibly know anything about it, and in ex-
> change for this we acquire the wretched privilege of similarly interfer-
> ing with the self-government of our fellow citizens. The absurdity of
> such a system is so self-evident that the mere statement of it would
> seem to be sufficient to insure its removal. . . . Our very municipal-
> ity is merely the creature of the legislature, which may abolish it
> altogether at any moment or interfere in the minutest details of its
> organization.[84]

Patronage provided another way in which Philadelphia's political system was
penetrated by external authorities. The state appointed port wardens, physicians, prison and bank inspectors, public notaries, and the city recorder, as
well as county inspectors to regulate trade, weighers of merchandise, measur-

ers of grain, and so forth. The governor controlled more than 660 appointments in Philadelphia in 1876.[85] The national government had even larger patronage resources at its disposal. In addition to the customs house, the federal mint, the Schuylkill and Frankford arsenals, and the Southwark Navy Yard, there were the jobs controlled by the U.S. Marshal in the city—the subtreasurer and postmaster, all of whom were federal appointees.[86]

The limited capacity of city government and the potential intervention of state and national government meant that local politicians were forced to go outside the city itself to achieve their aims. Working for local goals at the state or national level required them to seek allies outside the city. Conversely, the size and importance of Philadelphia led those political actors in the state arena to ally with politicians from the city. Although Philadelphia was the smallest of the sixty-three counties in Pennsylvania in terms of size, its population of 674,022 in 1870 was well over double that of its nearest rival, Allegheny County, which had only 262,204 inhabitants. As the state's second largest city, Pittsburgh's population was only 53,000 in 1870. Philadelphia's political importance can be judged by the fact that in 1870 it accounted for approximately one-quarter of the state's electorate and provided 6 of Pennsylvania's 27 congressmen, 4 of its 31 state senators, and 18 of its 100 state representatives. It also provided 16 members of the Republican State Central Committee formed in 1868, while every other county in the state was restricted to just one representative.[87] Philadelphia was so powerful politically that the *New York Times* claimed that "it was the state." Similarly, the *Harrisburg Patriot* called the state capital "Philadelphia's thirtieth ward."[88] While these claims are exaggerated, they do testify to the crucial significance of Philadelphia in state and national politics. State and federal political actors therefore needed to accommodate the city's politicians if they were to increase their power in the state and federal arena. In the process of jostling for supremacy, they were to change the configuration of political forces in the city in a fundamental way.

3

The Politics of Protest and Reform

The immediate postbellum period marked not only the ascendance of the career politician in Philadelphia's politics but also the beginning of a bitter local struggle that was characteristic of struggles that took place in many other cities nationwide. This conflict has absorbed the interest of the public and scholars ever since. Begun in earnest in the late 1860s, the classic duel between reformers and bosses in Philadelphia dominated local politics for the best part of the next century. But what was the nature of political reform in Philadelphia at the time of its inception, and what role did the city's men of substance play in postbellum Philadelphia?

Two quite different, indeed conflicting, answers to this question have already been provided. Sociologist E. Digby Baltzell and historians Sam Bass Warner Jr. and Russell Weigley have argued that the city's men of wealth (in particular the new business and banking elite that displaced the old colonial gentry at the top of the city's social structure at the time of the Civil War) abandoned local affairs and politics. But contemporary observers, such as George Vickers, Alexander McClure, James Bryce, E. V. Smalley, and subsequently Henry Lea's biographer, Edward S. Bradley, have claimed that reform groups organized by the city's "best men" scored a series of stunning reform victories against "bossism" in the 1870s, culminating in Stokley's defeat in 1881.[1]

Neither interpretation is accurate. The city's businessmen did continue to participate in local affairs, but because reform politics was limited to groups that were few in number, short-lived, poorly organized, and unrepresentative, they did not enjoy the degree of success that contemporary publicists maintained. The reform groups the city's businessmen organized actually played only a peripheral role in the postbellum election and government arena. In fact, they closely resembled the early reform groups that have been categorized as "indigenous" responses to local conditions, that in the absence of a national social-scientific approach to the theory and practice of urban government drew entirely from resources and values already in place and addressed the municipal condition as purely a local one.[2] Reform politics, then, was similar to machine politics at this time in Philadelphia's political development—neither well organized nor centralized.

The "Best Men" in Retreat?

Although the exodus of the wealthy from political life is a familiar theme in the literature on nineteenth-century urban politics, the assertion that Philadelphia businessmen "abandoned the city's affairs and its politics" was misleading, in the sense that their retreat from political office was a postbellum rather than antebellum phenomenon and that it was as much a change forced on them as it was a voluntary gesture on their part.[3] It is necessary, however, to qualify this claim further, for as it stands it bears little relation to historical reality.

That businessmen had not become "ignorant of their city and abandoned its politics" in the postbellum period can be demonstrated in a number of ways. If we take the city's postwar social elite, for instance, an analysis of the thirty-nine men in the city whose income exceeded $25,000 in 1864 reveals that ten, far from "abandoning the city's affairs," were actively engaged in local reform politics (see Table 6). Moreover, these men of wealth were not just members of reform groups; they were prominent activists who occupied important posts of responsibility, and often the prime movers in their formation. For instance, Henry C. Lea, ably supported by Wheeler, Baird, Drexel, and Lippincott, was largely responsible for the organization of the Citizens' Municipal Reform Association (CMRA) in June 1871 and the Reform Club in spring 1872.[4]

The Citizens' Municipal Reform Association was set up in response to the establishment of the Public Buildings Commission by the state legislature in the summer of 1870. Reform publicist George Vickers pinpointed the act creating the commission "as the origin of the reform movement in Philadelphia." He said:

> By creating a body with unlimited tenure of office, with power to fill all vacancies, with authority to tax the community and to spend the public money without restriction or supervision, this act was so subversive of all the principles of self-government that when its provisions came to be fully understood, it aroused general indignation.[5]

The citizens indignant enough to join the reform effort included the city's most prominent bankers, lawyers, manufacturers, and merchants. Of the 75 CMRA activists listed in Appendix 1, for example, 25 were manufacturers, 17 were lawyers, 16 were merchants, and 4 were bankers; 4 publishers, 2 stockbrokers, 2 physicans, and a railroad president, newspaper publisher, hotel proprietor, and painter made up the remainder. These reformers varied in background as well as in occupation. Some, such as "gentlemen lawyers" Clement Biddle, Theodore Cuyler, and William Rawle, were descendants of the city's "first families" of the Revolutionary period, while others, such as Irish immigrant and locomotive manufacturer Matthew Baird, ironmaster Charles Wheeler, and publisher Joshua Lippincott, had worked themselves out of poverty to establish million-dollar businesses. Still others, such as publisher Henry C. Lea, ironmaster J. Vaughan Merrick, and bankers Anthony J. Drexel and Edward W. Clark, had inherited their respective family businesses.[6] The reformers also differed in their political allegiance. While the majority of them were strongly Republican, the group did include conspicuous Democrats, such as Lehman Ashmead, James Dougherty, William Massey, and Colonel James Page.[7]

As a whole, then, the reform group included an impressive cross section of the city's best citizens. Given the differences between them, such unity would be remarkable had they not been accustomed to joint intervention in local politics in the past—for instance, in sponsoring the political consolidation of Philadelphia and the chartering of the Pennsylvania Railroad, on the basis that it would be for the general good of the business community and the

Table 6.   Elite Philadelphians and Their Political Activities, 1871–1886

Name	Occupation	CMRA	Reform Club	Comm. of 100	Other
Matthew Baird (2nd)[a]	Locomotive manufacturer	Central Council	M	—	UL
Charles Wheeler (5th)	Ironmaster	Tr.	M	M	CSRA, UL
Anthony J. Drexel (6th)	Banker	Finance Comm.	VP	Tr.	CSRA, UL
Edward W. Clark (14th)	Banker	—	—	M	CMA
J. Vaughan Merrick (17th)	Ironmaster	Central Council	—	—	CMA, CSRA
Joshua B. Lippincott (18th)	Publisher	Central Council	VP	—	UL
Clarence H. Clark (21st)	Banker	—	—	—	CMA
Henry C. Lea (27th)	Publisher	VP	P	M	CMA, CSRA, UL
John Wanamaker (33rd)	Dry-goods merchant	—	—	M	CSRA
Clement Biddle (39th)	Lawyer	M	M	—	MC 1871, UL

SOURCES: E. Digby Baltzell, *An American Business Aristocracy* (New York, 1958), 108; Howard F. Gillette, "Corrupt and Contented: Philadelphia's Political Machine, 1865–1887" (Ph.D. diss., Yale University, 1970), 53–54; Citizens' Municipal Reform Association, *Committee and Membership* (Philadelphia, 1871); *Committee of One Hundred* (Philadelphia, [c. 1882]); Citizens' Municipal Association, *Constitution. By-Laws, and List of Members* (Philadelphia, 1886); Civil Service Reform Association of Philadelphia, *First Annual Report of the Executive Committee* (Philadelphia, 1882), 37–48.

NOTE: One elite Philadelphian actively engaged in politics but not included in this table is Thomas Dolan (11th), on the grounds that as chairman of the state Republican party in 1882 he was an associate of Matthew Quay and the state Republican machine, and not a participant in reform activities. See Chapter 7.

[a]The figure in parentheses indicates the position of the elite member in Baltzell's table of the wealthiest individuals in the city in 1864.

CMA = Citizens' Municipal Association; CSRA = Civil Service Reform Association; M = Member; MC 1871 = Democratic party candidate in 1871 mayoral election; P = President; Tr. = Treasurer; UL = Union League; VP = Vice-president.

city as a whole.[8] This tradition, by which government and business formed a partnership for the public good, provided the common ground for businessmen reformers.[9]

Unity among businessmen was also fostered by such organizations as the Commercial Exchange and the Board of Trade. Founded in 1854 by merchant reformer George L. Buzby, precisely for the purpose of bringing businessmen of all types together, the Commercial Exchange listed among its membership in 1871 manufacturers from the reform groups—for example, William Massey (brewer), Barton Jenks (textiles), and Israel P. Morris (iron), and merchants Henry Winsor (shipping) and John Wetherill and Amos R. Little (dry goods). Links between merchants and manufacturers were strengthened further through exclusive social clubs, such as the Union League, of which at least thirty of the seventy-five CMRA activists were members.[10] What brought businessmen together in the immediate postwar period was not a scheme for internal improvements, for instance, but a common threat to the security of their wealth—in this case the career politician who had taken control of the local Republican party organization and city government.

The sense of injustice men of wealth felt at the loss of their social and political leadership was aggravated by the economic consequences of the influx of "fourth rate political ward jobbers into Councils who go there not for the honor but for the plunder."[11] Businessmen reformers were particularly alarmed on two counts. On the one hand, they believed the city's finances were out of control and that escalating levels of taxation, expenditure, and indebtedness had to be arrested, or else the "inevitable result [will] be the destruction of our credit and a crushing burden of taxation that will destroy the sources of our prosperity."[12] On the other hand, they were aggrieved that, in spite of "the vast sums which have been levied upon us," basic city services were still poor and inadequate.[13] The CMRA maintained:

> The sums so recklessly squandered during the past ten or twelve years should have given us the best ordered, cleanest, best-paved, best-lighted city in Christendom, with exhaustless supplies of pure water, a model police force and a school system unapproachable in its excellence and completeness. Yet there is not a third-rate city in Europe that is not our superior in most of these necessary adjuncts to modern civilization. Our streets never were filthier nor so constantly in need of repair, breeding pestilence and wearing out horses and vehicles. Our gas never was so poor or so dear; our water supply so indifferent in quality and insufficient in quantity; our school system manifesting

so alarming a tendency to extravagance and corruption; our police force so passive in maintaining order and so active in perpetrating election frauds.[14]

The reason "we are so deficient in nearly all the comforts and adornments which befit a great metropolis" is "the culpable neglect of the authorities"— in particular, "fraud and extravagance" on the part of "a few hundred idle and worthless politicians [who] grow rich, while the people are plundered and receive comparatively nothing, either in good government or necessary improvements."[15] The reformers identified the two "sources of evil from which we suffer"[16] as being "the fact that the people of our large cities really do not govern themselves"[17] and

> the heated partisanship which has led our citizens to sacrifice their better judgement and independence to the dictates of party discipline, and to support the "regular nominees" of their political faith irrespective of the character and qualifications of candidates. . . .
> . . . Corruption, incapacity and self-seeking have become recommendations for office, and our municipal government has thus necessarily passed into the hands of the corrupt and incapable.

The remedy for the city's problems, the reformers believed, "lies in emancipating ourselves from the bonds of party discipline."

> It lies in recognizing the difference between the business of supplying our community with water, gas, cleaning, paving, schooling, and justice, and the great questions of statesmanship which divide the country at large into political parties.
> Between these there is no necessary connection, and the object of the Reform Association has been to form an organization through which men of the most opposite political convictions could unite in the work of securing an honest, efficient and economical transaction of municipal business without thereby proving false to their political allegiance or endangering the success of their respective parties throughout the nation.[18]

The reformers set themselves a simple general objective: "to reform, if possible, existing abuses and to prevent their reoccurrence by causing honest men to be elected to legislative and municipal office."[19] They set about achieving this objective, in the first instance, by attempting to secure additional support from the rest of the business community. At Henry Lea's instigation, they organized the Reform Club, designed to counteract the feeling among businessmen that independent voting in local elections would aid Democratic attempts to lower tariffs. The Reform Club's constitution, like the CMRA's charter, prevented it from participating in state or national politics, and consequently the reformers confined their activities to municipal affairs, which they regarded "as simply a matter of business and not of politics."[20]

In order to secure the election of capable, honest men, irrespective of party, the reformers reasoned that it would be necessary initially "to arouse public indignation."[21] Accordingly, they sought to demonstrate to the electorate, by way of pamphlets, tracts, addresses, and public meetings, that "we were being most frightfully robbed and misgoverned."[22] For example, they issued tracts purporting to show the prevalence of ballot fraud under the existing registration and election laws, the reckless extravagance of the "Row offices" and the fee system, how funds were misappropriated by the city treasurer, and how levels of taxation and expenditure were outstripping the growth of population and the value of property.[23] In a similar vein, Henry Lea published a political satire in September 1872 entitled *Songs for the Politicians,* which included "The Respectable Man" and "The Educated Hog," ridiculing respectable middle-class citizens who, driven by conformity or self-interest, always voted for the "regular" ticket. The hired thug who intimidated the voter at the polls was the subject of "The Battle Song of the Rounder," and "The Lament of the Taxpayer" was devoted to citizens, who always ended up the loser.[24]

For all their propaganda, however, the reformers failed miserably in the electoral arena. The maximum number of votes they collected when they presented their own ticket for county officers, for example, was in 1872, when they received just 13,000 votes out of the 90,000 cast.[25] The reformers blamed national issues, ballot fraud, and the novelty of independent voting for their poor performance.[26]

Although frustrated in their electoral efforts, they were more successful in their attempt to curb state legislative interference in local affairs. In this respect, they were beneficiaries of (as well as participants in) the successful campaign for constitutional revision launched in the early 1870s, following the widespread publicity given to allegations of political corruption in the state government.[27] In presenting the reformers' proposals in January 1873 to the state convention that was given the task of drawing up a new constitution, Lea argued that responsible local self-government in Philadelphia could be realized only if the way the state legislature enacted special and local legislation was ended, the voter registration and election laws were changed, the system of administering justice in petty cases was reformed, the fee system was abolished, and provision was made for the punishment of bribery of public officials.[28]

By stripping the Republican-dominated Board of Aldermen of supervisory control of the voter registration system, forbidding special and local legislation, and replacing fees with a salaried system and making bribery punishable, the convention accepted every one of the reformers' suggestions except for the proposal that elected aldermen be replaced by magistrates appointed by the governor.[29] With the adoption of a new state constitution in 1874, reform activity subsided as the city's "best men," confident that the foundations for responsible local government had been laid, turned their attention to the effort to bring the nation's centennial celebration to Philadelphia.[30] A new era in Philadelphia politics failed to materialize, however, and when the opportunity arose to exploit the factional rivalry within the Republican party, the city's businessmen, inspired by paper manufacturer E. Dunbar Lockwood and dry-goods merchant Amos Little, mobilized in November 1880 "to give the Gas Trust its death blow."[31]

The Committee of One Hundred closely resembled earlier reform groups in both its membership and objectives. Indeed, thirteen former members of the CMRA—including Lea, Drexel, and Wheeler—were members of the original committee set up on November 26 (see Appendix 2). Of the 137 members who participated between 1880 and 1883, a substantial majority listed their occupations within the business community as merchants (45), manufacturers (30), or professional men (13).[32] Like their predecessors, committee members also pursued their business interests in civic and social organizations, for 56 of them belonged to the Board of Trade and 70 belonged to the Union League. The committee's high social status can be adjudged from the fact that two-thirds of its members (90) were listed in Boyd's Blue Book, which described itself as a "society directory containing a list of the names and addresses of the elite of the city of Philadelphia."[33] In a subsequent review of early reform groups, the Municipal League of Philadelphia depicted the Committee of One Hundred as being "a select body of men" that represented "in its personnel many of the city's commercial and professional interests."[34]

Initially conceived as an Independent Republican body "seeking to reform the management of the Republican party," the Committee of One Hundred quickly abandoned the notion of "reform within the party" in favor of an "effort on behalf of the whole people."[35] "Believing in the principle that party interests must be subordinate to those of the whole city," the committee sought to "restore the honest administration of the early days of the municipality" and thereby to make "the government of the city . . . a model of efficiency and economy."[36] The reformers, like their predecessors, believed this could be achieved by securing "the nomination and election of a better class of candidate for office," maintaining "the purity of the ballot," prosecuting those "guilty of election frauds, maladministration of office and misappropriation of public funds," and promoting "a public service based upon character and capability only."[37] In pursuit of the latter, sixty-three (41 percent) members of the committee also enrolled in the local Civil Service Reform Association.[38]

The reformers met with instant success in the first election they contested, for the joint ticket they presented with the Democrats defeated the regular Republican ticket headed by Stokley. The election of Samuel G. King as mayor and John Hunter as receiver of taxes in February 1881 marked the beginning of the committee's five-year involvement in local politics.[39] The reform group confined itself largely to endorsing candidates for public office who "at the very least [were] law-abiding citizens, known for their sobriety, morality, trustworthiness and general fitness."[40] To ensure that only the most suitable candidates for the Councils and for ward offices were selected, a subcommittee on ward organization was instructed to set up "auxiliary committees of citizens in every ward" made up of "all persons desirous of cooperating with the Committee of One Hundred."[41] The reformers' commitment to nonpartisanship in local affairs meant that they endorsed candidates irrespective of party, and sometimes candidates of neither party.

A further subcommittee, on legislation, was set up "to promote such measures as are necessary in the interest of reform."[42] It reported in favor of civil service reform and structural changes in the system of city government, and when these proposals were incorporated in the Bullitt Bill, the reformers sent a delegation to Harrisburg to support the measure.[43] With the adoption of the Bullitt Bill as the new city charter in 1885, the Committee of One Hundred formally disbanded in January 1886.[44]

So, contrary to received wisdom, the city was still important to local businessmen in their daily lives and the latter had not abandoned its affairs or its politics in the postbellum period. Indeed, the idea that the wealthy would abandon local politics solely for profits does not square with common sense. For instance, businessmen as local residents were the wealthiest city-dwellers and therefore had a vested interest in city politics and government because of taxation. Besides, city government was charged with important housekeeping functions that determined everything from the value of real estate to the use of police as strikebreakers; and men of wealth, like citizens in general, also cared deeply about the provision of basic city services—water, gas, street lighting, parks, and police and fire protection—particularly at a time of rapid urban growth.

It was a mixture of resentment at the deterioration of municipal services, amid fears that the rapid growth of the city budget was endangering the security of wealth against taxation, that prompted men of substance to organize the first of a series of reform groups aimed at improving local government. In December 1869, for example, a number of local businessmen set up the Citizens' Association for the Improvement of Streets and Roads of Philadelphia to pass on complaints about the city's streets to the appropriate authorities.[45] And in June 1871 the CMRA was organized in response to the creation of the Public Buildings Commission, which the reformers pointed out, was "empowered to tax us without limit, and to spend our money without supervision, to hold office without restriction of time, and to fill all vacancies in their own body, [thus] inflicting on us all the evils of taxation without representation."[46]

The received wisdom makes sense only if by "the city's affairs and its politics" it is referring to "public office," for in this respect the retreat of the wealthy is marked. Even such a committed reformer as Henry C. Lea could not be persuaded to enter formal politics. For example, in November 1878, when Joseph Caven suggested that he put his proposals for the reform of the gas works into effect by running for the office of trustee, Lea replied:

> Mr. Henry assures me that I could be of substantial service, owing to the factions within the trust, and that it would enable you to overthrow the "Gas Ring" which has so long exercised a baneful influence over our politics . . . [but] . . . I long ago determined never to accept public office of any kind, and the one in question would be especially distasteful to me as a proper performance of its duties would involve labor incompatible with my other engagements.[47]

The Committee of One Hundred prided itself that "not a single member was a politician or an aspirant for office."[48] Anxious to avoid the fate of its predecessor, the CMRA—which was dismissed as a "mere party of office seekers [who] have no right to reproach others on the same account" when it placed its own members on an election ticket—the committee's Articles of Association provided

> that no person holding any important office under the national, state or city government shall be eligible for membership; and that any member becoming a candidate for office shall cease to take an active part in the affairs of the Committee; and if elected shall cease to become a member.[49]

Although unwilling to run for public office themselves, the reformers were still committed to bringing about political change through the election of men "whom office seeks, rather than those who seek office."[50] How successful were they?

The "Forward March of Reform"?

According to contemporary observers James Bryce, George Vickers, Liberal Republican Alexander McClure, newspaper reporter E. V. Smalley, and subsequently Lea's biographer, Edward S. Bradley, a well-organized reform movement was not only preeminent in local party politics in the immediate postbellum period but also scored a series of remarkable victories against "bossism." Beginning with the "practical political coup" by which the CMRA succeeded in defeating gas trustee William E. Rowan's election bid for the office of sheriff in 1876, the reformers made a "break in Bossism's Wall" by electing, and reelecting, the Democrat Robert E. Pattison to the post of city controller in 1877 and 1880.[51] "This evidence of Independent strength so encouraged the remnant of the old Reform Association," Bradley suggests, "that E. Dunbar Lockwood convened a Committee of One Hundred leading citizens of Independent sympathies to put in nomination at coming elections [February 1881] a slate of local officers who should have at heart the best interests of the city." He continues: "Thus began a movement which continued with increasing success until 1886 when the passage of the Bullitt Bill assured the end of the Gas Trust."[52]

In the wake of Stokley's defeat in February 1881, contemporary journalist E. V. Smalley noted:

A great change has recently been brought about by the sincere, courageous, and persistent efforts of a few businessmen acting in the field of politics but outside of party lines. These men successfully appealed to the conscience, self-interest and public spirit of the best classes of their fellow citizens.[53]

Similarly, Alexander McClure in his autobiography subsequently claimed:

The Committee of One Hundred came into power and found it possible to enforce something approaching honest elections, and they thoroughly revolutionized the city. It was the best-directed reform movement of modern times. It was made up of practical businessmen who understood that idealism in politics was good in theory, but utterly valueless in practice, and they not only defeated the notoriously corrupt machine men of the city, but they defeated men of the highest standing who adhered to and sustained the organization, thereby giving it the benefit of their reputations. . . . For a full decade, the Republican leaders were under fair notice that Machine candidates would be made to bite the dust.[54]

These claims about the reformers' achievement neatly complement the standard history of the Committee of One Hundred written by George Vickers in 1883, in which Vickers gives a passionate account of how the city's businessmen brought about the fall of bossism in Philadelphia. The impression that bossism was dead and that the city's businessmen were responsible for it was also conveyed in James Bryce's analysis of the Philadelphia "Gas Ring," which relied heavily on Vickers's "little book" for information on local politics and reiterated Vickers's claims.[55]

These claims are, however, similar to the claims the same observers made about the degree of clout allegedly exercised by "bosses" McManes and Stokley—that is, exaggerated. A closer examination of the evidence suggests that contemporary observers not only overstated the role these early reform groups played in local political affairs but also credited them with successes they did not merit.

In the first instance, it is difficult to see how Rowan's defeat in 1876 and Pattison's victories in 1877 and 1880 can be attributed to the efforts of the CMRA, because there was no organized reform activity in the city at this time. Although Vickers and Bradley both argued that the CMRA's work did not come to an end until 1878, there is reason to believe that the group suffered a lingering death and had ceased to be an influential force in local politics since the adoption of the new state constitution in 1874. Vickers himself admitted that "the CMRA although not disbanded, ceased to act politically as an organization after February 1877"—that is, nine months before Pattison's victory later that year.[56]

It seems that the only work carried out under the auspices of the CMRA, after the constitutional reforms it had advocated had been adopted, were Lea's three exhaustive reports on the operation of the gas works under the gas trust, published in 1874.[57] Lea appears to have been an isolated crusader, for as Howard Gillette has pointed out, "his continued activity in the name of reform, publicized as it was after 1875, simply did not represent the existence of any organized reform effort."[58]

This is also suggested by Bradley, who attributes the demise of the CMRA to Lea's enforced absence from the city on the grounds of poor health.[59] In retrospect, Lea himself suggested to Frank W. Leach in March 1905 that the reform group went into decline primarily because

> the task was endless. . . . The essential weakness of all such [reform] efforts is that the powers of evil are untiring and always at work, for they make their living by it, while the volunteers for good have something else to do, in time their energies are spent, they disband and the enemy reoccupies the field. . . . Then came the end, not abruptly, sensationally, as the result of some great catastrophe, which disrupted the organization and ground it into powder. But the simple silent processes of nature were at work. . . . One by one those who labored dropped out and there were none to take their places, and the association quietly went out of existence, having opened the path for those who might come to take up the burthen when a recrudescence of misrule might call for new effort.[60]

The challenge of organizing the forthcoming Centennial Exposition provided the reform volunteers with "something else to do." CMRA member John Welsh, for example, quit his position as the first president of the Reform Club to become chairman of the Centennial Board of Finance. Joseph Patterson, John Wetherill, Nathan Parker Shortridge, Henry Winsor, and Amos Little, of the reform group, also joined the board.[61] Other reformers, including Henry Lea, Clement Biddle, Barton Jenks, Henry Lewis, and William Massey, recognizing the financial boom that America's first world's fair would bring to the city, led fund-raising efforts and "mobilized the financial community with the same spirit as they devoted to the Union League in the Civil War."[62]

Another important factor in accounting for the demise of organized reform activity in the mid-1870s was the serious division reformers suffered within their ranks over the question of partisanship. This was particularly notable in the case of the Reform Club and the Union League. Problems arose over the Reform Club's role in local politics because of the contradiction inherent in its constitution. On the other hand, the club's constitution declared that its "fundamental object . . . is to advance its principles by mutual intercourse and discussion and not as a political or partisan body," but, on the other hand, it was also committed

> to associate . . . for the purpose of aiding in the reform and improvement of the municipal government of the city of Philadelphia, in the election of honest and capable men to fill its offices and represent it in the State legislature, irrespective of their views on national and State politics; in the punishment and prevention of fraud and corruption in municipal officers; and in guarding the rights and privileges of the city of Philadelphia from legislative encroachment.[63]

Consequently, friction developed between reformers who were committed to active intervention in local politics and those who sought political change only through "mutual intercourse and discussion." Indeed, at the very time when the reformers were supposed to have scored their first notable victory over "bossism," the Reform Club had "irreparably split" over the issue of partisanship.[64]

In November 1876, for example, while Rowan failed in his bid to become sheriff, J. V. Ingham filed a suit against the Reform Club in the Court of Common Pleas. The court upheld Ingham's claim that the resolution passed at the club's annual general meeting calling for a "political" assessment of three dollars to be levied on every member for the year 1876–77, to form a special fund to aid municipal reform, was an infringement of the first article of the club's constitution.[65] By the time of Pattison's victory, members who wanted the club to be "a purely social organization" were in the majority, but the acrimony between the two factions persisted to such an extent that the Reform Club was forced to disband in May 1880.[66]

The split in reform ranks over the degree to which they should participate in local affairs emerged even earlier in the case of the Union League. In April 1875 internal dissension erupted among the League's membership when the watchdog committee appointed by the Board of Governors to oversee local elections refused to endorse the Republican party ticket for the forthcoming county election.[67] Since the League was pledged to use its influence to secure the nomination of men who placed the welfare of the people above party interests, the Committee of Sixty-Two reasoned that because Henry Bingham and David Lane were members of the Society of Mysterious Pilgrims they were unfit to hold public office. Furthermore, the committee publicly condemned the Pilgrims as, "that dictatorial band of men, nominally of both parties, but without true allegiance to either, which now rules and oppresses our city and is disgracing and destroying the Republican organization."[68] Some members were outraged by this stand, particularly since Bingham was a director of the Union League. Others felt that by making its conclusions public knowledge the watchdog group had exceeded its responsibility. At the subsequent annual general meeting, a majority of the League's members voted in favor of an amendment to the bylaws that "the League as a body should not hereafter take part in municipal politics unless otherwise directed by members in General Meeting."[69] By 1876, then, the League had effectively withdrawn from municipal politics and in the future would concentrate only on national affairs.

If Rowan's defeat and Pattison's success did not mark "the beginning of the forward march of reform," how can we account for these election results? In short, a combination of party factionalism and independent voting, rather than the efforts of a well-organized reform movement, was responsible for Rowan's failure and Pattison's victory. As noted in the last chapter, the Republican party was rent by factionalism in the 1870s, as three loose coalitions of politicians led by McManes, Stokley, and Disston, respectively, contended for power within the party. The fact that Rowan was the only citywide Republican candidate who failed to be elected in November 1876 suggests that his defeat was due to party factionalism. While City Treasurer Delos Southworth and Presidential candidate Rutherford B. Hayes obtained majorities of 14,720 and 15,427 votes, respectively, Rowan lost to the Democratic candidate William Wright by 6,227 votes. Because he consistently polled fewer votes than Southworth in the election returns for Disston's twenty-ninth ward (10.6 percent), Leeds's tenth ward (13.0 percent), Stokley's ninth ward (8.3 percent), and Martin's nineteenth ward (6.6 percent), it seems likely that Rowan was cut by the supporters of McManes's factional rivals within the party (see Figure 4). Suspicion of party treachery is also suggested by the fact that Disston was the nephew of the Democratic candidate and that Wright's chief supporters were Lewis Cassidy and Thomas

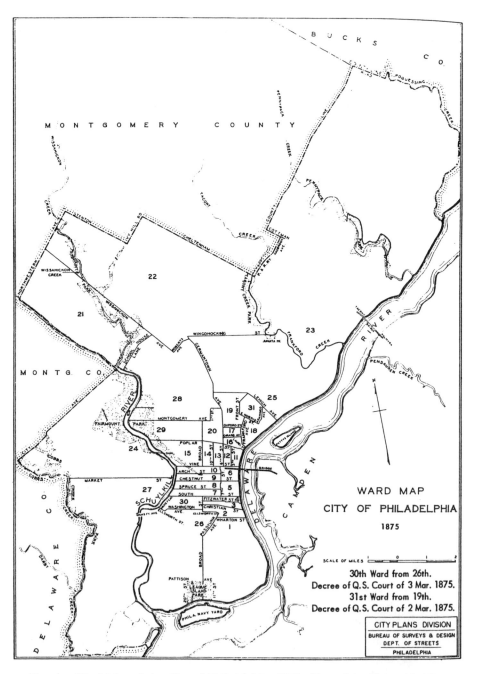

Fig. 4. Ward Map of the City of Philadelphia, 1875. (From John Daly and Allen Weinberg, *Genealogy of Philadelphia County Subdivisions,* 2nd ed. [Philadelphia, 1966], 72.)

Barger, who were both Pilgrims and allies of Stokley on the Buildings Commission.[70]

Rowan's close association with McManes, and his reputation as a "jobbing politician," also apparently cost him the support of many traditional Republican voters. E. V. Smalley reported before the election:

> The Republicans of Philadelphia are loaded with a candidate for Sheriff in the person of the regular nominee Mr. Rowan, whom many thousands of them are refusing to carry. For many years he has been a prominent spoilsman in the corrupt councils ring and his reputation is so bad that before the County Convention met, every decent Republican paper in the city attacked him.[71]

The returns of traditional Republican suburban wards such as the twenty-second ward (Germantown) and Caven's fifteenth ward, where Rowan polled 14 percent and 11.3 percent less votes than Southworth, respectively, indicates that Smalley's assessment may well have been accurate.[72]

Party factionalism also seems to have been responsible for Pattison's victory in 1877, even though reform publicists insisted it was another step in "the forward march of reform." By failing to stress that the CMRA, the Reform Club, and the Union League did not take any part in the election campaign, and that the whole Democratic ticket was elected, not just Pattison, the accounts of these contemporary observers give a misleading impression of Pattison's election victory. Pattison himself suggested to the Democratic convention that nominated him that "the signs of the times" such as "the dissensions of the Republicans, and their maladministration in office while in power," "point to victory." [73] Leach concluded that "the rampant factional strife within the ranks of the 'regular' Republican politicians" was the "determining" factor in the election.[74] The election returns also indicate that James Sayre, Russell Thayer, and Andrew J. Knorr suffered the same fate as Rowan had the previous year, for the Republican ticket was cut again by a combination of Disston and Stokley supporters.[75]

As Pattison was the only candidate on the Democratic ticket to be elected in November 1880, and since this year was also a Presidential election year, when party lines were traditionally more tightly drawn, it is Pattison's reelection, rather than initial election, that is remarkable. It appears that independent voting, rather than party factionalism, was the main factor responsible for his election victory. Pattison, a young lawyer and son of a Methodist preacher, had so impressed Independent councilmen and many of the city's "best men," in his role as guardian of the city treasury, that Joseph L. Caven organized a rally at which fifty of Philadelphia's leading businessmen who were "Republican in national politics" but "independent in local affairs" endorsed Pattison for reelection.[76] The president of Common Council explained:

> As a Republican I propose on next Tuesday to vote for Garfield because the best interests of the country demand that no change be made in the national administration; as a Republican I propose at the same time to vote for Robert Pattison for Controller because the best interests of Philadelphia demand that no change be made in the administration of that office.[77]

Thousands of Philadelphians seem to have followed Caven's line on election day, for while Garfield and three local Republican candidates carried the city by more than 20,000 votes, Pattison defeated Harper Jeffries by 13,593 votes.[78] Both Bradley and Vickers acknowledged that Pattison's victory was not due to the efforts of an organized reform movement. Bradley suggests that "Independent strength" in the form of a "public protest against corruption overwhelmed the bosses," while Vickers notes that the spontaneous bolt against the Republican candidate was "by the people unorganized, by popular sentiment crystallized into tangible opposition."[79] Similarly, the *North American* regarded Pattison's victory as "unmistakably the result of independent personal effort by citizens of character, property, education and responsibility."[80]

The election returns reported in Table 7 suggest that Stokley's defeat in the mayoral election of February 1881 was due to a combination of the independent voting and party factionalism that had characterized local elections over the previous five years. A comparison of the percentage of votes polled by Stokley in 1881 with those received by W. Nelson West, the successful Republican candidate supported by both McManes and the Committee of One Hundred, indicates a repetition of the spontaneous independent bolt in the traditional Republican suburban wards (15, 21, 22, 23, 24, 26, 28, 29) that had brought about Pattison's victory, the previous year. The ward returns from North Philadelphia (13, 14, 16, 17, 18, 19, 20, 31), where McManes's support was particularly strong, also suggest that Stokley was a victim of party factionalism (see Figure 4).

That Stokley's defeat was in part attributable to a suburban protest against the misuse of city funds is also suggested by the fact that ring wards (15, 20,

Table 7. The Republican Party Vote in Selected Philadelphia City Elections (by ward), 1877, 1881 (as % of total vote)

Ward	W.S. Stokley Mayor, 1877		W.S. Stokley Mayor, 1881		W.N. West City Solicitor, 1881
1	58.2	−9.0[a]	49.2	+6.8[b]	56.0
2	40.9	−2.5	38.4	+4.0	42.4
3	40.9	−6.2	34.7	+0.9	35.6
4	53.3	−14.1	39.2	−0.1	39.1
5	60.4	−5.8	54.6	+2.3	56.9
6	45.0	−4.9	40.1	+1.9	42.0
7	61.9	+2.2	64.1	+5.2	69.3
8	58.3	+3.3	61.6	+5.4	67.0
9	52.8	+2.6	55.4	+5.5	60.9
10	63.5	−1.7	61.8	+7.2	69.0
11	34.5	−4.4	30.1	+3.8	33.9
12	49.2	−8.0	41.2	+5.1	46.3
13	51.3	−2.8	48.5	+10.4	58.9
14	52.3	−4.4	47.9	+10.3	58.2
15	46.5	+2.6	49.1	+12.0	61.1
16	48.1	−10.7	37.4	+6.1	43.5
17	35.2	−2.8	32.4	+4.1	36.5
18	50.0	−3.5	46.5	+13.5	60.0
19	46.2	−1.5	44.7	+8.5	53.2
20	49.6	+0.1	49.7	+9.9	59.6
21	52.2	+0.4	52.6	+8.9	61.5
22	53.9	−6.6	47.3	+14.8	62.1
23	53.5	−6.2	47.3	+15.9	63.2
24	47.7	−5.6	42.1	+14.2	56.3
25	42.8	−2.5	40.3	+7.3	47.6
26	57.8	−9.3	48.5	+9.4	57.9
27	65.4	+1.7	67.1	+7.4	74.5
28	52.7	−0.8	51.9	+10.0	61.9
29	50.1	−0.2	49.9	+12.2	62.1
30	50.9	+0.9	51.8	+8.5	60.3
31	50.1	+0.4	50.5	+12.5	63.0

SOURCES: *Inquirer*, February 21, 1877; *Manual of Councils, 1881–1882*, 111; George Vickers, *The Fall of Bossism: A History of the Committee of One Hundred and the Reform Movement in Philadelphia and Pennsylvania*, vol. 1 (Philadelphia, 1883), 129–32; Frank W. Leach, "Twenty Years with Quay," *North American*, March 5 and 12, 1905.

[a]The figures in this column represent the percentage difference between the votes cast for Stokley in the 1877 election, when he was supported by James McManes, and those he received in the 1881 election, when he was opposed by both the Committee of One Hundred and the gas trust leader.

[b]The figures in this column represent the percentage difference between the votes cast for Stokley in the 1881 election and those received by Nelson West, a party candidate supported by both McManes and the Committee of One Hundred.

22, 24, 28, and 29), which consistently provided Republican majorities in mayoral elections between 1865 and 1884, failed to do so in 1881 (see Table 8).[81] The idea that Stokley's defeat was also due to McManes supporters "cutting" his candidacy is not too surprising when we recall that the mayor had used similar tactics in previous years to prevent the election of party nominees endorsed by the gas trust faction. Moreover, publication of the political satire *Solid for Mulhooly* by one of Stokley's close associates, along with the mayor's campaign pledge to abolish the gas trust, suggests that the "ticket-cutting" was probably an important feature of the election, as the *Times* maintained.[82]

Attributing Stokley's defeat to the intervention of the Committee of One Hundred was not the only error these reform publicists committed. They also made the mistake of assuming that, simply because the Committee of One Hundred endorsed the Democratic candidate, Samuel G. King, for the mayoralty, the reform group must have been responsible for his victory. They wrongly credited this "reform success" to the committee, when by their own admission the "strength of the city's Independent voters" to which they referred, was an "unorganized" phenomenon that had emerged as a significant factor in local elections before the reform groups had even been set up.[83]

Furthermore, the notion that the Committee of One Hundred was even capable of, let alone solely responsible for, dealing bossism a stunning blow in February 1881 is difficult to sustain. The committee did not really have sufficient time to mobilize the "Independent strength" of the electorate, since it was only actually organized on November 26, 1880, and did not finally agree on a mayoral candidate until just two weeks before the election day.[84] And because "not a single member" of the committee "was a politician or an aspirant for office," as E. V. Smalley emphasized, it is also debatable whether these businessmen had the necessary expertise to organize a great political movement.[85] Even more serious, however, was that the reformers were divided over what tactics should be employed to secure a reform victory. The committee was badly split over whether to seek reform "within the (Republican) party" or outside party lines.

Given the failure of past nonpartisan reform groups, such as the CMRA and the Reform Club, the Committee of One Hundred was initially set up purely as an Independent Republican body "seeking to reform the management of the Republican party."[86] However, the group's executive committee "caused consternation" at the general meeting of December 20, 1880, when, after "considering the subject of the nomination of proper candidates for municipal offices to be chosen at the February election," it recommended

Table 8. Philadelphia City Wards Returning a Majority for Republican Mayoral Candidates, 1865–1884

Year	Candidate	50–55%	55–60%	60% +
1865	McMichael	9	8	1 7
(26)[a]		16 19	13 15	10 14 18
		20 23 24	21 22	26
1868	Tyndale	1 7 8 9		
(28)		13 19	14 15 18	10
		20 24 27	21 22 23 26	
1871	Stokley	8 9		1 7
(29)		16	13 14 15 16 19	10 18
		24	20 27 28 29	21 22 23 26
1874	Stokley	9	5 8	1 7
(29)		12 13	14 16 18 19	10 15
		20 21 24 25 28	26 29	27
1877	Stokley	4 9	1 8	5 7
(31)		13 14 18		10
		21 22 23 28 29	26	27
		30 31		
1881	Stokley	5	9	7 8
(31)				10
		21 28		27
		30 31		
1884	Smith	5 9	1 8	7
(31)		13 14 15 19	10 18	
		20 22 24	21 23 28 29	26 27
				30 31

SOURCES: Election statistics published in the *Inquirer*, October 11, 1865; October 14, 1868; February 18, 1874; February 21, 1877; February 16, 1887; and *Manual of Councils, 1881–1882*, 111.

[a]The figure in parentheses represents the total number of wards in the city at the time each mayoral election was held. Ward 27 was subdivided from ward 24 in 1866; 28 from 21 in 1867; 29 from 20 in 1871; and 30 from 26 and 31 from 19 in 1875. See John Daly and Allen Weinberg, *Genealogy of Philadelphia County Subdivisions*, 2nd ed. (Philadelphia, 1966), 69–72.

that the Committee of One Hundred should actually endorse Stokley for the mayoralty.[87] The "general uproar" subsided only after executive member James A. Wright explained to the meeting that Stokley's nomination was recommended because the mayor had promised the committee he would support certain reform measures, such as transferring the gas works to the city and establishing a police force free of political influence.[88] The general meeting eventually voted in favor of Stokley's nomination, 52 to 30.[89] (That 40 members of the committee, one-third of the entire body, were absent from the meeting also calls into question whether the businessmen were genuinely committed to political reform.)

Convinced that the group had made a fatal error in endorsing Stokley, Rudolph Blankenburg and John Verree resigned and organized a rival Businessmen's Committee to promote the nomination of manufacturer Edward T. Steel for mayor.[90] That Blankenburg and Verree were correct in their assessment was soon confirmed, for when Stokley secured the Republican nomination for mayor on January 13, 1881, he reneged on his promises to the reformers and ignored their request that he endorse the Committee of One Hundred's Declaration of Principles.[91] Consequently, the committee withdrew its nomination of Stokley and, recognizing that it had been "deluded" by the notion of "reform within the party," amended its Declaration of Principles to permit "a union of all the elements of opposition to the Ring, irrespective of party."[92] This about-turn on how best to achieve political reform in local politics was sufficient to woo Blankenburg and Verree back to the group, but the subsequent endorsement of Select Councilman Samuel G. King, the Democratic nominee, for the mayoralty, on January 30, 1881, led several prominent members—among them Anthony J. Drexel, Henry Winsor, William Sellers, Benjamin Comegys, Oliver Evans, Frederick Loeble, James Dobson and R. H. Griffith—to resign from the committee in protest at its betrayal of the Republican party.[93]

The division between reformers over the question of partisanship continued to undermine the effectiveness of the Committee of One Hundred in local elections, however. For example, in the 1884 mayoral campaign, twenty-three members, led by Edward R. Wood, John P. Wetherill, and Lemuel Coffin, resigned from the committee when the group voted to endorse Samuel King for reelection, in preference to the Republican nominee, Independent Republican Councilman William B. Smith.[94]

Apart from the "internal weakness manifested in the ranks of the organization itself," the Municipal League later attributed the committee's lack of "vigor and success" to the fact that the group was not "thoroughly representative" and not "well-organized in every ward of the city."[95] With reference to the former, we have already noted that the members of the Committee of One Hundred, like their predecessors in the CMRA and the Reform Club, were a socially exclusive group, but since almost half (forty-two) of them lived in fashionable neighborhoods, such as Rittenhouse Square (eighth ward) in Center City, or in prestigious suburban districts, like Chestnut Hill and Germantown (twenty-second ward), they were also residentially segregated from the bulk of the city's population. Moreover, as one-third of the city's wards (10 out of 31) were not represented on the committee at all, the group's geographical isolation was accentuated even more (see Appendix 2).[96]

Because the Committee of One Hundred was also a self-constituted body that conducted political affairs in an autocratic manner, there is reason to believe that the efforts of the city's "best men" had little impact on the city's electorate.[97] As the *Times* suggested, the committee, like its predecessor the CMRA, was composed of men who "sat in their cosy parlours and cooked up tickets for others to vote and issued flaming manifestos to the public but like the Pope's bull against the comet, these paper bulletins amounted to little or nothing because the masses of people were not taken into account."[98] Similarly, committee member George H. Earle Jr. later conceded to Frank W. Leach that the reform group had "perished" because it "was essentially aristocratic in temperament," while former CMRA executive officer John J. Ridgway even suggested that the committee's "entire course [had] alienated the public."[99]

The reformers' influence in local elections was also hampered by their poor organization and their dislike of political activism. The committee's participation in local elections was limited merely to endorsing candidates on the recommendation of the group's executive committee for citywide offices, or on behalf of its "auxiliary committees of citizens in every ward" for district offices.[100] Contemporary newspapers judged the committee's success or failure in local politics on this basis. For example, in February 1882 they heralded a "reform victory" since three-quarters of those elected to the Councils had been endorsed by the Committee of One Hundred, whereas in February 1884 they deemed the successful election of all regular Republican nominees to be a "Reform Waterloo."[101] Consequently, the impression the reader gets is that the committee played a dominant role in local elections— for example, the committee was solely responsible for the election of forty-two of the fifty-four councilmen elected in February 1882 and therefore fully deserved its reputation as being the "conqueror of the bosses."[102] While we cannot be certain about the extent to which the Committee of One Hundred influenced local elections, opposition to boss rule was never matched by comparable political organization.

Historian Philip S. Benjamin attributes the reluctance of the "gentlemen reformers" to build an effective political organization to the strong Quaker

influence on the Committee of One Hundred. He points out that although
the Quaker portion of the city's population was less than 1 percent, almost
one-fifth of the group's members were prominent Friends. [103] Even though
"the operations of boss rule clearly violated standards basic to the Quaker
ethos," Benjamin argues, "the Quakers proved hesitant and ineffectual as
political reformers" because they were "unable to resolve the dilemmas posed
by . . . the Friends' tradition of avoiding active participation in politics and
of their [usual] attachment to the Republican party." [104]

The committee disliked political activism and organization so much that
they refused to endorse William B. Smith for the mayoralty in February 1884
even though they had supported his election to Select Council in two earlier
campaigns and had applauded his stand against McManes, as president of the
upper chamber, from 1882 to 1884. The reformers believed Smith's method
of campaigning was "undignified" and "unethical" because he conducted a
personal canvass of the city and made a direct appeal to the party's division
workers. [105]

Even if the reformers could have overcome their "distaste for organization
on the ward and precinct level," they would have had difficulty establishing a
"viable base to launch their challenge to the machine" because as vehement
opponents of the spoils system they had no way to reward reform volunteers. [106] As McClure pointed out, "the labor of the reformers is a thankless
task. It is all work and no pay beyond the gratification of having performed a
duty to the public." [107] In sum, then, since the reformers both lacked experience and were weakened by divisions over partisanship, and formed groups
that were poorly organized and unrepresentative, they were not capable of
achieving the electoral victories that had traditionally been accorded them.

Finally, reform publicists misrepresented the real significance of the new
city charter when they depicted it as the culmination of the reformers'
achievement, for it was the leaders of the state Republican party—Simon
Cameron and his chief lieutenant, Matt Quay—who were responsible for the
passage of the Bullitt Bill. [108] Their motivation, however, was not to bring
about better urban government but to extend their influence over Philadelphia City Council and the local Republican party organization. [109]

Because of the size of its population, Philadelphia was extremely powerful
politically, particularly in terms of its electoral and representational strength.
Indeed, the city's politicians had played a key role in the factional struggle
between Cameron and Andrew Curtin for control of the state Republican
party organization. Only after allying with "Ring" leader James McManes
and Sheriff William Elliott, for instance, was Cameron able to pressure

William Mann, one of Curtin's most faithful allies, into accepting his leadership of the party.[110] The alliance with McManes, Elliott, Mann, and ultimately Stokley, combined with the deployment of superior patronage resources and the successful conversion of key leaders (such as Quay and Wayne MacVeagh) away from the opposition camp, enabled the resourceful Cameron to establish himself as the undisputed leader of the state Republican party, and also, by attracting Philadelphia's full electoral strength, to withstand the Liberal Republican revolt of 1872.[111]

But Cameron's efforts to control the state legislature were soon handicapped, and the electoral success of the Republican party was at risk, when Philadelphia politicians he had accommodated—Stokley and McManes—began to publicly question his authority[112] and he was forced to take steps to curb their power. His uncompromising insistence, as a senatorial oligarch, on complete loyalty from his personal following placed him in the position of having to eliminate those who stood in his way.[113]

The passage of the Bullitt Bill in 1885 represented the culmination of Cameron and Quay's efforts to eliminate Stokley and McManes as significant political actors in the city's political arena, not of the reformers' achievements. They had begun this process almost a decade earlier, when in the wake of the defeat of the mayor's ally Wilson Henszey for the presidency of Common Council in January 1876 they had supported, through loyal subordinates led by twentieth ward leader and councilman David H. Lane, adoption of a tight spending policy by the new president, Joseph L. Caven, and his Independent associates.[114]

This economy drive, combined with the "Pay-as-You-Go" Act of 1879 (a state legislative bill, sponsored by Caven and again supported by Cameron Republicans, that restricted Philadelphia's debt limit and required each city department to make requests for funds within limits set in advance by the tax rate), had the desired effect not only from the reform perspective of bringing an "end to profligacy" in the administration of city finances, but also from Cameron's viewpoint in the sense that Stokley was seriously weakened as resources for local patronage and opportunities for "honest graft" declined.[115] The policy of retrenchment returned Cameron a handsome dividend for those who suffered most from the misuse of city funds—suburban residents in the city's fastest growing wards expressed their displeasure by switching from their usual Republican allegiance and voting in favor of Stokley's Democratic opponent, Samuel G. King, in the 1881 mayoral election. The strength of the suburban protest vote ultimately cost Stokley the election, and with this defeat he ceased to be a significant factor in the city's politics.[116]

Collaboration with Independent councilmen also played a part in Cameron and Quay's efforts to undermine McManes's position in the city's politics. Joint action in the Councils to secure the election of gas trustees who would be hostile to the "Ring" leader, and the appointment of a committee to investigate alleged mismanagement of the gas works, met with only partial success on this occasion, however.[117] What provided Cameron and Quay with the decisive breakthrough in curbing McManes's power were not the efforts to challenge his leadership of the gas trust or to improve the trust's account-ability, but rather the initiatives they made aimed at diminishing his influ-ence within the local Republican party and also city government.

With regard to the former, the state leaders in May 1883 attempted to lure Independent Republicans back to the ranks of the regular party by organizing a new political club, the United Republican Association (URA) of Pennsylvania. Headquartered in the Betz Building on the northwest corner of Broad and Chestnut streets, adjacent to the new City Hall building, the URA was "brought into being to attract," as Leach put it, "all local elements thought to be in antagonism to the McManes dynasty."[118] That the state leaders were successful in their goal is suggested by the fact that the URA managed to woo not just local party activists who were opposed to McManes, but also prominent businessmen, such as Edward C. Knight, George A. Boker, and Colonel A. Louden Snowden, men who were "staunch Republi-cans in national affairs but not necessarily conspicuous in municipal politics." Independent Republicans, such as Joseph L. Caven and John J. Ridgway, and members of the Committee of One Hundred reform group, like Francis B. Reeves, George D. McCreary, Thomas Learning, H. W. Bartol, Nathaniel E. Janney, and Thomas W. Barlow, also joined the new organization.[119] The *North American* commented that the members of the URA included

> many active young men thoroughly acquainted with political affairs but who have never been attached to the cliques whose power brought the party organization into contempt; and considering the condition of the party at present, it will not be long before the association will exert a powerful influence in shaping the political affairs of the city.[120]

The paper's prediction proved accurate, for by the end of the year the URA, led by Ridgway and supported by Lane, had secured the nomination of "a vigorous opponent of McManes" for the mayoralty: William B. Smith, Independent Republican and president of Select Council.[121] Smith's subsequent victory in the election in February 1884 meant that, for the first time since Cameron's senatorial triumph in 1867, the mayoralty of Philadelphia lay with entirely loyal interests. Henceforth, the *Times* suggested that the local Republican party would be controlled by Quay, Smith, and Lane, "who turn in with the Cameron element."[122]

Cameron and Quay attempted to attract Independent Republicans back to the party organization, not just through the creation of a new political club but also by supporting reformers' efforts to establish a new system of government in Philadelphia. This initiative "startled Independents everywhere," not least because businessmen reformers regarded the provisions of the Bullitt Bill (such as the application of civil service rules to all city employees, the reduction of city departments from thirty-two to nine, and granting the mayor the power of appointment and removal of department heads) as the key to combating "bossism" in local politics. Yet here, ironically, were in their view two of its most conspicuous practitioners supporting the same reform principle they did.[123]

Cameron and Quay supported the same goals as businessmen reformers because it was politically expedient for them to do so, not because of any sincere commitment to reform. For example, it placed them in a positive light in the eyes of reformers and Independents (as they intended), and the Bullitt Bill, if implemented, would (by placing the gas trust under the new Department of Public Works, whose director would be held responsible by appointment to the mayor) abolish McManes's "center of power." Cameron and Quay also favored centralizing power and responsibility under a strong mayor; it would strike a decisive blow against councilmen and ward "bosses" because the practice of having executive departments controlled and administered by committees of the Councils would be eliminated. Philadelphia State Representative Boies Penrose, for example, advised Quay that "the ward and district leaders" who were fighting the Bullitt Bill were "losing influence":

> They're moss covered and sawdust stuffed. They're years behind the times. Younger men who will be more vigorous and harder to control will take their place unless the independent power of those local bosses is taken away and concentrated in a single head. You can control one man, particularly if you've been careful to select a tame and respectable one, but a dozen ignorant saloon-keepers can raise hell.[124]

The irony of Cameron Republicans supporting the same legislation as such reform groups as the Committee of One Hundred and the Civil Service Reform Association did not escape the attention of some contemporaries who recognized the political advantages the former could gain from the bill. In an editorial entitled "Boss Rule in Reform Disguise," McClure's *Times* argued that "the sweeping absolutism of the Bullitt Charter" would produce "an absolute Boss Restoration."[125] The paper claimed:

> Every facility is given for the Bosses to organize the whole city government under their dependents, and when thus organized there will be no power of removal or possibility of reform except by another appeal to a future legislature. With all the audacious villainry of Tweed, no such reckless violence to public rights was ever dreamed of.[126]

In a similar vein, George H. Earle of the Committee of One Hundred predicted that the Bullitt Bill would "create the worst ring which ever ruled the city."[127] Other "highly reputable and well-known citizens," including John Wanamaker, John W. Patton, A. Louden Snowden, Louis Wagner, and George S. Graham, also had doubts about the proposed new charter. They were wary of "the danger of sudden and sweeping change" that would occur if the bill was passed. Since "the Mayor has almost despotic powers," they were also concerned about "the difficulty of electing a good Mayor and the risk of electing a bad or unfit one."[128]

Despite the reservations some of the men of substance had, and the bitter opposition of the "Gas Ring" and the Councils, the Bullitt Bill was passed by the state legislature in May 1885 and went into effect in April 1887.[129] As it transpired, the fears of the minority of the city's best citizens were well founded, for the structural changes in local government implemented under the new city charter did not bring about "the fall of bossism" reformers had anticipated. James Bryce, for instance, subsequently acknowledged that the Bullitt Charter,

> has worked for good . . . [in that] . . . it extinguished the separate gas trust, and therewith quenched the light of Mr. McManes, who ceased to be formidable when his patronage departed, and has now become a "back number" . . . [but] . . . in the stead of Mr. McManes, the State Boss now reigns.[130]

In the process of curbing McManes's power and extending his influence over Philadelphia City Council and the local Republican party, Quay by "turning reformer" also managed to undermine the bonds that held the reformers together. Lucretia L. Blankenburg later recalled: "Senator Cameron stood back of Quay; together they worked to defeat all reform movements in Philadelphia and Pennsylvania. They enmeshed different members of the Committee of One Hundred until they ceased to be reformers and finally were largely the cause of the Committee's dissolution."[131] Thus, political expediency on Quay's part yielded a handsome return: the abolition of McManes's "center of power" and the demise of organized reform activity in the city.

Contrary to the opinion of reform publicists, the new city charter then represented more a triumph for Cameron and Quay than a triumph for genuine political reform. By consolidating power and responsibility in local government, the new charter paved the way "for the worst ring which ever ruled this city," as some men of substance had forecast—a "ring" that was to be controlled not by city politicians, as in the past, but by the state Republican party leader, Matthew S. Quay.

4

Centralization of the Philadelphia Republican Party Organization

During the years immediately following the collapse of the "Gas Ring," the organization and structure of Philadelphia's politics were transformed. Political power that had been fragmented among a number of rival formations was consolidated, and political competition came to be dominated by, and centered on, the struggle between two new protagonists: a full-fledged political machine and a well-organized reform movement. Put another way, power within the city's Republican party was centralized, and the control it in turn exercised over Philadelphia's government expanded to such an extent that the "Organization" emerged as the dominant institution in the local polity. It maintained that position of hegemony, despite concerted reform opposition, for more than thirty years, until the early 1930s.[1] How can we account for this emergence, or institutionalization, of the Republican machine as the central force in the government and politics of turn-of-the-century Philadelphia?

Conventional wisdom suggests that the centralization of political machines was dependent on the ability of a would-be political boss to acquire a monopoly over the distribution of patronage within his domain. Such a mo-

nopoly would enable an aspiring party leader to establish a reliable system of
control and discipline because he would quickly be able to reward politicians
who were loyal to him and starve out those who were not.[2] This is precisely
what happened in the case of Philadelphia. The administrative consolidation
and centralization of authority under the new city charter of 1887 made
available just such a large pool of patronage, and the Organization's leadership established a monopoly over its distribution. That monopoly proceeded
to operate in exactly the manner conventional theorists suggest. Indeed, the
threat of dismissal from public office was regarded by one contemporary
observer, Clinton R. Woodruff, secretary of the National Municipal League
(1894–1920), as the linchpin of "the Philadelphia system."[3]

Even so, the monopolization of patronage distribution cannot by itself
fully explain how the Organization's leadership managed to establish a reliable system of discipline. The difficulties McManes and Stokley faced in
disciplining their subordinates, even when they did control substantial
amounts of patronage in the city, indicate that the explanation conventional
wisdom offers is, at best, only a partial one.

In fact, the emergence of a full-fledged political machine in Philadelphia
came about as a result of a series of innovations initiated by state and local
Republican party leaders, and those innovations transformed the way the
Republican party organization *functioned* at both the state level and the city
level at the turn of the century. This transformation, which was the result of
replacing the Republican "feudal regime" of the 1870s and 1880s with a
centralized political structure, was not simply a natural and automatic consequence of the monopolization of patronage distribution. It was also due to a
number of changes in party methods, rules, recruitment, and finance implemented by the state and city party leadership in a deliberate attempt to
centralize power within the Republican party. How, then, did the respective
party leaders manage to establish a reliable system of control and discipline?

Quayism and Philadelphia

In order to provide a satisfactory explanation, it is necessary first to focus on
developments at the state level. Matt Quay's ability to influence party affairs
in Philadelphia to his own advantage rested on his success in consolidating
power within the state Republican party, a task he undertook in the wake of
James G. Blaine's defeat in the Presidential election of 1884. James Kehl,

Quay's biographer, identifies this election as a key turning point in the development of the state Republican party, because Blaine's defeat finally convinced Quay that the machine Cameron, like other senatorial oligarchs, had operated since the Civil War was inadequate.[4] A variety of factors—the reluctance of Grant's successors to supply adequate amounts of federal patronage to the Camerons; implementation of the Pendleton Civil Service Act in 1883; the party factionalism that resulted from the reliance on patronage; and the twin threat posed by the growing power of business and the rapidly increasing size of urban constituencies—led Quay to conclude that a power base in central government was "too vulnerable for effective boss rule."[5]

With Simon Cameron's approval, Quay therefore decided, in Kehl's words, "not to repair the Cameron machine but to design a new model that shifted the locus of power from Washington to the individual states," and in Pennsylvania, he "personally became the connecting link between the 'interests' and legislative approval of their growing demands."[6] In order to function as an efficient political broker, it was necessary for Quay to control the flow of legislation and appropriations through the state legislature, and this in turn was contingent on his ability to subject party subordinates who staffed the state government to his discipline.

What enabled Quay to establish a reliable system of discipline among his followers was not just the monopoly of federal and state patronage at his disposal (which he regarded as a curse as much as a blessing) but also a regular and independent (of business interests) supply of money.[7] This "income," derived from manipulating public funds in the state treasury, enabled Quay to become

> the new proprietor of Pennsylvania. . . . While governors and legislators directed the affairs of Pennsylvania, . . . Quay manipulated the affairs of governors and legislators. The power of the treasury often elected the officials who came to Harrisburg and just as often despatched them to their homes when they ceased to fulfill the purposes that Quay . . . had designed for them. The treasury made and unmade men; by juggling the state's millions it could arrange personal successes or frame personal tragedies.[8]

While treasury funds enabled Quay to influence the outcome of local elections to state office, it was the power to withdraw patronage and to reduce or withhold state appropriations (as well as the threat to make public any personal or political indiscretion a legislator may have committed) which provided him with the means to ensure that subordinates remained loyal to him during their term of office.[9] Quay was so successful in inducing subordinates to accept his leadership that Independent Republican gubernatorial candidate John Wanamaker claimed in 1898:

> The Republican party of Pennsylvania has well nigh lost its identity. So completely has Quayism taken possession of it that we almost look in vain for any semblance to its former self. . . . The single aim of those who control its organization has been to drive principle, conscience and righteousness out and to let Quayism in.
>
> The party organization has been thoroughly subjugated and is now officered and directed for the benefit of one man and not the Republican party.[10]

The internal consolidation of power within the state Republican party, and the control it in turn exercised over Pennsylvania government, had important consequences not just for reform insurgents but also for the structure and organization of party politics in Philadelphia. We have already seen how Quay, through the creation of the URA and by securing passage of the Bullitt Bill, managed, at McManes's expense, to increase his influence over the Philadelphia Republican party and city government. The establishment of a reliable system of discipline within the state Republican party, combined with the ability to control the flow of legislation and appropriations through the state legislature, enabled Quay to extend his influence over the city's political affairs still further, to the point of being able to impose his personal choice as leader of the local Republican organization.

"From his seat in the U.S. Senate," as Steffens put it, Quay chose "David Martin for boss. . . . [He] raised up his man and set him over the people. . . . Boss Martin picked up and set down from above was accepted by Philadelphia and the Philadelphia machine."[11] Martin was "accepted" because Quay, by discriminating in granting or withholding support for appropriations to public agencies, and for legislation designed to meet the needs of corporate interests, made it clear to Philadelphia businessmen, financiers, social service agents, and politicians that the nineteenth ward leader was the correct local "political channel" to use to ensure that their claims for government support would receive preferential treatment.[12]

Martin was not plucked from political obscurity by Quay, as Steffens implies. He had held a variety of public offices, such as county commissioner, mercantile appraiser, and sergeant-at-arms in the state and national

House of Representatives, and was as well a local Republican party ward leader, when Quay "declared" him "to be the boss of Philadelphia."[13] Martin was, however, a Quay-made man in the sense that his promotion to city boss was due to the state party leader who subsequently made the former garbage collector "a full-time member of his state organization and even advanced him to the Republican National Committee in 1891."[14] It was also through Quay's intervention that Martin was appointed to the prestigious federal office of Collector of Internal Revenue by President Harrison in May 1889. Indeed, it was through the judicious distribution of federal and state patronage that Martin struck the final blow against McManes by establishing control over the Republican City Committee. In gratitude for his elevation, Martin, as local party leader, willingly took orders from state boss Quay—until 1895, when he felt independent enough to turn against his benefactor and join (with "Boss" Chris Magee of Pittsburgh) in an unsuccessful statewide bid to wrest control of the Republican machine from the party leader.[15]

The way Quay responded to Martin's refusal to endorse Boies Penrose, his choice as Republican mayoral candidate in 1895 ("one of the dirtiest and basest exhibitions of treachery in the history of the city's politics," according to the *Times*), illustrates well the methods the state boss could use to deal with potential rivals to his leadership and also at the same time influence political affairs in Philadelphia to his own advantage.[16] Initially he attempted to embarrass and discredit his political opponents, first by launching a scathing "personal attack" on the Philadelphia party leader "from the floor of the U.S. Senate," accusing him of being a tool of big business, and then by persuading the state legislature to set up a Committee of Inquiry to investigate (and confirm) allegations of misgovernment in Pennsylvania's two largest cities.[17]

He then sought to undermine their political influence locally by redistributing federal and state patronage positions in Philadelphia and Pittsburgh in favor of subordinates who had remained loyal to him, and by attempting to revise the respective charters of these two cities in a way that benefited his embattled supporters.[18] Finally, he astonished his opponents (and supporters) by adopting yet again the role of reformer. On this occasion, Quay committed himself to implementing (but ultimately not delivering) civil service reform in all branches of government in the state. The adoption of a reform strategy, though, was sufficient to boost his own personal popularity with the electorate at the expense of his opponents.[19] Indeed, this strategy, combined with the other initiatives, eventually enabled the "master of corrupt politics" not only to emerge triumphant in the struggle with "his recalcitrant pupils" but also, in the process, to install seventh ward leader Israel ("Iz") W. Durham, Penrose's campaign manager, as the new Philadelphia Republican party leader.[20]

Iz Durham and Organizational Change

Unlike Martin, "Iz" Durham and his associate "Sunny Jim" McNichol were quite content to reap the rewards that political control of a burgeoning metropolis like Philadelphia had to offer, while submitting to the dictates of Quay and Penrose in the state arena. Penrose's biographer maintains that Iz was "the kind of subordinate with whom a state boss could feel comfortable. Unlike McManes and Martin, he had no ambitions to enlarge his kingdom but demonstrated an indefatigable dedication to success at the local level."[21] Such was Durham's preoccupation with local politics that even though he attended every Republican National Convention between 1896 and 1908 as a city delegate, he was often quoted as saying, "What do I care who is President, so long as I can carry my ward?"[22]

Under Durham's regime there were a number of innovations in the way the Republican party conducted its affairs, changes that were to transform fundamentally the way the party organization functioned. The first organizational change involved an alteration in the party rules that radically affected the membership of the Republican City Committee and made it, rather than the wards, the prime unit of the organizational structure. When Stokley and McManes were engaged in their struggle for factional superiority, Republican party rules provided that representatives on the City Committee were to be elected at the ward level and that they could be removed from office only by a two-thirds majority vote of their respective ward executive committees.[23] In the wake of Martin's demise at the turn of the century, Durham altered these rules so he could dictate who should sit as ward representatives on the City Committee. This was achieved by dropping the requirement that ward representatives had to be existing members of their ward executive committees, and by extending the eligibility of those entitled to sit on the party's central body to all public officeholders and party workers. The practical consequence of these changes in the party rules was that the party leadership could impose its own representatives on the City Committee by designating as ward leaders the party workers it favored, rather than those who believed themselves to be the legitimate agents of Republican interests in the various wards.[24] The *Press* pointed out:

> Under the rule, the City Committee is vested with power which stifles independence in ward politics. The City Committee has had power, in fact, to step in and dictate the affairs of any one or all of the 42 ward organizations. This power was finally extended so that the City Committee was able to say who should and who should not sit in its Councils as the representative of a ward.
>
> The rules of the Organization were drafted and amended from time to time, to fortify Durham against possible attack. He personally dictated the changes to the rules. It was the fountain-head of his system of making and unmaking ward leaders in a single night. Under his system, a ward leader was a ward leader only when the City Committee said so.
>
> Old ward leaders of known strength in their respective wards were gradually crowded out at the direction of Durham and their successors seated in the City Committee by that body itself. Without the approval of the City Committee, a ward was barred from naming its representative in that Committee. The City Committee was Durham: Durham was the City Committee.[25]

Under the amended party rules, Durham and McNichol purged recalcitrant politicians from the Organization. A comparison of the City Committee's membership for 1905 with that of 1895 (the year of the Martin-Magee revolt) reveals that only eleven of the thirty-seven ward representatives survived the leadership purge (see Table 9).[26] Independent "freewheeling types" such as Charles Kindred, Edward W. Patton, and Theodore Stulb, were replaced on the City Committee by new "organization men" such as Peter E. Smith, George J. Van Houten, and John Klang. Other examples of the new generation of politicians, handpicked by the party leaders to sit on the City Committee, included John K. Myers, Elias Abrams, Samuel Sutcliffe, Charles T. Preston, William McKinley, Thomas S. Wiltbank, Frank H. Caven, and Oscar Noll.[27]

In order to ensure that these new representatives remained loyal to the Organization and would not resist dictation from the center, Durham insisted that most of them be given appointive positions on the public payroll.[28] An examination of the Republican City Committee for 1905 shows that (besides Durham and McNichol), twenty-three ward representatives

Table 9. The Republican City Committee, Philadelphia, 1905

Ward	Representative	Elective Office	Appointed Position	Occupation
1	William S. Vare	Recorder of deeds		Contractor
2	Harry C. Ransley	Pres., Select Council	Pres., Mercantile Appraisers	Store merchant
3	Harry J. Trainer	Select councilman	Mercantile appraiser	Horseshoer
4	Robert J. Moore*	Magistrate	Clerk, "Row" office	
5	Samuel G. Maloney		Harbor master	
6	Charles Getzinger		Clerk, city controller's office	
7	Israel W. Durham*	State senator	State insurance commissioner	
8	Edward A. Devlin*	Former magistrate	Mercantile appraiser	
9	John K. Myers		Assistant chief, Highways Bureau	
10	James P. McNichol*	State senator		Contractor
11	Joseph H. Klemmer*	Register of wills	Former tax auditor	
12	John Klang	Select councilman		Saloonkeeper
13	James L. Miles	Sheriff		Attorney
14	Jacob Wildemore*	City commissioner		
15	Charles L. Brown	State senator	Counsel, State Dairy & Food Commission	Attorney
16	Elias Abrams		Assistant highway inspector	
17	David S. Scott*	Magistrate	Clerk, City Hall	
18	Samuel Sutcliffe*		Chief, Street-Cleaning Bureau	
19	David Martin*	State senator		
20	David H. Lane*		Educational commissioner	
21	Charles T. Preston		Assistant Chief, Highways Bureau	

No.	Name			
22	Jesse S. Shepard	State senator		
23	William McKinley		Collector	
24	Thomas S. Wiltbank	Select councilman		Real estate broker
25	Wilbur F. Short	Select councilman		Hosiery mfgr
26	Arthur R.H. Morrow		Assistant director of supplies	Journalist
27	George J. Van Houten	Common councilman	Court officer	
28	George Sterr Jr.		Assistant chief, Highways Bureau	
29	Peter E. Smith	Sergeant-at-arms, Select Council		
30	John Smith*		Assistant engineer, Bureau of Fire	
31	Horatio B. Hackett*	State senator		
32	William H. Berkelbach		Inspector, Street-Cleaning Bureau	
33	John B. Lukens*		Mercantile appraiser	
34	Frank H. Caven	Select councilman		Upholstery mfgr
35	George A. Castor	Congressman		
36	Hugh Black	City commissioner		Teamster
37	Oscar E. Noll		Assistant Chief, Highways Bureau	
38	James E. Walsh	Select councilman		Insurance agent
39	George A. Vare	State senator		Contractor
40	Harry D. Beaston	Receiver of taxes	Supervisor of the census	Coal merchant
41	Peter E. Costello		Director of public works	Contractor
42	Henry Homiller		Inspector, Water Bureau	

SOURCES: *Press*, January 12, 1895; *Public Ledger*, June 18, 1905; *North American*, June 19, 1905; *Record*, June 20, 1905; *Gopsill's Philadelphia City Directory for 1905* (Philadelphia, 1905).

*Members of the Republican City Committee in 1895.

held appointive positions, while only fifteen had recognized occupations outside of politics (see Table 9).

The control the party leadership exercised over the membership of the party's local units extended to the division level, since division leaders, even though elected by the party's registered voters, were in practice subservient to the selected ward leaders. Ward leaders, by the judicious distribution of minor patronage positions and campaign funds, and the exercise of careful discrimination in responding to requests for favors from voters, could usually ensure that their particular choices as committeemen were adopted as the party's divisional representatives.[29]

The second of the party leadership's innovations resulted in party nominations for public office being subjected to strict control by the City Committee and the various ward committees. One of McManes's and Stokley's main weaknesses, it will be recalled, was their inability to ensure that their particular followers would be nominated for public office, and they were not able to prevent their opponents from securing the party's nominations. The reason for this weakness was that the City Committee did not function as a centralized and powerful institution. It was not capable of extinguishing dissent or controlling the candidate-selection process, either citywide or at the ward level.

Consequently, party conventions were arenas of intense rivalry as the various factions struggled to secure party nominations for public office. As a successful nomination depended on factions obtaining the largest number of delegates, conventions were occasionally rowdy and violent as disputes arose, particularly over the admission of delegates when seats were contested by the rival factions.[30]

In order to resolve such disputes, the party rules provided for boards to try contests. These boards were comprised of the president and secretary of the local party association, and the other three divisional officers who had been responsible for compiling the register of those eligible to vote in the divisional primary elections.

It was often because these divisional boards failed to function as impartial tribunals for the settlement of contested seats that party nomination conventions subsequently became rowdy and violent.[31] Contemporary political scientist Walter Branson pointed out that these boards were "characterized by incompetence and venality" and tended to "create rather than decide contests."[32]

Given "the notorious partiality of the contest boards," the party's rules were ultimately amended, in May 1898, in order to grant the City Committee and ward committees the right to issue tickets of admission to the convention hall to the primary delegates *whom they considered* to be properly elected.[33] Although "this practice" was "apparently begun in good faith," according to Branson, it "opened the way for flagrant abuses. It has enabled the faction in control of the party organization to make up the roll of a convention in an arbitrary manner, giving itself a majority even when defeated at the primaries."[34] Divisional representation at nomination conventions was thus rendered an "abstract principle," in the words of Frank W. Leach.[35]

This alteration to the party rules provided the party's leadership with the institutionalized means to control the candidate-selection process for public office. Because the party leadership controlled the membership of the City Committee and the various ward committees, implementation of the new party rule meant that, in practice, any Republican politician who desired public office in Philadelphia could not get it without the endorsement of the "boss." So long as a prospective candidate obtained an endorsement "from the proper source" (Durham), Leach suggested, "the thing is done. His nomination is assured." He "can rusticate in Florida or luxuriate at the Hot Springs until the convention adjourns."[36]

Reformers protested that the Republican party organization, under Durham and McNichol, had become "a system of absolute despotism, a menace to free government" that "totally destroys and makes subservient the popular will."[37] The Municipal League of Philadelphia also complained:

> Party primaries and nominating conventions have been made a farce. They are in no sense representative, they simply register the wishes of the "bosses" declared days and weeks beforehand. Deliberation has been abolished, as has consideration. Automationism has taken their place and independence of thought and action by party men has been almost unheard of, or where manifested has been speedily punished.[38]

The party "bosses" could guarantee not only the party nominations but also—because the Organization was able to control the electorate (as we shall see in Chapter 6)—almost certain victory in the general election to public office. The Organization was able to virtually guarantee that (unlike the 1870s and early 1880s, when a Republican politician could win office by running as an independent candidate) its endorsement alone was not only necessary but also sufficient for a party supporter to hold public office in Philadelphia. By the late nineteenth century, then, the Republican party boss, unlike his predecessors, was for the first time able to enjoy a monopoly over the recruitment of candidates to public office.

A third organizational change, which stemmed directly from the first two, was the systematization and centralization of party revenues. For example, the city "boss," like Quay, became a political broker, the connecting link between corporate interests and legislative approval of their growing demands.[39] When businessmen or corporations needed legislative privileges from city government, they channeled their requests and "contributions" (the "routine graft" or oil that kept the machine in running order) through the office of the city "boss" in the Betz Building, adjacent to City Hall. Because the "boss" was able to control the flow of legislation and appropriations through City Council, they no longer used lobbyists to bribe legislators or government officials on an individual basis, as they had done in the past. This new arrangement represented an important shift toward party centralization, for the money or company stock that private interests had formerly paid for favors or protection no longer went to party subordinates but went directly into the pockets of the party "boss."

Also important were the exorbitant profits party leaders enjoyed as a result of the virtual monopoly that firms they controlled or invested in exercised over public contract work.[40] The consistent regularity with which these favored firms obtained contract work was, like the ability of the "boss" to function as a political broker, a direct consequence of the establishment of a reliable system of discipline within the Organization.

The willingness of public officials to divide the perquisites of office with the Organization, and the insistence of party leaders that they should do so, reflects this important shift toward central control of party revenues. For example, when the Organization was hard-pressed, as during the period of City Party insurgency (1905–7), public officeholders were obliged to raise a campaign "pot" among themselves. In 1906 William S. Vare and Joseph Klemmer donated their annual salaries of $10,000 and $5,000, as recorder of deeds and register of wills, respectively, to the Organization's coffers. State Senator Clarence Wolf and Insurance Commissioner David Martin both gave $5,000 each, and before the pot reached the twentieth contributor more than $100,000 had been collected for the election campaign.[41] This gesture by various public officeholders indicates that party workers—unlike in the earlier period of "individualism and ring rule"—were more inclined to accept that their commitment and obligation to the party organization was not exhausted once they were elected to office. In sharp contrast to individuals who collected fees on State House Row in the 1870s, Organization men at the turn of the century regarded public office not so much as their own personal property but as something they occupied on behalf of the party leadership. It was not just coincidence, it would seem, that the Bardsley treasury defalcation scandal of 1891 was the last occasion, under Organization rule, that an elected official was removed from office for abusing his position for *personal* financial gain.[42]

The systematic and comprehensive way in which the Organization levied "political assessments" on patronage-holders was also indicative of the centralized control over party revenues. In the first decade of the twentieth century approximately 94 percent of all city employees paid assessments to the Republican Organization, even though it was against the law to solicit these subscriptions.[43] These "voluntary contributions" were either deducted at source from wages or collected by way of the postal service.[44] They ranged from $350,000 in 1903 to $500,000 in 1910, and totaled more than $3 million between 1903 and 1913. The Organization employed a "progressive system of taxation," requiring the lowest-paid jobholders, at $900 a year or less, to contribute 1 percent of their salary to the City Committee twice a year before each election, and the highest paid, earning $6,000 a year or more, to contribute 4 percent. Jobholders also gave an additional sum to their ward committees, equivalent to half the amount they had donated to the City Committee.[45]

The rigor with which these extralegal income taxes were collected was such that reformers proclaimed them to be "one of the vicious features of machine control."[46] City employees were subject no less to "the galling yoke of the political gangster," as Rudolph Blankenburg put it.[47] There is a certain irony about these comments, because they are actually an unintentional compliment on the way the leadership of the Organization financed party operations. We should not find this too surprising, however, for reformers saw no contradiction in their condemnation of political machines both for the grand inefficiencies of spoils and for the extraordinary efficiency with which they levied political assessments.

The fourth and final innovation of the party leadership involved a shift in the how the functionaries who staffed the party apparatus were compensated. The changes were intended to maintain the Organization in a healthy state of efficiency. For instance, in the 1870s and 1880s, when the majority of the thirty separate government agencies responsible for city services reported to the Councils, political appointments were parceled out by the majority party, regardless of faction, to all councilmen on an individual basis.[48] The introduction of the Bullitt city charter in 1887, however, had important consequences for the control and distribution of political appointments. The new system of government was characterized by administrative consolidation and the centralization of power and authority in the mayor. It also made the chief executive, in conjunction with the other eight heads of department, responsible for formulating rules prescribing a uniform and systematic method governing the selection and promotion of city officials. In addition, the mayor was also given the power to appoint the civil service examining board, whose duty it was to implement these recruitment procedures. The mayor's power of appointment also extended to the key position of secretary of the civil service examining board, the official who was responsible for coordinating the activities of the various subcommittees of the board and for drawing up the lists of eligible applicants who had achieved the required standard to be employed by the city.[49]

So long as the mayor remained faithful to the Organization, party leaders were in a position to exercise strict control over the appointment of city officials. That they invariably did so (apart from Mayor John Weaver's temporary break with Durham in 1905) is reflected in the character of the appointments they made to the civil service examining board itself. After 1887, the key position of secretary, for instance, was usually filled by a senior figure on the Republican City Committee, such as the former clerk of the Quarter Sessions Court, James W. Latta, twenty-sixth ward leader Arthur H. Morrow, or Rolla Dance, a protégé of McNichol's who had succeeded "Sunny Jim" as select councilman for the tenth ward.[50] Such stalwarts of the City Committee as Harry C. Ransley and Walter T. Bradley were also appointed as civil service examiners and were responsible for interviewing prospective public employees, such as policemen, park guards, prison officers, messengers, doorkeepers, janitors, and watchmen.[51] Given the enduring loyalty of successive mayors to the Organization, local reformers could legitimately claim, as indeed they did, that the function of the civil service examining board was not to insulate public office from party influence but "to keep out those who were objectionable to the bosses."[52]

The establishment of a virtual monopoly over public patronage meant that party leaders could now control the distribution of political appointments. Instead of distributing these appointments in equitable fashion among individual councilmen, the party leadership introduced a new criterion for their distribution: they were to be doled out on the basis of the number of Organization votes each ward leader could produce. In other words, the amount of patronage a ward leader could receive was to be performance-related.[53] This system of distribution was adhered to so rigidly that records of the political residence of every city employee were kept in government departments, and employees were not allowed to move from one division to another until permission was obtained from the chief of the bureau in which they worked. That permission was not granted until it had been approved by the head of the department, after he had taken the issue up with the ward leader where the employee happened to live.[54] This method of distribution may not have produced the most suitable appointments for the city, but it maintained the Organization in a constant and healthy state of efficiency because its emphasis on productivity had a galvanizing effect on ward leaders and committeemen.[55]

Positions on the public payroll were not the only incentive the party leadership used to encourage dedication to duty among the rank-and-file. Public office also seems to have been a reward for those who labored long and hard for the Organization. For instance, one-third of the Republican delegation to the state House of Representatives in 1920 were lawyers, and the majority had a long record of service to the Organization. They included Leopold Glass, counsel for the City Committee; such ward leaders as Sigmund Gans, Matthew Patterson, and John K. Scott; and John Drinkhouse and Richard Curry, who had each served on their respective ward committees for more than twenty years.[56] In sharp contrast, a similar survey of the delegation in 1890 shows four school directors, six ward committee members, and one former magistrate among the twenty-nine Republican representatives. The other eighteen were engaged in a wide cross section of occupations and did not have any record of service to the party, though two did have distinguished war records.[57] The monopoly the Organization established in the 1890s over the recruitment of candidates to public office cannot by itself account for the differences in the length of party service between the two delegations. What also seems to have been significant is the reluctance of party "bosses" in Philadelphia to permit significant positions (except on occasions when political tickets required hasty "window dressing" or the unusual luster of some amateur's reputation) to go to men with less than a decade of party experience.

In addition to the incentives provided by political appointments and public office, members of the Organization were also compensated for their loyalty by the opportunity to participate in what George Washington Plunkitt termed "honest graft."[58] The planning and development of the ten-mile-long Northeast (Roosevelt) Boulevard through open farmlands to the isolated suburb of Torresdale provides a classic example of "honest graft" in practice. In 1902 the Philadelphia Land Company was incorporated, and its

representatives, employed by John Mack, began to buy up cheap land between Torresdale and the city center. Meanwhile, Peter Costello, forty-first
ward leader and chairman of the Councils Finance Committee, who owed his
position to Durham and McNichol, introduced an ordinance for the construction of a boulevard from Broad and Cayuga streets to Torresdale, even though
there was no apparent need for such a thoroughfare. The thirty-fifth ward,
the main beneficiary of the proposed boulevard, contained almost 25 percent
of the city's land area, but it had only 8,614 inhabitants, of whom fewer than
one in five lived or owned property close to the route. However, the route cut
through the farm property that had recently been acquired by the Philadelphia Land Company, and after the ordinance was passed the company's
associates made a handsome profit through the sale of their land to the city.[59]
For example, in September 1903 the company bought 105 acres from Mary J.
Anderson for $23,550 and 212 acres from Henry C. Thompson for $99,700.
These 317 acres were assessed in 1908 at $93,550, a rate of $300 per acre,
yet the city paid $50,496 for 20 acres, a rate of $2,500 per acre.[60]

In addition to the sale of land, damages totaling $1,380,000 were also
awarded by road juries, often up to fifteen times in excess of the assessed
value of property along the route. This was an outright gift inasmuch as the
improvements, instead of damaging the property, actually increased its
value. The *North American* was convinced that

> these land operations . . . have, in fact, followed the lines of a defi-
> nite system. . . . A combination of land speculators and politicians
> operating through the scandalous road jury system dipped into the
> city treasury at a rate in excess of one million dollars a year.[61]

City Solicitor James Alcorn, and his assistant John Monaghan, legal counsel
to the Organization, as well as City Committee members Harry J. Trainer,
Harry C. Ransley, James B. Anderson, Charles F. Kindred, Kennedy
Crossan, and James Dorney, all received large awards.[62]

The Organization's control over the boulevard venture was such that it was
possible to change the proposed route at will almost overnight. In 1903, for
example, David Martin reconciled his differences with the Organization the
same time Mack fell out with Durham and McNichol.[63] To mark the occasion, the original line of the Boulevard was changed by about one and a half
miles so as to include some of Martin's property at the expense of John Mack's
(see Figure 5). When land was taken by the city for the Pennypack Creek
Park, which was part of the general Northeast Boulevard scheme, 30 acres on

Martin's 202-acre property, which he had bought in 1895 for $65,374, were condemned. Martin received $77,980 in damages, and his remaining property was assessed at $103,100.[64] It is not surprising that these activities prompted Blankenburg to regard the Northeast Boulevard as

> the culmination of Organization effrontery and thievery . . . which . . . is open to curves as crooked as its projectors. Boulevards are generally supposed to run in a straight line, but this scheme of the grafters is planned to run for ten miles at all kinds of angles in the direction of and past the lands acquired by the "Gang," increasing the value of their holdings immensely.[65]

As McNichol received the $1.4 million contract for building the boulevard by the same unscrupulous methods he obtained other public contract work, Blankenburg dubbed the enterprise the "McNichol Boodlevard" and concluded: "The Torresdale Boulevard was conceived for graft purposes solely, and when completed will be one of the most striking, as well as costly, monuments of the phenomenal graft administration of Samuel H. Ashbridge."[66]

Opportunities to participate in "honest graft," and the prospect of public office or positions on the public payroll as rewards for hard work on behalf of the party, not only provided incentives that kept the Organization in a healthy state of efficiency but also encouraged a strong sense of loyalty among the rank-and-file. This is not surprising, because party workers were far more likely to support a political structure that rewarded its members in a "democratic fashion" on the basis of their performance than one that elevated politicians because they had personal resources (such as wealth, social standing, or popularity) that could be utilized in election campaigns.

Over time, the disbursement of rewards by the Organization on a productivity basis led to recruitment and promotion of leaders who were different from the people who had played a dominant role in Republican politics during the factional era. The Organization's monopolization of recruitment to public office, and its ability to control the electorate, converted a prospective career in local politics from a high-risk one into a low-risk one, because the Organization could guarantee favored candidates virtually an unlimited tenure of office.[67] This fundamental change in the condition of local politics had important consequences for the character of the men who sought and were elevated into public office. Not least, independent "freewheeling types" who chafed under any restraint tended to be weeded out in favor of "organiza-

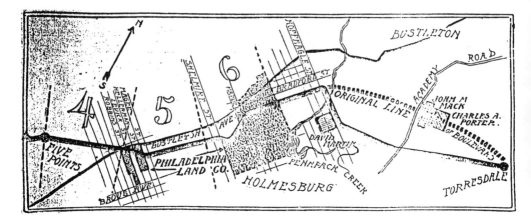

Fig. 5. The "McNichol Boodlevard," showing the change in the original line of the Boulevard to benefit Martin at Mack's expense, and also the lots owned by the Philadelphia Land Company. The numbers 4, 5, and 6 refer to the construction of the Boulevard. All these contracts were ultimately awarded to D. J. McNichol and the McNichol Paving & Construction Company, even though the work was given out on a sectional basis. Hence, Blankenburg's derisive nickname for the thoroughfare. (*Sources: The Bulletin*, October 11, 1911, Committee of Seventy Scrapbook, Urban Archives Center, Temple University; City Contracts 20037, 20704 [1903]; 21566 [1904]; 25528 [1907]; and 26883 [1908]; Records Center, City of Philadelphia.)

tion men," party workers who accepted political loyalty and regularity as primary virtues over and above their own individual feelings.

By the time William Vare became party leader in the 1920s, the politicians who staffed the Republican Organization were of a new political generation. Formed under Durham's reign, this generation's members did not find the notion of party discipline so novel and hence so chafing. One contemporary political scientist, John T. Salter, pointed out that "the most striking single identifying quality" of Republican party division leaders was their loyalty.

> These men are loyal to their leaders, just as their leaders are in turn loyal to their own leaders and the Organization. It is personal rather than civic loyalty. This loyalty pattern is a habit of mind among the overwhelming majority of the members of any successful party organization. It is so implicit in normal times, that one must turn in nature to a highly trained bird dog to find its counterpart, or to a young child's faith in its parent.

In a free moment, these men unhesitatingly describe themselves as "order men." They take orders and ask no questions.[68]

The establishment of a strict system of control and discipline within the Organization had important consequences not only internally, on the character of the men who staffed the party apparatus, but also externally, for the rest of the Philadelphia community. In essence, the institutionalization of the Republican machine paved the way for genuine boss rule to emerge in the city for the first time.

5

The Characteristics of Republican Boss Rule in Philadelphia

The consolidation of power within the Republican party in Philadelphia in the late nineteenth century did not just herald the establishment of machine politics as both a centralized political *structure* and a political *style*. It also enabled the career politicians who became Republican party leaders subsequent to the machine's institutionalization—David Martin and his ally Charles A. Porter, Israel W. Durham, James P. McNichol, and the Vare brothers—to exercise a degree of clout in local affairs that was far greater than that of their predecessors.

The Sphere of Boss Influence

But what evidence do we have that the Organization did function as its centralized and hierarchical structure suggested it should? Did Republican party leaders after 1887 really have more clout than McManes and Stokley?

The legitimacy of these claims is clear when we note the characteristics Martin and his successors had in common but that at the same time distinguished them from their predecessors.[1] The first distinguishing feature of boss rule after 1887 was that Martin and his successors were chosen to run the city Republican party organization by the state party leader (or "boss"), Matthew S. Quay. Quay and his successor, Boies Penrose, had a firm grip over the Republican party organization in Philadelphia. James Bryce observed: "In the stead of Mr. McManes, the State Boss now reigns supreme through his lieutenants."[2] Muckraker Lincoln Steffens even suggested that Quay was "the proprietor of Pennsylvania and the real ruler of Philadelphia, just as William Penn, the Great Proprietor was."[3] This led Steffens to conclude:

> The Philadelphia Organization is upside down. It has its roots in the air, or rather like the banyon tree, it sends its roots from the center out both up and down and all around, and there lies its peculiar strength. . . . The organization that rules Philadelphia is . . . not a mere municipal machine, but a city, State, and national organization.[4]

A second characteristic that Martin and his successors had in common, and that also distinguished them from their predecessors, was that they did *not* occupy any public office in city government when they held the position of city boss. Apart from McNichol's six-year spell as select councilman and Bill Vare's four-year term in the upper chamber, local Republican party leaders after 1887 avoided city government office altogether. Instead, they opted for public positions in county or state government (see Table 10). This preference may well have been a reflection of the close links between the city boss and the state boss, or it may have been a recognition of where power actually lay, since the city of Philadelphia was merely a legislative agency of the state and not an independent sovereignty. However, it is particularly significant that, unlike McManes and Stokley, the power of Martin and his successors did not stem only from the public offices they personally occupied. That is, after 1887, local party leaders were able to subject their followers to a system of control and discipline regardless of the public office they themselves occupied.

In the case of party office, the city boss firmly controlled the internal affairs of the Republican party organization For example, in 1905, when ward leaders Charles F. Kindred, Theodore B. Stulb, and Alexander Crow Jr. questioned Durham and McNichol's authority during a period of reform insurgency, they

Table 10. Political Base, Occupation, and Public Offices of Republican Party Leaders, Philadelphia, 1887–1934

	David Martin (1845–1920)[a]	Charles A. Porter (1839–1907)	Israel W. Durham (1856–1909)	James P. McNichol (1864–1917)	George Vare (1859–1908)	Edwin Vare (1862–1922)	William S. Vare (1867–1934)
Political base	19th ward, N.E. Phila.	8th ward, downtown	7th ward, downtown	10th ward, downtown	1st ward, South Phila.	1st ward, South Phila.	1st/26th ward, South Phila.
Occupation	Garbage collector	Contractor	Flour dealer	Contractor	Contractor	Contractor	Contractor
Public office	1889–91, collector of internal revenue for 1st district of Pa. 1897, secretary of the Commonwealth 1898, state senator, 8th district; 1905–9, state insurance commissioner 1909–13, register of wills 1916–20, state senator	1862–66, supervisor of streets 1872–74, state representative 1890, state senator	1885–95, police magistrate 1897, state senator 1899–1905, state insurance commissioner; 1908–9, state senator	1898–1904, Select Council 1904–17, state senator, 3rd district	1890–96, state representative 1896–1908, state senator, 1st district	1897, state representative 1908–22, state senator, 1st district	1898–1902, pres., Board of Mercantile Appraisers 1899–1902, Select Council 1902–12, recorder of deeds 1912–26, U.S. House of Representatives 1926–29, U.S. senator-elect

SOURCES: John A. Small, *Small's Legislative Hand Book 1900* (Harrisburg, Pa., 1900), 1161, 1164; *1910*. 974–75; *1920*. 1098–1100; *Manual of Councils. 1898–1904*; "The North American," *Philadelphia and Popular Philadelphians* (Philadelphia, 1891), 18, 27–29; Harold Zink, *City Bosses in the United States* (Durham, N.C., 1930), 206–29; William S. Vare, *My Forty Years in Politics* (Philadelphia, 1933).

[a]Years in parentheses are birth and death years.

were automatically replaced on the Republican City Committee by Peter E. Smith, John Klang, and Charles L. Brown.[5] Reform leader Rudolph Blankenburg wryly observed: "Disobedience to the orders of the 'Organization,' whether from the rank and file or those higher up, is meted with instant punishment. . . . It cannot and does not brook insubordination, which, in fact, is about the only 'crime' it is unwilling to tolerate."[6]

Bill Vare was also able to dictate his choice of ward leaders. Contemporary political scientist John T. Salter noted: "When Vare says 'There is your leader—elect him,' the ward committee follows orders."[7] This kind of obedience prompted the *Sunday Dispatch* to remark: "The Republican Organization is a good deal like an army. It obeys the wishes of the general staff."[8]

Local elections provide a good example of the smooth efficiency of the machine and of the tendency of party workers, throughout the city, to carry out the boss's orders. The September primary election of 1925 (the "Shoyer stickers election," as it became known) provides a dramatic illustration of the boss's ability to subject party subordinates to a strict system of control.[9] John M. Patterson, the Organization candidate for the Republican nomination for district attorney, fell ill just before the primary and on election day was believed to be dying. At 3:00 P.M., the Vare leaders went into conference at Republican party headquarters and decided to defeat their own candidate. Given that voters had been going to the polls since 7:00 A.M. to vote for Patterson, and there were only four hours left before the polls closed, this decision was quite remarkable. Ward leaders were summoned by telephone to party headquarters and given bundles of stickers printed on the eve of election day and held in readiness in the event of Patterson's death. Bearing the name of Former City Treasurer Frederick J. Shoyer, the stickers were distributed by car to polling places throughout the city, where election officials placed them over Patterson's name or in a blank space on the ballot paper. Soon after the polls closed, Patterson died, but the Vare forces were unable to rob him of victory; he received 168,795 votes. Yet in an incredible feat of organization, the Vare machine had managed to cast 124,895 votes for a man who had not previously been discussed as a candidate for district attorney and whose name had not even been printed on the ballot paper.[10]

The system of control the city boss exercised over subordinates in party office also extended to followers who occupied public office.[11] For example, in 1901 State Boss Quay punished an ungrateful Peter B. Widener for his lack of support during a political crisis. Quay had supervised the passage of legislation creating a new category of street railway company specifically directed toward destroying Widener's monopoly of the transit industry in Philadelphia. While Widener set sail for a European holiday, two of Quay's supporters introduced the necessary bills, without notice, in the state legislature on May 28, 1901. They were whisked through the House and Senate by June 5 and passed by Governor Stone on June 7, when charters were issued for roads in Scranton and Pittsburgh and for thirteen companies in Philadelphia.

The machine in Philadelphia was equally effective. Under instructions from Iz Durham, James L. Miles, president of Select Council and chairman of the Republican City Committee, called a special session of the Council for Monday, June 10, to consider the thirteen franchise ordinances. The forty-member Council included nineteen ward leaders, and it quickly referred the bills to the Street Railroads Committee chaired by Watson D. Upperman, the thirty-first ward representative on the Republican City Committee. It is significant that Charles Seger, the machine's "whip," appointed by Durham, also sat on the Railroads Committee, and it took just one hour to approve these ordinances that affected nearly two hundred miles of the city's streets as well as the rights and interests of existing transit companies. The bills were then passed by the Councils on June 12, sent to Mayor Ashbridge the following day, and initialed shortly after midnight on June 14, but not before the mayor had publicly refused to veto or accept an offer to the city of $2.5 million for the same franchises from store merchant John Wanamaker.[12]

The street railway franchise grab was widely condemned by the forces of good government, but what is remarkable about this incident, from the perspective of political organization, is the speed with which the ("macing") conspiracy was executed. That this legislation could be passed through both the state legislature and City Council in just over two weeks is testimony to the superb way in which Quay and Durham were able to marshal their troops in the respective legislatures.[13]

Local party leaders managed to maintain control of their followers in City Council, even when they were starved of patronage resources. For example, the Vare and McNichol forces in the Councils successfully combined to thwart Blankenburg's reform initiatives by employing obstructionist tactics to undermine his mayoral administration (1912–16). Morris L. Cooke, Blankenburg's director of public works, acknowledged that "the real stumbling block" to reform was "the openly antagonistic attitude of our City Councils." He said: "The whole body is organized so that a very few strong-willed and corrupt men at points of vantage arrange everything. A bare half dozen absolutely dictate to twenty times their number."[14]

The "Contractor Bosses"

The monotonous regularity with which successive party leaders secured public contract work suggests that the city boss's ability to control the behavior
of his followers was not confined to unusual or special occasions. On the
contrary, the remarkable way firms that party leaders invested in, or associated themselves with, prospered indicates that the city boss was able to
subject subordinates in public office to control and discipline on a *consistent*
and *regular* basis. For example, David Martin, Charles Porter, and John Mack
were nicknamed the "Hog Combine" because "they hogged everything in
sight and more!"[15] Between 1887 and 1894, companies they controlled
completed nearly $5 million worth of business with the Department of
Public Works (see Table 11). After 1894, Martin and Porter's Vulcanite
Paving Company received 736 contracts worth approximately $4 million,
and John Mack's businesses acquired more than 4,000 contracts for at least
$33 million worth of public work.[16]

Similarly, McNichol and the Vare brothers were labeled "the contractor
bosses." James P. McNichol and his brother Daniel inherited the family
building firm and completed more than $6 million worth of municipal work
in the form of street-paving and repair contracts in the 1890s.[17] Their
company, in which Durham was made a secret partner, then undertook more
ambitious projects. They built the $25 million Torresdale water-filtration
plant (1899–1907) and the Roosevelt Boulevard (1903–14), which opened
up the northeastern section of the city to automobile traffic and residential
development, as well as the subway tunnel (1907–8) for the Market Street
transit line, and the Ben Franklin Parkway (1918), which linked Fairmount
Park to the city's center.[18]

"Sunny Jim's" other interests included the Pennsylvania Company, which
controlled a half-a-million-dollar garbage disposal business, and the Filbert
Paving and Construction Company, which netted 310 city contracts worth in
excess of $3 million between 1903 and 1911. He was also the major stock-
holder in the Millard and Keystone construction companies, which obtained
a $3 million contract for new high-pressure fire mains, the largest single
contract awarded by the Department of Public Safety during the Reyburn
administration of 1907–11.[19]

The Vare brothers—George, Edwin, and Bill—initially set up a small
contracting business in South Philadelphia, hauling ashes and collecting and
dumping the city's garbage. The company, however, quickly developed into

Table 11. Philadelphia City Contracts for the Department of Public Works Awarded to the "Hog Combine," 1887–1894

Year	Bureau of Highways	Bureau of Water	Bureau of Surveys	Misc.	Total
1887	$ 102,178	$ 227,360	—	—	$ 329,538
1888	141,461	252,145	—	—	393,606
1889	109,323	352,029	—	—	461,352
1890	354,562	4,249	$ 73,175	—	431,986
1891	244,626	59,555	15,916	—	320,097
1892	174,157	23,148	271,759	—	469,064
1893	956,272	1,851	—	$ 24,303	982,426
1894	307,560	1,038,000	72,080	83,481	1,501,121
Total	$2,390,139	$1,958,337	$432,930	$107,784	$4,889,190

Year	Vulcanite Paving Company (152 contracts)	Filbert & Porter (16 contracts)	Charles A. Porter (16 contracts)	Total
1887	$ 102,176	$ 227,360	—	$ 329,536
1888	156,505	237,101	—	393,606
1889	126,024	328,199	$ 7,128	461,351
1890	358,812	—	73,175	431,987
1891	304,182	—	15,916	320,098
1892	197,305	—	271,759	469,064
1893	982,427	—	—	982,427
1894	391,041	1,110,080	—	1,501,121
Total	$2,618,472	$1,902,740	$367,978	$4,889,190

Major Items:

Paving Broad Street	$700,406
Lining East Park Reservoir	$792,660
North Pennsylvania Junction	$263,400
Queen Lane Reservoir	$1,038,000

SOURCES: *Mayor's Annual Register of Contracts,* 1887–1894, Department of Records, City Hall, Philadelphia; City Contracts, Records Center, City of Philadelphia; Anti-Combine Committee, *For Good Government* (Philadelphia, 1895), 15–21. (The *Mayor's Annual Register* lists the number of contracts awarded to the above firms during the period 1887–94. The value of those contracts was calculated from the individual contracts stored at the Records Center, 410 North Broad Street, Philadelphia.) The Anti-Combine Committee was a local nonpartisan reform group set up in 1895 with the aim of electing former Democratic governor Robert E. Pattison "as Mayor, to secure a business administration of city affairs."

a major street-cleaning operation, and between 1888 and 1921 they collected $18 million from fifty-eight street-cleaning contracts, usually covering the first, second, and third districts of the city. In 1905, and from 1909 to 1911 inclusive, they managed to obtain the contract for cleaning the entire city, at a cost of $950,000 in 1905 to $1,372,000 in 1911. The Vares also carried out $10 million worth of other public work, including sewer construction, bridge-building, resurfacing work, and the development of League Island Park. In total, Vare interests received 341 public contracts worth more than $28 million (see Table 12).[20]

Private work was also important to the "contractor bosses." In public testimony, Edwin Vare admitted that by 1911 he had undertaken $50 million worth of work for the city, $15 million from public contracts, $35 million from subcontracting work for private parties. The largest private contract the Vares got was with the Bell Telephone Company and involved digging and laying conduits throughout the city. McNichol enjoyed a similar deal with the United Gas Improvement Company. The "contractor bosses" could insist on a monopoly arrangement in private contract work, for these large utility companies could not complete any project without approval from City Council and the Department of Public Works.[21]

The procedure by which city contracts were awarded shows that the city boss controlled subordinates in public office. First impressions suggest that public contracts were awarded on an impartial basis, since it was the Councils that determined (except when the state legislature dictated otherwise) what work would be done within the city and either granted permission to utility companies to proceed or appropriated the necessary funds to government departments. Heads of departments, appointed by the mayor, were then responsible for awarding public contracts and overseeing the satisfactory completion of both private and public work on behalf of the city.[22]

In practice, however, this procedure was so tightly controlled by the Organization that fair and open competition among contractors was stifled and only those firms favored by the city boss prospered. For example, because the bulk of the Councils' work dealt with matters of business routine and not general public policy, and because (prior to 1919) it was a large and unwieldly body, all bills, resolutions, and petitions were considered by committees first, before open discussion in the chambers.[23] If any committee did not favor certain bills, it obstructed them by simply holding them back. In 1912, for instance, although 311 bills were reported out for action by the Councils, 2,084 had actually been referred to committees. And committee recommendations were almost never changed by the Councils. Of the 254

Table 12. Public Contracts Awarded in Philadelphia to Vare Interests, 1888–1928

	No. of Contracts	Total Amount	No. of Contracts/ Value Unknown	Estimated Value[a]	Grand Sum
Wilson & Vare (1888–95)	14	$ 830,419	3	$ 227,000	$ 1,057,419
W.S. Vare (1891–93)	—	—	3	5,000	5,000
George Vare (1894–1904)	98	816,149	28	326,452	1,142,601
Edwin Vare (1890–1922)	157	21,324,120	27	3,110,000	24,434,120
Vare Construction Co. (1923–28)	11	1,409,042	—	—	1,409,042
Totals	280	$24,379,730	61	$3,668,452	$28,048,182

SOURCES: *Mayor's Annual Register of Contracts*, 1888–1928, Department of Records, City Hall, Philadelphia; City Contracts, Records Center, City of Philadelphia.

[a]Because of theft or fire it is not possible to trace all the individual contracts at the Records Center. In such cases, an estimated value has been calculated, based on the average value of contracts awarded to the firm in the particular year when the individual contract could not be found.

bills reported favorably by committee in 1912, only 4 were rejected and 200 were passed unanimously.[24]

The Organization always controlled the most important of the twenty-seven Council committees—the Finance Committee, the Highways Committee, and the Surveys Committee—which dealt with 75 percent of all Council work. In 1910–11, for example, 22 of the 53 councilmen who occupied the 72 positions on the three committees were members of the City Committee. Ward leaders Frank H. Caven, Harry J. Trainer, Peter E. Costello, and John P. Connelly sat on all three committees, with the latter being chairman of the Highways Committee. The chairmanship of the Finance Committee was held by first ward leader Joseph R. C. McAllister, who relied on an appointed position as a real-estate assessor for his livelihood and owed his political career to the Vares.[25] Similarly, in 1911, when Vare received a contract to clean the entire city for $1,372,000, seven ward leaders sat on the Councils Street-Cleaning committee, which determined the size of the appropriation to the Street-Cleaning Bureau. They included Neil MacNeill, Ferdinand G. Zweig, Harry J. Trainer, and Kennedy

Crossan—all members of Vare's mayoral campaign committee for the Republican primary election in 1911.[26]

More than 50 percent of the appropriations allocated by the Councils went to the Department of Public Works and the Department of Public Safety, the two largest departments in city government. In theory, the mayor appointed the heads of departments, but in practice, because he owed his election to the party, they were selected by the City Committee, because the Organization had to be certain they would follow their instructions with regard to awarding contracts and appointment or removal of subordinates.[27] These positions were sometimes filled by committee members. For example, David Smyth, James B. Sheehan, Joseph H. Klemmer, Henry Clay, Arthur R. H. Morrow, and Peter Costello all served as either director or assistant director of Supplies, Public Works, or Public Safety under the Weaver and Reyburn administrations of 1903–11.[28] Ward leaders also occupied lucrative and influential offices within these departments. For example, when Morris L. Cooke took over as director of public works in the Blankenburg reform administration (1912–16), he discovered that all the assistant commissioners of the Bureau of Highways, drawing $2,500 a year, were ward leaders who had no knowledge of highway engineering.[29]

It was these party workers in public office that ensured that city contracts were placed with firms favored by or controlled by party leaders (see Figure 6). Edwin Vare, for example, was awarded a $950,000 contract in 1905 to clean the entire city by forty-first ward leader Peter Costello, director of public works, on the recommendation of eighteenth ward leader Samuel Sutcliffe, chief of the Street-Cleaning Bureau. Both these party workers had been elevated to the City Committee by McNichol in the 1890s. In addition, eighth ward leader Robert Scott, Magistrate Dennis F. Fitzgerald, and State Representatives Joseph MacIvor and Henry S. Myers were employed as district inspectors to see that Vare carried out the work properly.[30]

A conspiracy to defraud the city in the construction of the smallpox wing of the new municipal hospital, which was uncovered in October 1905, shows just how much the awarding of contracts was a tightly knit Organization affair. Those charged included Abraham L. English, the director of public safety under Mayor Ashbridge (1899–1903), who awarded the $1 million contract in 1903; city architect Philip H. Johnson, who was Durham's brother-in-law; and two representatives of Henderson & Company, of which McNichol was a director. It was shown that they acted together to change the specifications of the contract after it was awarded and carried it out in their

THE
VICIOUS CIRCLE
OF
"POLITICAL CONTRACTOR"CONTROL   ("P.C")
IN
PHILADELPHIA'S
CURRENT MIS-GOVERNMENT

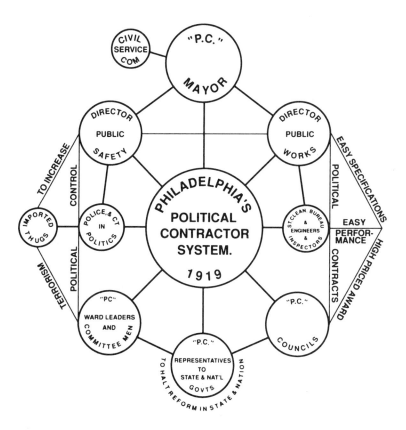

Fig. 6. Philadelphia's Political Contractor System, 1919. This chart, illustrating how the "contractor bosses" were able to maintain a tight grip on the awarding of contracts for public work, was used by the Philadelphia Charter Revision Committee in its publicity campaign to secure the passage of a new city charter in 1919. (From Neva R. Deardorff, "To Unshackle Philadelphia," *The Survey* [April 5, 1919], 21.)

own way, with the aid of the building inspector, James D. Finley, a flour merchant who also happened to be Durham's cousin.[31]

The construction of the Torresdale water filtration system, between 1899 and 1907, provides the best illustration of the methods successive administrations used to stifle fair competition among contractors; all but two of the major contracts for this $25 million enterprise were awarded to D. J. McNichol & Company.

In June 1905, Mayor John Weaver had a falling-out with Durham over the boss's proposal to lease the city's gas works to the United Gas Improvement Company. Weaver "turned reformer" and appointed "two of the country's foremost engineers," John Donald Maclennan and Major Cassius E. Gillette of the War Department, to head an inquiry into the awarding of contracts for the construction of the filtration plant. The engineers reported back to the mayor that the favored contractors, in collusion with city officials, had robbed the treasury of $6 million of the $18 million spent on the filtration scheme by 1905, even when allowing the contractors a 20 percent profit margin.[32]

Their investigation into this "graft operation" revealed that a variety of methods had been used to "guide the contracts into the 'right' hands," as the *Public Ledger* put it.[33] These included inadequate advertising for bids, the insistence on lump-sum bids (rather than itemizing bids so competitors could have made intelligent bids on the different classes of work at unit prices), and the Filtration Bureau's withholding (except for the favored contractor) of information needed to calculate such an estimate; the awarding of contracts to McNichol's company on the basis that it was the "best" or most "responsible" bidder, rather than the "lowest" bidder, and on the grounds that his firm would complete the work in the shortest time; the readvertisement of some contracts when other competitors were the lowest bidders; and, finally, the intimidation of competitors by contract specifications that "gave excessive and unnecessary power to city officials."[34]

In the case of the latter, the filtration contracts contained a clause that gave the director of public works authority to change the plans and specifications of contracts to an unlimited extent, and to fix the price of work as charged. The engineers claimed that the main purpose of this provision was to permit city officials to harass an unwelcome contractor without the latter being able to prevent it or to secure legal redress.[35]

The experience of George C. Dietrich, who managed to obtain one of the two large contracts that eluded McNichol, suggests the engineers were correct in their assessment. Dietrich attempted to build Lardner's Point Station

No. 2 for $532,000, leaving himself a margin of $120,000 as protection against accidents and delays and to provide a reasonable profit, but because he had successfully underbid the McNichol firm he incurred the wrath of the Organization. The chief of the Filtration Bureau, John W. Hill, who had been specially imported from Boss Cox's Cincinnati, told his inspectors to "keep after that Dutchman [Dietrich]—you must nail him down to a hair." In fact, sixty-two material changes were made to the specifications of his contract, and eighty-nine supplementary sheets of drawings were issued after the contract was let. Dietrich was forced into bankruptcy and left Philadelphia for Seattle a ruined man.[36]

In these circumstances, it is not surprising to find that there was no competition for the five largest contracts awarded for constructing the filters and providing sand and gravel to fill them. Contemporaries such as reformer Rudolph Blankenburg, however, were still bewildered that city work totaling $9,400,000 could not attract other bidders: "It is an astonishing feature of the bidding for the sand contracts, which were the largest that had ever been awarded in Philadelphia or elsewhere in the U.S., that not a single firm of sand-dealers participated in the bidding, although there were a dozen or more reputable and thoroughly competent dealers in the article in the city."[37]

The Vares apparently obtained their street-cleaning contracts like McNichol secured the filtration contracts. Street-cleaning contracts were awarded on a yearly basis only, which meant that prospective bidders had to take the risk of purchasing expensive vehicles and machinery without any guarantee that their contract would be renewed. They were also not awarded until late November, which did not allow sufficient time for a new contractor to establish his own dumping stations throughout the city.[38] In addition, bidders were discouraged by two specifications that were never enforced when Edwin Vare was awarded the contract: the contractor had to "employ an extra 195 men as 'block men' to clean each city square" in the downtown district and make sure there was "a sufficient number of men maintained on all asphalt, brick and wood block streets to keep them clean at all times."[39]

The wide interpretation that could be placed on the latter specification meant that officials of the Street-Cleaning Bureau could easily harass an unwanted contractor. This occurred in the case of Daniel Dooley, an independent contractor who suffered a fate like that of George C. Dietrich. In 1903 Dooley obtained the street-cleaning contract in the third district for $59,000, underbidding the Contracting Combine by $112,000. From the outset, he was harassed as numerous complaints were filed with the bureau that he was not fulfilling the contract specifications. He was compelled to pay fines totaling $9,084.50, or 15 percent of the contract value. Dooley was again successful in bidding for the 1904 contract, but the strain of events took their toll, for he died in March of that year, a victim of what his widow and the *North American* called "gang persecution."[40] After the Dooley episode, the Vares picked up street-cleaning contracts on a regular basis, and by 1911 they were the only bidders, offering to clean the entire city for $1,340,000. The *North American* called the charade of awarding contracts "a Reyburnian Joke."[41]

An important consequence of the ability of successive party leaders to subject subordinates, both in party office and in public office, to a reliable system of control was that the city boss was able to regulate the legislation that did (or did not) pass through City Council. As George W. Norris, Blankenburg's director of wharves, docks, and ferries, complained, "The legislation that the Mayor wanted, the [Councils] refused. The legislation that he did not want they passed over his veto."[42] For example, when reformers persuaded the state legislature to pass a new housing code in 1913 that regulated health and safety standards in Philadelphia, the Councils, guided by Edwin Vare, voted insufficient funds to pay for the one hundred sanitary inspectors that would have to be hired to ensure that the act was enforced.[43]

In a similar vein, a decade earlier, Israel Durham repeatedly blocked the efforts of utilities financier John Mack to secure a Council ordinance that would have allowed him to break the Philadelphia Electric Company's local monopoly on electric lighting. Mack, a railroad financier and street-paving and garbage disposal contractor, had been a close associate of Durham's at the turn of the century. He was also president of the Keystone Telephone Company and interested in using the company's extensive underground conduits to establish a new electric company.[44] Fearful of a potential rival, Joseph McCall, president of Philadelphia Electric, attempted to take over the Keystone Company in 1904. Durham acted as an intermediary for Mack and negotiated a deal with McCall whereby Philadelphia Electric would purchase the Keystone conduits for $2.5 million. In addition, Durham promised McCall that the Councils would approve an ordinance prohibiting the further stringing of electric-light wires within the districts covered by the Keystone's conduits, thereby safeguarding the company's future interests.

On returning from holiday, Mack rejected the agreement and demanded that Philadelphia Electric pay $3 million for the underground conduits. When McCall refused to increase his offer, Mack announced his intention to compete against Philadelphia Electric and promised prospective consumers a

20 percent reduction in electric rates. Meanwhile, Durham, humiliated at the way Mack had canceled his agreement, vowed that no ordinance giving Mack electric privileges would ever pass the Councils. Mack attempted to secure an ordinance on several occasions, but he never succeeded. He was eventually forced to accept McCall's original offer, and, worse still, his contract work for the city was substantially cut. Durham contemptuously dismissed him with the expression "Why, that man doesn't know what division he lives in and could not carry it with a million dollars."[45]

Because the boss's approval was necessary to pass legislation in the Councils, communication and payment passed through him rather than directly from private interests to subordinates. That is, when businessmen, or big corporations such as the Pennsylvania Railroad, sought legislative privileges, they channeled their requests and "contributions" (the "routine graft," or oil that kept the machine in running order) through the city boss's eleventh-floor office in the Betz Building. They rarely attempted to bribe councilmen on an individual basis, as they had done in the past, nor did they bother to lobby the mayor, the official head of government. Instead, private interests found that their needs were more easily met by dealing with a single overall boss, a leader of unofficial executive status who could guarantee results because of his ability to control city government.[46]

For example, when the Mutual Automatic Telephone Company secured franchise privileges in July 1894, it was obliged to distribute $363,000 of its stock to the Organization. Seventy-five members of Common Council were each allocated six $50 shares, and twenty-five Select Council members were allocated twenty shares each. This share distribution guaranteed a three-fifths majority in each Council chamber, enough to secure passage of the franchise in the event of a mayoral veto. Almost half the shares, however, went to David Martin and his associate Charles A. Porter, who each received 1,525 shares valued at $76,250.[47] The local reform watchdog group, the Citizens' Municipal Association, acknowledge that, as state senators, Martin and Porter had "no official connection with Councils" but that as leaders of the Republican party organization "possessed notorious influence with members."[48]

The "influence" David Martin and his successors as party leaders exercised was, as we have seen, the ability to subject subordinates, in both party office and public office, to a strict system of control. It is this increased discipline within the internal party organization that distinguishes genuine "boss" rule in turn-of-the-century Philadelphia from the party factionalism and ring rivalry that prevailed in the 1870s, when McManes and Stokley struggled for supremacy within the Republican party. Under Martin and his successors, the Organization exhibited the internal cohesiveness and discipline that was characteristic of the mature political machine—that is, the Republican party organization functioned as its centralized and hierarchical pyramid structure suggested it should. Because this transformation in the way the Organization functioned was dependent on its ability to command the support of the electorate on a regular basis, we need to look at who supported the Republican political machine and why.

6

Electoral Foundations and Functions of the Republican Machine

To provide a fully satisfactory explanation for the increased internal discipline within the Republican party organization, it is also necessary to see how the Organization was able to overwhelm its external electoral opponents, for as Edward Banfield and James Q. Wilson have pointed out, the former was dependent on the latter: "The existence of the machine depends upon its ability to control votes."[1]

The Organization's ability to control the electorate was impressive. Apart from the occasional defeat in 1905 and 1911, when reform elements were successful, the Republican party secured all city and county offices in Philadelphia (except where statute in the form of minority representation required otherwise) between 1887 and 1933.[2] Indeed, it was not unusual for the Organization to roll up enormous majorities in local elections. For example, mayoral candidates Ashbridge, Weaver, Moore, and Kendrick in 1899, 1903, 1919, and 1923, respectively, all polled well over 80 percent of the votes cast (see Table 13).

The question that presents itself, then, is how the Organization was able

Table 13.   The Republican Party Vote in Philadelphia Mayoral Elections,
1887–1931

Year	Candidate	% of Total Vote	Total Vote in Election
1887	Fitler	58.7	155,045
1891	Stuart	60.9	178,891
1895	Warwick	63.8	215,981
1899	Ashbridge	84.7	167,745
1903	Weaver	83.7	201,550
1907	Reyburn	57.6	211,585
1911	Earle	49.4	265,579
1915	Smith	63.4	265,067
1919	Moore	80.5	283,094
1923	Kendrick	86.5	330,970
1927	Mackey	66.8	444,215
1931	Moore	90.2	407,343

SOURCES: Election statistics published in the *Inquirer*, February 16, 1887; February 21, 1895; February 22, 1899; February 19, 1903; February 20, 1907; November 9, 1911; and the *Manual of Councils, 1916*, 301–37; *1920*, 274–75; *1927*, 285–86; *1931*, 297–98; as well as the *Eighteenth Annual Report of the Registration Commission* (Philadelphia, 1923), 18–19.

to get the support of the electorate so regularly. Conventional wisdom attributes the electoral success of political machines to their ability to attract disproportionate support from critical social groups (such as the poor and the foreign-born) in city populations[3]—that is, from voters who, for one reason or another (disorientation in a new environment,[4] unfulfilled "needs,"[5] or a particular "political ethos"[6]) were especially susceptible to the kind of inducements, such as patronage, favors, or services, the machines offered. To what extent was this the case in Philadelphia?

In the first instance, the institutionalization of the Organization did coincide with significant changes in the size and composition of the city's population. Up to the 1920s, the city's population continued to grow at approximately the same rate (20 percent) as in the early postbellum period. As a result, Philadelphia's population almost doubled, from just over 1,000,000 in 1890 to almost 2,000,000 by 1930 (see Table 14).

Immigrants too had made a significant contribution to this increase in numbers. In fact, one in two Philadelphians was either a first- or second-generation immigrant in the period between 1880 and 1930, and the foreign-born population alone accounted for almost 25 percent of the city's total population between 1880 and 1920 (see Table 15). The composition of

Table 14.   Population of Philadelphia, 1880–1930

Year	Total No.	% Increase
1880	847,170	—
1890	1,046,964	23.6
1900	1,293,697	23.6
1910	1,549,008	19.7
1920	1,823,779	17.7
1930	1,950,961	7.0
1880–1930	—	130.3

SOURCES: Census Office, *Census of Population, 1880*, 1:454–65; idem, *Vital Statistics of Boston and Philadelphia Covering a Period of Six Years Ending May 31, 1890* (Washington, D.C., 1894), 118–19; idem, *Census of Population, 1900*, 1:241–42, 677; U.S. Bureau of the Census, *Census of Population, 1910*, 3:605–8; idem, *Census of Population, 1920*, 3:896–99; idem, *Census of Population, 1930*, 3:688–707.

Philadelphia's ethnic population had also changed markedly over the period 1880–1920. For example, the proportion of the city's foreign-born population that was either Irish or German fell from more than 75 percent in 1880, to just over 25 percent by 1920. By this time, Russian Jews were the largest foreign-born group in the city, and there were almost equal numbers of foreign-born Italians and Irish (see Table 16).

When compared with other large northern cities, though, Philadelphia did not receive its proportionate share of new immigrants. In spite of its size and industrial importance, the percentage of foreign-born residents in Philadelphia was the lowest of all large northern cities, averaging 25 percent of the total population from 1870 to 1920, compared with 35 percent in Boston, 40 percent in New York, and even higher percentages in newer cities, such as Cleveland, Detroit, and Chicago.[7] Philadelphia's black population, by contrast, was large: almost 5 percent of the city's total population in 1900, and more than 10 percent by 1930 (see Table 15). Indeed, in 1900 Philadelphia housed a larger black community than any other northern city, and by the 1920s had a greater percentage of blacks than any other large city in the country, except for St. Louis and Baltimore.[8]

The data in Table 17 enable us to assess the importance of ethnicity and social class in accounting for the distribution of the Organization's electoral support. The entries in the table are unstandardized partial-regression coefficients (and the accompanying standard error) generated by a series of multiple-regression equations for the Philadelphia mayoral elections from

Table 15. Ethnic Composition of Philadelphia, 1880–1930 (as % of total population)

	1880	%	1910	%	1920	%	1930 (%)
Blacks	31,669	3.7	84,459	5.5	134,229	7.4	11.3
Ireland							
Born	101,803	12.0	83,196	5.4	64,590	3.5	2.7
2nd	126,655	15.0	115,809	7.5	—	—	6.8
Stock	228,463	27.0	199,005	12.9	—	—	9.5
Germany							
Born	55,769	6.6	61,480	4.0	39,766	2.2	1.9
2nd	80,700	9.5	89,187	5.8	—	—	—
Stock	136,469	16.1	150,667	9.8	—	—	—
Italy							
Born	1,656	0.2	45,308	2.9	63,723	3.5	3.5
2nd	—	—	28,942	1.9	—	—	5.8
Stock	—	—	74,250	4.8	—	—	9.3
Russia							
Born	276	0.03	90,697	5.9	95,744	5.3	4.5
2nd	—	—	45,650	3.0	—	—	5.3
Stock	—	—	—	8.9	—	—	9.8
Other Foreign							
Born	45,826	5.3	104,026	6.7	134,104	7.4	—
2nd	48,366	5.7	217,197	14.0	—	—	—
Stock	94,192	11.0	—	20.7	—	—	—
Total Foreign							
Born	205,330	24.1	384,707	24.7	397,927	21.8	18.9
2nd	255,721	30.2	496,785	32.1	591,471	32.4	31.7
Stock	460,056	54.3	881,492	56.8	989,398	54.2	50.6
Total Population	847,170		1,549,008		1,823,779		1,950,961

SOURCES: Census Office, *Census of Population, 1880,* 1:454–65; idem, *Vital Statistics of Boston and Philadelphia Covering a Period of Six Years Ending May 31, 1890* (Washington, D.C., 1894), 118–19; idem, *Census of Population, 1900,* 1:241–42, 677; U.S. Bureau of the Census, *Census of Population, 1910,* 3:605–8; idem, *Census of Population, 1920,* 3:896–99; idem, *Census of Population, 1930,* 3:688–707; Theodore Hershberg (ed.), *Philadelphia: Work, Space, Family, and Group Experience in the Nineteenth Century* (New York, 1981), 465.

NOTE: "Born" = the number of foreign-born in specified country; "2nd" = second generation, native born with fathers born in specified country; "stock" = foreign-born plus second generation.

1865 to 1931.[9] The dependent variable in each equation is the percentage of the ward's total mayoral vote in the general election that was cast for the Republican party's candidate. The independent variables in these equations measure the demographic characteristics of the ward. For instance, the variables German, Irish, Italian, and Jewish indicate what proportion of each

Table 16.   Ethnic Groups in Philadelphia, 1880–1920 (as % of total ethnic population)

	1880	1890	1910	1920
Foreign Born:				
English	12.9	14.4	9.6	7.8
German	27.3	27.8	16.1	10.0
Irish	49.8	41.2	21.8	16.2
Italian	0.8	2.5	11.8	16.0
Russian	0.1	2.9	23.7	24.1
Other	9.1	11.2	17.0	25.9[a]
Second Generation:				
English	—		4.2	
German	29.0		18.0	
Irish	45.5		23.3	
Italian	—		5.8	
Russian	—		9.2	
Other	25.5		39.5	

SOURCES: Census Office, *Census of Population, 1880,* 1:454–65; idem, *Vital Statistics of Boston and Philadelphia Covering a Period of Six Years Ending May 31, 1890* (Washington, D.C., 1894), 118–19; idem, *Census of Population, 1900,* 1:241–42, 677; U.S. Bureau of the Census, *Census of Population, 1910,* 3:605–8; idem, *Census of Population, 1920,* 3:896–99; idem, *Census of Population, 1930,* 3:688–707; Theodore Hershberg (ed.), *Philadelphia: Work, Space, Family, and Group Experience in the Nineteenth Century* (New York, 1981), 465.

[a]The largest ethnic group in this residual category were the Poles who comprised 7.8 percent of the city's foreign-born population in 1920.

ward's population had mothers who were born in Germany, Ireland, Italy, and Russia—the percentage of the ward's population that is first- or second-generation German, Irish, Italian, or Jewish. The "other foreign" variable is a residual category that indicates the percentage of the ward's population whose mothers were born in a foreign country other than Germany, Ireland, Italy, or Russia. (The "all foreign" variable has been used in equations where the information provided by the decennial census permitted only a limited breakdown of the population based on color and nativity.)[10] The final independent variable, "social class," is a measure of the class composition of the ward's population.[11]

These regression coefficients estimate the impact (controlling simultaneously for all other variables included in the equation) of a unit change in the variable in question on a ward's voting behavior. A coefficient of .63 on the Italian variable in the 1919 election, for example, indicates that, holding all other independent variables constant, as the first- and second-generation

Table 17. Ethnicity, Social Class, and the Republican Party Vote, Philadelphia Mayoral Elections, 1865–1931

Year	Blacks	Germans	Irish	Jewish	Italians	Other Foreign	All Foreign	Social Class	R^2
1865 [26]*							-.96[b] (.30)	.65 (.81)	.37
1868 [28]							-.83[b] (.27)		.32
1871 [29]	-.48 (.36)						-.92[b] (.29)	-.42 (.64)	.34
1874 [29]	.23 (.31)						-.73[b] (.25)	-.69 (.54)	.31
1877 [31]	.43[c] (.23)	-.39 (.49)	-.31[c] (.13)			-.47 (.30)		-.15 (.11)	.54
1881 [31]	.26 (.23)	-.59[b] (.19)	-.23 (.14)			-.82[c] (.31)		-.18 (.12)	.58
1884 [31]	.88[b] (.28)	-1.55[c] (.60)	-.29 (.16)			-.59 (.37)		-.42[b] (.13)	.57
1887 [31]	.20 (.19)	-1.41[a] (.21)	-.45 (.38)			-1.36[a] (.22)		.51 (.50)	.82
1891 [35]	.41[c] (.18)	-1.68[a] (.18)	-.68[c] (.32)			-1.03[a] (.20)		.20 (.46)	.83

Year									R^2
1895 [37]	.29 (.22)	-.58ᶜ (.22)	-.62 (.38)			-.68ᵇ (.24)		.47 (.56)	.41
1907 [45]	.52ᶜ (.24)	.21 (.36)	-1.07 (1.07)	.39ᶜ (.18)	.29 (.30)	.86 (.57)		-.61ᶜ (.23)	.61
1911 [47]	.80ᶜ (.32)	.31 (.46)	1.80 (1.42)	.43 (.24)	.31 (.40)	1.04 (.74)		-.26 (.29)	.63
1919 [48]	.43ᵇ (.15)	.27 (.96)		.15 (.21)	.63ᶜ (.27)	.78ᵇ (.28)		.11 (.24)	.38
1923 [48]	.23ᶜ (.10)	-.20 (.69)	-.18 (.69)	.12 (.17)	.43ᶜ (.21)	.48ᶜ (.20)		-.50ᵇ (.16)	.40
1927 [48]	.64ᵃ (.13)						1.68ᵃ (.33)		.65
1931 [48]	.86ᵃ (.04)						.37ᵃ (.09)	-.83ᵃ (.06)	.52

NOTE: The figures in this table are regression coefficients; those in parentheses are standard errors.

*The number in brackets following the year is the total number of wards (N) in the city at the time each mayoral election was held.

ᵃ$p < .001$.

ᵇ$p < .01$.

ᶜ$p < .05$.

Italian proportion of a ward's population increased by 10 percent, the Republican share of the ward's mayoral vote increased by 6.3 percent. Conventional methodological wisdom suggests that unstandardized regression coefficients are the measures least likely to run the risk of ecological fallacy. The table also reports the explained variance when all variables are entered in the equation.

What conclusions can be drawn from an examination of the coefficients? First, a knowledge of the class and ethnic composition of the city's wards enables one to explain in the usual statistical sense (R^2) from 31 percent to as high as 83 percent of the variation among the city's neighborhoods in the votes cast for the Republican party's candidates.

Second, the regression coefficients in these equations indicate a watershed at the turn of the century in the distribution of electoral support for the Republican party. The coefficients in the equations for 1865 to 1895, for instance, indicate that ethnicity is strongly negative and independently related to Republican party voting while social class is not. The coefficients of the "all foreign" variable in the equations for the elections held between 1865 and 1874 are all very large, negative, and significant at the .01 level. Similarly, the coefficients of the ethnicity variables in the equations for the elections held between 1877 and 1895 are again generally large, negative, and (in almost two-thirds of the cases) significant at the .05 level.[12] By contrast, in only one (1884) of the ten elections held between 1865 and 1895 does a regression coefficient of the social-class variable pass this test. From these results we can infer that up to 1895 the Republican party was supported overwhelmingly by the native-born population, irrespective of social class, and vigorously opposed by the ethnic population, which during this period was composed largely of Irish and German immigrants.[13]

The regression coefficients in the equations for 1907 to 1931 reveal a marked change, however, in the distribution of the party's electoral support. Contrary to the earlier pattern of support, they indicate that social class is strongly negative, and independently related, to Republican party voting, while ethnicity is (for the most part) not. The coefficients of the social-class variables in these equations, for example, are generally large, negative, and in three out of five elections significant at the .05 level.[14] By contrast, only one-third (7 out of 21) of the coefficients of the ethnicity variables manages to pass this test. The coefficients of the remaining independent variable in the equations (that is , the "black" variable) are different again from those of the social-class variables and the ethnicity variables in that they are generally large and positive, and all of them are significant at the .05 level.

These results suggest that by the turn of the century the electoral base of the Republican party did bear some resemblance to that of the classic political machine, as portrayed by conventional wisdom. The Organization was supported by the poor and the black population of the city, if not by voters of immigrant stock. However, the claims of contemporary Republican party leaders that "Poles, Hungarians, Italians and other foreigners when they come here vote for the Republican ticket," as well as the fact that seven of the coefficents of the ethnicity variables in Table 17 are moderate to large, positive, and significant at the .05 level, suggest it would be premature to conclude that the Organization was not supported by the "new" immigrant population in Philadelphia.[15]

How can we reconcile this apparent paradox between the assertions of contemporary machine politicians that there was a clear relationship between the Organization and immigrant voters, and the failure of Table 17 to show such a relationship? The answer lies in the fact that (contrary to the presupposition on which Table 17 is based) ethnic voting behavior, as John Shover has demonstrated, was not uniform across the city as a whole.[16] Shover shows that immigrants who resided in Philadelphia's urban core early in the twentieth century were much more likely to vote for the machine in significantly greater proportions than their counterparts in outlying suburban districts, a characteristic that was reflected in the Organization's ability to secure (from 1903 onward) a consistently higher level of support in the city center and in South Philadelphia ("The Neck")—the area sandwiched between the Schuylkill and Delaware rivers (see Figure 7)—than in any other section of the city (see Table 18).[17]

Since Philadelphia's immigrants also differed from one another in terms of their backgrounds, their reasons for emigrating, and in such matters as religion, language, and dress, this divergence (by location) in ethnic voting behavior not only accounts for the failure of Table 17 to show a meaningful relationship between immigrant voters and the Organization, but also suggests that it must have been *environmental* factors, rather than *cultural* ones, that induced ethnic voters in the inner city to support the Republican political machine.[18] That is, it was the postmigration problems of adjustment to a new alien environment which drove immigrants, along with the poor and black population of the urban core, to support the Republican Organization in return for the "personal service" it rendered.[19] Put another way, the relationship between the Republican Organization and its supporters conforms to that suggested by scholars—Richard Wade, Oscar Handlin, William Whyte, and Robert Merton—who argue that the machine should

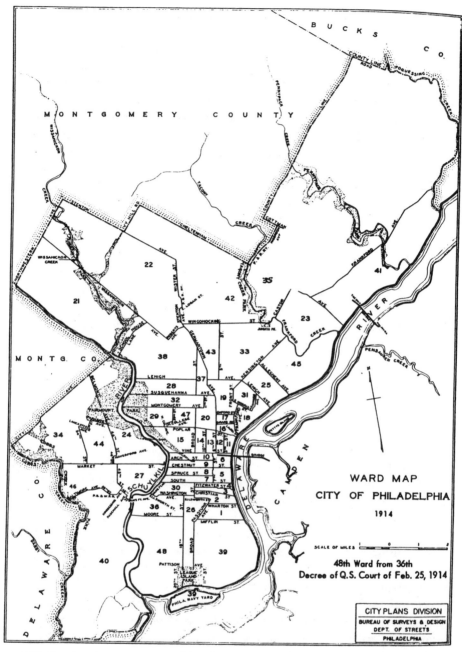

Fig. 7. Ward Map of the City of Philadelphia, 1914. (From: John Daly and Allen Weinberg, *Genealogy of Philadelphia County Subdivisions*, 2nd ed. [Philadelphia, 1966], 84.)

be viewed as an expression of the patterns of social life in the city's tenement districts: as a defensive reaction against discrimination and as a natural product of the social structure of the inner city.[20]

Robert Merton and the Latent Functions

Although this postmigration theory helps us to identify why immigrants supported the machine and which immigrants were especially likely to vote for the machine, the scholars who subscribe to this view are not just concerned with accounting for the distribution of electoral support for the urban political machine. Robert K. Merton, in particular, has been responsible for establishing a more positive image of the role the political machine played.[21] And Oscar Handlin, Eric McKitrick, Elmer Cornwell, Alexander Callow, Seymour Mandelbaum, Zane Lee Miller, and John Allswang have all incorporated Merton's functional model in their analysis of the political machine— so much so, in fact, that in the last thirty years bosses and reformers have undergone a role reversal in the literature on urban politics.[22] The urban bosses are now depicted as "good guys" who served the needs of the otherwise unorganized urban poor, while the reformers were allegedly business and professional men intent on imposing economic and cultural control over the lower orders.

But how valid is Merton's analysis of the relationship between the machine and its supporters? Did the machine fulfill the "latent" functions Merton suggests it did? How well does Merton's model fit the reality of Republican Organization rule in Philadelphia?

The short answer is: not very well at all. The current preference for bosses over reformers is rooted in the conviction that the reformers were unresponsive to the poor when they championed programs from motives of efficiency, and bosses won the support of the poor whose lives they understood when they attacked reformers' programs. The problems with this approach, however, are illustrated in John F. Baumann's study of the Philadelphia Housing Commission between 1909 and 1916.[23] Baumann criticizes the reformers for imposing efficiency on slum-dwellers when they secured the Heidinger Housing Act of 1913, which created one hundred sanitary inspectors to regulate health and safety in Philadelphia's poor housing. Edwin Vare, popularly known as "the apostle of the poor," then served his constituents—Baumann

Table 18. The Republican Party Vote in Philadelphia Mayoral Elections, 1887–1931 (as % of total vote in district)

District	1887	1891	1895	1899	1903	1907	1911	1915	1919	1923	1927	1931
Center	66.4	69.7	66.8	87.8	89.1	68.9	78.0	88.0	93.1	95.7	86.8	96.1
South	52.0	58.1	58.5	81.3	87.9	70.9	60.8	79.0	84.7	93.5	85.6	94.1
West	64.4	65.3	62.5	82.5	75.6	46.7	42.2	52.4	72.8	85.0	59.8	89.1
Northwest	63.5	63.2	64.3	86.5	81.8	51.7	45.1	58.6	82.8	85.6	59.4	91.8
Northeast	53.4	56.1	65.5	84.4	82.5	58.1	44.2	62.6	77.6	88.4	65.2	91.3

SOURCES: Election statistics published in the *Inquirer*, February 16, 1887; February 21, 1895; February 22, 1899; February 19, 1903; February 20, 1907; November 9, 1911; and *Manual of Councils*, *1916*, 301–37; *1920*, 274–75; *1927*, 285–86; *1931*, 297–98; as well as the *Eighteenth Annual Report of the Registration Commission* (Philadelphia, 1923), 18–19.

NOTE: The five districts into which the city has been divided for the purposes of this analysis are the same as those used by John Daly and Allen Weinberg in their *Genealogy of Philadelphia County Subdivisions*, 2nd edition (Philadelphia 1966), 98–100; that is, Center City comprising of wards 5,6,7,8,9 and 10; South Philadelphia (1,2,3,4,26,30,36,48), West Philadelphia (24,27,34,40,44,46), and that area to the Northwest (13,14,15,20,21,22,28,29,32,37,38,42,47) and Northeast (11,12,16,17,18,19,23,25,31,33,35,41,43,45) of the downtown core. For the precise location of these forty-eight individual wards see Figure 7.

appears to argue—by blocking funds to pay the inspectors and by emasculating the housing law in the next legislative session.[24] The reformers may have wanted to inspect housing because they were inspired by the need for efficiency, but it does not follow that poor slum-dwellers opposed inspections that would improve the health and safety of their homes. Indeed, since the Housing and Sanitation Division of the city's Health Bureau was at this time receiving two hundred complaints a day concerning violations of existing laws, it seems more plausible that poor slum-dwellers would have welcomed inspections as a way of improving housing conditions.[25]

Baumann's argument, however, leaves us with having to accept the highly improbable assertion that the urban poor preferred the boss's system of regulation whereby slumlords and manufacturers could provide unsafe and unhealthy living and working conditions in exchange for buying off the machine's inspectors. If we were to extend Baumann's argument to other issues raised during Blankenburg's reform administration (1912–16), for example, the reformers' efforts to lower food and gas prices in the city, and to institute a public works program during the depression of 1914 to 1915 (initiatives that were all thwarted by the Organization[26]) we would be left with the incongruous proposition that the urban poor preferred a system of boss rule that maintained high food and gas prices and unemployment.

Baumann's study does demonstrate that bosses gave as much aid to slumlords and manufacturers who got rich off the urban poor as they gave to the poor themselves. Indeed, in the case of Philadelphia, the Republican Organization, at the same time it was providing a "personal service" for the immigrant poor, was also aiding and abetting those interests—the saloon, gambling-house, and tenement-house owners, the utility entrepreneurs, the land developers, and the manufacturers—who were making large profits as a result of urban growth, often at the expense of the working classes.[27]

The "personal service" the Organization provided was, moreover, simply that: favored individuals received such benefits as buckets of coal, Christmas turkeys, summer trips to Atlantic City, or jobs on the public payroll, but these favors constituted the sum total of the Organization's welfare program.[28] In other words, the Organization's petty welfare system provided a social service only on a sketchy, unsystematic, and haphazard basis.

The Organization actually did little to promote genuine social reforms that would have met the real needs of its constituents—for example, programs that would have provided decent housing, good schools and hospitals, clean water, full employment, and racial integration.[29] Instead, it focused its energies on "giving the people something they could see." Essentially practical, the Organization reasoned that ordinary citizens judged a government by tangibles they could see with their own eyes, so it supported ambitious building projects—such as the Ben Franklin Parkway, the Roosevelt (Northeast) Boulevard, the League Island Park, and the Municipal Stadium—which were aimed at promoting civic improvement while at the same time beautifying the city. Such schemes provided the Organization with new allies in the business community and led to more jobs, patronage, and profit for the machine.[30]

Some contemporaries were not beguiled by the Organization's strategy. Political satirist Edmund Sage noted in his novel *Masters of the City,* published in 1909, that the products of Organization rule lay "in driveways and distant parks, in Temples of Justice and public buildings, in fanciful lamps and freak decorations." But, he continued, "All of these things do not reach the mass of the people. It does not give seats in schools, take the dirt from off the streets, give the tired man and woman a rest in the trolley or train, keep down rents, abolish crowded tenements, provide playgrounds, supply drinking fountains and public lavatories for the people."[31] Most projects were downtown-oriented, in order to bring traffic to the downtown, to beautify it, and to raise or maintain downtown business property values. Too little funds and too little energy remained for other things.

The tradition of the "boss" from Vare down to Daley has been that of "giving people what they wanted," but in practice this meant what the machine has perceived as what the people wanted. The real question is whether the needs of a large urban center and its people would not have been better met if more money had been spent on less glamorous programs, such as proper police and fire protection, better housing, and sanitation.

In the 1960s, Sam Bass Warner Jr. conducted an examination of Philadelphia's urban development in an attempt to understand why contemporary America was facing an urban crisis. His conclusion was that the long tradition of excessive reliance on private institutions and private wealth as the basic mode of social organization in the city was responsible for the ills that afflicted contemporary urban America. "Privatism" (which was, Warner subsequently explained, actually "capitalism" and the culture it spawned) was the enduring legacy "each Philadelphia" had bequeathed its successor.[32] Ultimately, "in the end," according to Warner, "the failure of the industrial metropolis was political." Local and state professional political leaders, Warner said,

utterly avoided dealing with the mounting social welfare and economic and physical development issues which constituted both the
disorders and the potential of the metropolis. . . . The whole negative attitude toward government which characterized the Republican . . . leadership encouraged a least-cost, low-quality orientation
toward all public institutions and programs whether they were police
departments, or schools, hospitals or highways.[33]

"The most conscientious research," Warner suggests, "would be required to
arrive at a judicious estimate of which of these two groups of professional
political leaders did the most damage to the city of Philadelphia."[34]

It is difficult to disagree with Warner's assessment, for the tradition of
"privatism" dovetailed neatly with the self-serving instincts of the Organization. That is, the Organization was unlikely to undermine the traditional
reverence for private enterprise because, as we shall see, it was in an ideal
position to cultivate and benefit from quid pro quo arrangements with
private interests.[35] Besides, bossism as a political situation was innately
conservative and defensive and by its very nature tended to avoid controversy
and division. Thus, ideological issues and the public interest were placed
well behind the need for political organization and self-preservation, a viewpoint that is nicely encapsulated in Durham's "What do I care who is
President, so long as I can carry my ward."[36]

The North American's obituary for Iz Durham emphasizes the self-serving
nature of bossism and its failure to promote the public welfare:

> Of the qualities of statesmanship he had none. He had no ideals. His
> ambitions were all selfish. He leaves no monument in the shape of a
> good statute or ordinance or any piece of constructive legisla-
> tion, . . . no civic improvement or betterment.[37]

According to Warner, the Vare brothers too, "after almost forty years of
power and effort, . . . could boast of very little constructive results for
Philadelphia."[38] Harold Zink credits the brothers for encouraging all sorts of
public works measures that benefited their South Philadelphia constituents,
and for their support as state legislators of such progressive reforms as child
labor laws, limitations on women's hours of work, worker compensation, and
mothers' assistance welfare payments. He also praises Edwin Vare for his

personal generosity to various charitable institutions and to individuals seeking aid.[39]

But a closer examination of the Vare brothers' activities reveals that they supported these social reforms only in the final stages of their passage—an astute political ploy on their part, because not to have supported the legislation would have meant damaging their reputations with their local constituents. The brothers did not initiate any of these social reforms, probably for the quite logical reason that the legislation represented a direct threat to the Organization's system of "personal service."[40] With regard to their support for various local public-works measures, Zink neglects to mention that it was the Vares who benefited from such schemes in the form of public contracts and that they could well afford to be generous benefactors to the poor because they were making exorbitant profits from such work.[41]

If the biographers of the state political leaders are to be believed, Matt Quay and Boies Penrose also were no more useful to the city's welfare than Durham or the Vare brothers. Indeed, the former appear to be carbon copies of their urban counterparts. James A. Kehl concluded his assessment of Quay's career with the comment that although the state boss had been "bold and innovative in party methods," he "did not apply his creativity to policy issues." Kehl continued:

> If he had displayed the same vision toward the issues that he displayed toward party organization, he might have become a statesman. Quay and his fellow politicians preferred to treat social and economic dysfunctions with verbal patches and legislative bandages, instead of forward-looking statesmanship. By supplying superficial responses they permitted many of society's most crucial decisions to gravitate from the realm of party and government into the hands of the rising industrial complex. Thus the party system failed to function as an effective catalyst when the nation desperately needed solutions to basic problems.[42]

Like Quay, Penrose appears to have devoted himself to the service of his party and to have invested little energy in tackling the pressing social and economic problems of the day. Walter Davenport put it colorfully.

> You may scan the records of Pennsylvania's legislature until vertigo threatens and fail to find more than a meagre scattering of his personal contributions to the political or social fabric of his state.

As later in the U.S. Senate, Penrose originated little or nothing of importance. His whole energies went into the service of his party in its struggle to perpetuate itself; or to his faction of the Republican party; or to those great business interests which provided him and his following with the funds with which to smother opposition. Penrose as a legislator, a contributor to government, was as colorless and unappealing as a sleeping walrus. Potentially until dissipation, sloth, prejudice, and narrow partisanship crippled his fine mind he was a statesman. Actually he was a glorified district leader and he remained just that, even through all his years in the U.S. Senate. [43]

Few people will need convincing that bosses were self-serving and devoted to their party organization, but what these assessments of the city and state's political leadership also point to is that bossism was destructive of functioning government for the vast majority of immigrants and low-income people who needed government the most. While Merton argues that the machine was successful because it served functions that were "at the time not adequately fulfilled by other existing patterns and structures," I contend that in the case of Philadelphia its main contribution was dysfunctional. Rather than being a natural functional substitute for government as Merton, and Max Weber, have claimed, the boss and his machine effectively prevented political parties and governments from devising, initiating, and implementing programs that could have dealt with the critical social and economic ills that have so bedeviled the modern American city.

In Philadelphia and in Pennsylvania, the Republican party organization itself was the subject of local and state election campaigns as questions of honesty and propriety in government took precedence over such difficult and important matters as economic development and social welfare. [44] When in office, the Organization concentrated on "giving the people something they could see," rather than attempting to meet the real needs of its supporters. It also prevented other groups from implementing programs that attempted to meet those needs, as the Women's League for Good Government wearily pointed out in 1919:

> The Organization is a sinister force that forms part of our "invisible government." If we attempt to analyse it, it seems to be more than anything else a tacit understanding of mutual helpfulness between men who make a business of using the machinery of popular government for the furtherance of their own personal ends. It is difficult to

locate it. Like the hurricane, we cannot always tell whence it cometh or whither it goeth, but we see the results clearly enough. It results in filling public offices with men who are at the best poorly fitted for the place, sometimes actually dishonest: in extravagance and misuse of public funds; in the passing of unnecessary laws that create "jobs"; in the quiet thwarting of measures urged by the public for the public good. As often in life, the innocent suffer for the guilty.[45]

Indeed, though Merton has argued that the machine, centralized and disciplined, developed as an alternative to the confused, decentralized nature of formal government, in the case of Philadelphia the Republican Organization, rather than "bringing order" to the city, actually perpetuated the diffusion and fragmentation of power. This is evident in the Organization's reaction to structural reform. In 1919, for example, the Vare brothers unsuccessfully resisted the passage of a new city charter that set up a streamlined unicameral system of government in place of the large and unwieldly bicameral version that had developed under the Bullitt Charter of 1887.[46] What is surprising about the brothers' opposition, however, is that back in 1905 they had supported, for the city's education system, the very kinds of reforms they subsequently fought against in municipal government. For instance, the 1905 school law created for the cities and towns of Pennsylvania a modern, centralized, bureaucratic management of schools. In Philadelphia, power was taken from the forty-two ward school boards and placed in the hands of a small central Board of Education and a strong superintendent of schools.[47]

There is a simple explanation for the apparent paradoxical behavior of the Vare brothers in 1905 and 1919. In 1905, the brothers were faithful supporters of Durham and Penrose's campaign to maintain a centralized and citywide Republican party organization. Durham was a keen supporter of the 1905 school reform because by abolishing ward school boards, and with them the local public office of school director, the law helped the city boss centralize authority within the Republican party by breaking down the independent strength of the party's ward organizations.[48] By 1919, however, the Vares were engaged in factional warfare with Penrose's supporters for control of the Republican City Committee, and indeed it was the state boss who was largely responsible for the passage of the new city charter. The brothers opposed the new charter because it broke down their power base in the oldest parts of the city (as Penrose intended) and fixed accountability and responsibility in local government more rigidly.[49]

The actions of the state and local party leaders in 1905 and 1919 suggest that these bosses had a pragmatic approach toward reform. Some scholars, notably J. Joseph Huthmacher and John D. Buenker, have argued that urban political machines made a significant contribution to the social and structural reforms that characterized the progressive era in the United States. Indeed, Buenker suggests that political bosses were partly responsible for the development of a new ideology, which he terms "urban liberalism."[50]

To label party bosses in Philadelphia "urban liberals" would be both inappropriate and misleading. Their behavior seems to indicate that they were power brokers who were primarily interested in maintaining control over their affairs, and who were prepared to support, or oppose, reform measures when it was in their interest to do so. In other words, the selective approach Republican bosses adopted toward social and structural reforms illustrates that they were not so much "for" or "against" reform as they were concerned with their own self-interest and the life of their party machine. Calling these Republican bosses "urban liberals" would entirely miss the point of their activity. The same can be said of Merton's functional analysis, in the sense that it greatly exaggerates the importance of the boss's services to the immigrant poor, while failing to recognize that the political machine in fact functioned as a blight on the system of government.

Merton also suggests that one of the machine's latent functions was to operate as a channel of social mobility for the urban immigrant poor. Again, it seems that in Philadelphia the Republican Organization did not fulfill this role. For example, John L. Shover analyzed the relationship between ethnicity and voting behavior in Philadelphia and surveyed the recipients of political patronage positions in local government between 1916 and 1938. He discovered that county non-civil-service jobs requiring no special skills were overwhelmingly allocated to persons with English, Scottish, and German surnames. In 1916 only 5 percent of these positions were held by persons with Jewish or Italian names. By 1932, according to Shover, Jews and Italians still held only 8 percent of such jobs.[51]

The "representative sample" of division leaders published by "The Young Republicans" in 1926 also provides us with an insight into those who staffed the party organization at the grass-roots level when the Republican machine was at the peak of its power and when the city's Jews and Italians were well established as the largest foreign-born groups in Philadelphia. I found that 62 percent of these party committeemen were jobholders and that, like Shover, less than 5 percent of them had Italian, Jewish, or Polish names.[52]

So, far from providing a career ladder for the immigrant poor, the Republican Organization in Philadelphia seems to have slighted its strongest supporters: the city's Italian, Jewish, and black populations.[53]

Finally, Merton's claim, and Banfield and Wilson's suggestion, that the political machine facilitated the integration of immigrants into the community, and thus their consequent assimilation into the middle-class political ethos, is also not tenable in the case of Republican Philadelphia. Shover has demonstrated that ethnoreligious political consciousness, far from diminishing, actually flourished in the city in the 1930s. By 1936, when the Philadelphia version of the New Deal coalition had taken shape, with only native whites remaining Republican, the city's ethnic and religious groups, responded to vital political choices as blacks, Jews, Germans, or Catholics, even though they were acculturated in terms of language, value systems, and lifestyle, and not as Americans grouped cross-culturally by occupation, class, or neighborhood.[54]

At least in the case of Republican Philadelphia, then, Merton's functional analysis does not provide an accurate interpretation of the relationship between the political machine and its poor immigrant supporters. Moreover, his functional theory does not provide a satisfactory explanation for the functions of the political machine because it rests on a faulty premise: that the machine originated as a response to "needs" and demands that other institutions failed to satisfy. We have already seen, however, that by the time the bulk of the "new" immigrants were arriving in Philadelphia at the turn of the century, the Organization was already a full-fledged political machine—a political institution, in fact, that dominated the government and politics of the city.

Thus, the Republican machine was not the creation of the "new" immigrant masses, or a product of immigrant culture and ethnic conflict. It emerged as a consequence of changes in the organization and structure of party politics in the city, not in response to the "needs" of various social groups.[55] The Organization operated as a centralized political structure that assimilated most of the city's subgroups as they arrived in Philadelphia. In doing so, however, it exploited the urban immigrant poor as much as it helped them. Indeed, its role was of a dysfunctional nature, depriving immigrants and low-income groups of an effective local government that could cater to their real needs.

In arguing that the only needs the Organization served were its own, I am not suggesting that historians should again embrace the contemporary reform caricature of the political boss, but rather that the positive image of the boss in the current literature needs to be revised. Recognition that political bosses were not cultural pluralists, but as culturally narrow as the most nativist reformer, is long overdue.

One-Party Politics

The Republican party enjoyed an extraordinary degree of electoral success between 1887 and 1933. The key to its electoral supremacy was not just the "personal service" it provided to individual voters. It also rested on the Organization's ability to nullify electoral opposition by exploiting the weaknesses of, and divisions between, the Democratic party and the nonpartisan reform movement.

With regard to the former, the minority party experienced a phenomenal decline between the 1880s and 1920s, both in leadership strength and in grass-roots support. The Republican Organization benefited specifically from three major turning points in the fortunes of the Democratic party: two concerned with national party policy, and the other with a localized factional struggle. First, there was the nationwide shift toward the Republican party in 1894, for the Democrats, as the incumbent administration, were blamed for the severe economic depression affecting the country. In Philadelphia this was reflected in a major change in the voting pattern of the third congressional district, traditionally the bulwark of the Democratic party. In 1894, this normally Democratic stronghold returned a majority for the Republican gubernatorial nominee for the first time in the city's history.[56]

Second, the local consequences of the national party split over the free silver issue and Bryan's candidacy for the presidency in 1896 stripped the city's Democratic leadership of many socially prominent families, who could all trace their party lineage to before the Civil War. Local "blue-bloods" such as John Cadwalader Jr., George W. Norris, and John and William Bullitt, as well as such men of substance as company director Henry D. Welsh, newspaper publisher William Singerly, and lawyers Emmanuel Furth, George F. Baer, and Henry M. Dechert, all participated in the "Jeffersonian bolt" from the party in 1896.[57]

Finally, Samuel Jackson Randall's death in 1890 precipitated a factional struggle for control of the third district, which he had represented in Congress. The principal protagonists included Randall's staunch ally lawyer William F. Harrity, who was supported by the sixth ward leader, Thomas J.

Ryan, and by Charles P. Donnelly, chairman of the Democratic City Committee, against the combination of State Senator William McAleer and Judge James Gay Gordon.[58]

The Organization skillfully exploited this rivalry by initially supporting the Gordon-McAleer faction and then switching allegiance to the Harrity faction, while making inroads on them both and ultimately capturing the third congressional district for the Republican party.[59] In the 1890s David Martin successfully sponsored McAleer's bid for Congress against Harrity's nominees, and in return McAleer supported Republican candidates in local elections. The most infamous McAleer defections from the regular Democratic ticket occurred in the mayoralty election of 1895, and the shrievalty election of 1896, and as a reward McAleer was given the Republican nomination for Congress in 1898.[60] This proved to be his undoing, however, for with his own party hopelessly fragmented, McAleer polled more Republican than Democratic votes in every ward in the district. The Organization therefore decided to drop him from their ticket in 1900, as they no longer needed the support of a superannuated Democrat. In 1900 McAleer carried only the sixth and seventeenth wards, while Bryan gained a majority in the sixth ward in the Presidential election. By the turn of the century, the old Randall Democratic stronghold had disintegrated.[61]

Having dropped McAleer, the Organization negotiated a new arrangement with Tommy Ryan. Ryan agreed to aid the Republican Organization in exchange for political immunity for his sixth ward and control of minority patronage resources. The basis for this bipartisan agreement lay in the section of the state constitution that guaranteed minority representation.[62] Because the Organization could control the distribution of appointive minority posts and had sufficient votes at its disposal to determine which minority candidates would be elected, however, this type of bipartisan arrangement weakened the Democratic party, ultimately destroying its independence.[63] Reformer George W. Norris observed in 1915: "Under the vicious system of 'minority representation,' the Democratic party has become little more than a bi-partisan adjunct of the Republican Organization, trading votes in return for a few salaried positions." Consequently, "the straight Democratic vote has naturally shrunk to negligible proportions," from 39 percent of the total vote in the 1891 mayoral election to fewer than 4 percent in the 1915 election.[64]

The party's "redemption," and the reemergence of a competitive two-party system, did not occur until the municipal election of 1933; up to then, it continued to function as a "kept minority" or, as reformer Thomas Raeburn White put it, "a mere corrupt annex of the Republican Organization."[65]

When Ryan's successor Charlie Donnelly, for instance, proved wayward in his loyalty to the Organization, he was replaced in 1924 as chairman of the Democratic City Committee by John O'Donnell, one of Bill Vare's closest friends and a fellow South Philadelphian.[66] O'Donnell's response in 1932 to a fellow Democrat who suggested that he break with Vare indicates the extent to which the Democratic party was subservient to the Republican Organization during his tenure of office. The Democratic party chairman refused on the grounds that he could not "do that to my old friend who has kept me on his payroll for so many years. Vare has been paying the rent on Democratic Headquarters. I can't bite the hand that feeds me."[67] So the provision for minority representation, instead of strengthening the opposition party by guaranteeing that it would always have some patronage, fostered a system of politics that institutionalized the impotence of the Democratic party.

With the establishment, in effect, of one-party rule in Philadelphia from the mid-1890s to the early 1930s, the initiative among the Organization's opponents was seized by groups outside the party system, in particular by the nonpartisan reform movement. Again, though, the Organization was usually triumphant in overcoming this new source of electoral opposition. It employed a number of different strategies to undermine the strength of the reform movement. One of the Organization's favorite tactics was to emphasize the importance of national issues and national party policy at the expense of local affairs. In particular, it exploited the fears of the city's business community over such matters as the tariff and the currency issue by suggesting that voting any other way than for the Republican party in local elections would weaken the party nationally. A typical Organization circular published during the 1901 campaign, for example, addressed voters in the following terms:

> Dear friend, neighbor and businessman,
> . . . Prosperity over the last five years has been due to Republican principles, both nationally and in the city.
> Pennsylvania and Philadelphia are the greatest manufacturing state and city of a great country. Will you by your vote at the request and harangue of a few so-called reformers who have joined themselves together under various titles such as "the Municipal League," "Union Party," "Reform League" and other insidious and high-sounding titles be led astray into the camp of the enemy to give them aid and comfort in order to rejuvenate and encourage those who in the past have been most active in upholding Bryanism, free silverism, free

tradeism and the other isms so strongly advocated by the Democratic
party.

An examination of the names of the most prominent people who
head the opposition to the regular Republican candidates in this city
will show that it is the same old political fleas who jump from one
party to the other, one year supporting Lincoln and Grant, then Harrison and Cleveland, and finally the low estate of Bryanism. . . .[68]

In addition to appealing to national partisan sympathies, ward leaders, such
as David Lane, also suggested to party supporters that if they were dissatis-
fied with the leaders of the local Republican organization "the proper method
of procedure" would be to seek "reform within the party" and not to support
reform insurgency movements outside traditional party lines.[69]

This emphasis on party loyalty and national issues appears to have paid the
Organization handsome dividends, for on a number of occasions reformers
attributed their defeats to the syndrome of "party regularity."[70] It seems that
even the reformers themselves could be duped by the cry of "party regularity," as eminent publisher John C. Winston, chairman of the Committee of
Seventy, admitted to a City Party public meeting in 1905:

> I have tried, by hard work in the Committee of Seventy, to atone for
> all my folly as a blind voter. . . . Never again will I permit myself to
> be lulled into a political trance by the purring cry of "party regular-
> ity!" No man shall ever again make me believe that it is high treason
> to vote for a good man on any municipal ticket. I have sat on a low
> bench in a practical political school . . . and I wish every hide-bound
> "regular" could see the light as I see it now.[71]

The Organization also engaged in extralegal practices to thwart well-
intentioned reformers. These included the invasion of reform party ranks to
secure nominations the Organization could control, and ticket-splitting on
election days to give enough votes to the Democratic party to keep it, rather
than a reform third party, as the official minority party.[72] A good example of
the latter practice occurred in February 1905, when fifteen magistrates, or
more than half the entire minor judiciary, were due to be elected. On this
occasion, the Organization not only elected its own candidates but deliberately
and successfully transferred 55,000 votes, more than one-quarter of those
actually polled, to the Democratic ticket, thus ensuring its triumph as a
minority over the City Party ticket. The election returns indicate that the

"straight" ballot, based on the number of votes received by the Republican and Democratic candidates for the city solicitorship, was 180,000 and 24,000 votes respectively. However, in the magistrates contest the ten machine Republicans polled between 30,000 and 50,000 votes less (131,000 to 151,000), and the five Democratic nominees polled over 50,000 votes more (74,000 to 80,000), than their respective party candidates in the city solicitorship election. If a "straight" ballot had taken place in the magistrates contest, the City Party's nominees (29,000 to 36,000) would have been elected as the minor judiciary, rather than the Democratic party's candidates.[73]

The Organization repeated this ticket-splitting exercise again in 1921 to ensure that its subservient auxiliary, rather than the Independent Republicans, occupied the minor judicial offices once more.[74] It also implemented similar ticket-splitting schemes in 1899, 1923, and 1927 in order to make certain that its own favored candidate was elected to the minority county commissionership, particularly since the bulk of the minority patronage available in the city was at the disposal of this official.[75] In 1923, for example, the "straight" ballot, based on the number of votes polled by the Democratic party candidate in the mayoral election, was 37,000 votes, but in the minority county commissionership contest of that year, John O'Donnell outpolled Edgar Lank by 80,000 votes to 35,000, largely because the Organization switched over 40,000 Republican votes to elect the "Vare Democrat" to the office, rather than Charlie Donnelly's associate (see Table 19).[76]

Occasional ticket-splitting ventures and astute methods of campaigning provide only a partial explanation for the Organization's electoral success. According to Clinton Rogers Woodruff, secretary of the National Municipal League, the real "secret of the machine's ability to continue itself in power" was the control it had over the entire election machinery.[77] The Organization exercised this control through a variety of extralegal and illegal practices. The former included control over key public bodies that were meant to be impartial and were responsible for safeguarding the purity of the ballot—for example, the registration boards, whose duty it was to draw up lists of qualified voters; the divisional election boards, which were responsible for ensuring that proper procedures were adhered to on election day; and the county commissioners, who made all the preparations for the holding of elections, including the selection of polling places and the certification of watchers.[78]

Illegal practices usually involved registration frauds, such as the wrongful issue of poll-tax receipts to qualify voters for registration, and the padding of

Table 19. Ticket-Splitting in Selected Controlled Philadelphia Wards: County Commissioner and Mayoral Elections, 1923

Party Candidates	Wards and Vote Totals						Total Vote
	2	3	8	12	13	14	
Mayoral election (the "straight vote")							
Kendrick (R)	6,189	3,471	2,973	3,067	5,035	3,878	24,433
Raff (D)	110	70	101	73	89	186	629
County commissioner election (the "split vote")							
O'Donnell (D)	2,256	1,448	2,250	1,169	1,025	1,594	9,742
Lank (D)	107	62	87	58	71	169	554
Kuenzel (R)	6,132	3,449	2,769	2,182	4,079	2,472	21,083
Holmes (R)	4,036	1,992	651	2,860	4,979	3,871	18,389
O'Donnell's lead over Lank	2,149	1,386	2,163	1,111	954	1,425	9,188
No. of votes "dropped" by Holmes	2,096	1,457	2,108				
No. of votes "dropped" by Kuenzel			—	678	900	1,399	
Total no. of votes "dropped" by Holmes and Kuenzel both: 8,638							

SOURCE: *Eighteenth Annual Report of the Registration Commission* (Philadelphia, 1923), 18–21.

assessors' lists and registration books. Before the 1906 Personal Registration Act, local newspapers and reformers estimated that the number of fraudulently registered voters in the city varied between 30,000 and 80,000.[79] As late as 1926, however, the Reed Senate committee investigating William Vare's election to the U.S. Senate found almost 25,000 false entries in registration books across the city. The forged signatures included dead people, nonnaturalized foreigners, and children.[80] The Senate inquiry also found evidence of election fraud, such as voting by phantoms (nonregistered voters), multiple voting (repeating), the miscounting of votes, the altering of ballots, and ballot-box stuffing in election divisions throughout the city. Such malpractices, the Committee concluded, meant that the average chance of a Philadelphia voter having his vote in the U.S. senator contest properly recorded was one in eight.[81]

A final illegal practice was the coercion of voters as they entered polling places. Reform groups and contemporary observers, like political scientist Maynard Kreuger, maintained that it was "a notorious custom in Philadelphia for political workers to force voters who have no disability whatever to accept 'assistance' with the result that many ballots are marked by the same person and the secrecy of the ballot becomes a mockery."[82] An inquiry conducted in the wake of the 1909 city election by the "watchdog" reform group Committee of Seventy, for example, revealed that 38,000 votes, or more than 15 percent of the total votes cast, were marked by persons other than the voters.[83]

The Organization also benefited from the problems that beset its opponents, one of which was public apathy. The Municipal League even claimed that "the criminally indifferent citizen" was a "more formidable" problem than that of "fraudulent voting."[84] In its annual report for 1901–2 the League observed:

> The machine can always depend upon its vote, partly through the perfection of its organization; partly through its almost absolute control of the election officers; but its great source of strength, we might almost say its bulwark, is the indifference and apathy of the independent voter.[85]

League Secretary Clinton R. Woodruff also conceded that a "revival of interest on the part of the 'stay at home' voter" was a "greater need" than "protection from the fraudulent vote."[86] Woodruff and the Municipal League drew this conclusion from their observations on the voting turnout figures in local elections. They noted, for example, that in the mayoral elections of 1899 and 1903 only about half the electorate (47.6 percent and 57.6 percent, respectively) bothered to vote.[87] More significant, however, was the electoral survey they conducted in selected wards of the city, which revealed that in "respectable divisions" in "independent wards," "less than 50 percent of the voters took the trouble to vote," while in the "machine divisions" "the number of voters represent from 80 to 100 per cent of the assessment." "Throughout the city," the League concluded, "the day laborer and man of moderate means is much more diligent in the exercise of his franchise."[88]

Leading civic reformers, such as Rudolph Blankenburg and Herbert Welsh, and muckraking journalists, like Lincoln Steffens and Theophilus Baker, all agreed with the League's assessment.[89] For example, Blankenburg, writing in January 1905, suggested:

> One of the crying evils of the hour is the lamentable indifference of the average citizen to his public duties and the easy-going spirit with which he permits his municipal or State servant to become his master and ruler. . . .
>
> . . . We have in our midst a quarter of a million honest, well-disposed men who could rescue the city if they would cultivate and arouse the dormant public spirit within them, if they would once awaken from the political turpitude and moral lethargy, that has, almost continually for a generation, been their voluntary lot.[90]

As Steffens was carrying out his investigation of municipal corruption, fellow journalist Theophilus Baker was dissecting the "Philadelphia character," which he believed to be

> . . . [a] patent contradiction of a high private and low public morality. . . . There is what may be called, for want of a better name, a sort of moral *locomotor ataxia,* an inability to put into action the community's really high sense of right and wrong conduct. The citizens lack the virtue militant, that individually disagreeable, but socially valuable quality—pugnacity —the quality that leads an Englishman to spend £20 to avoid the illegal exaction of a shilling. They are law abiding, conservative to the point of allowing a rogue to rob them, if he only preserves the appearances and technicalities of legality.[91]

Such comments from outsiders helped give Philadelphia a national reputation, which still endures, of being a city that was conservative, complacent, and dull.

"Sinful contentment," as Blankenburg put it, proved to be short-lived, however, for the "better elements" were shaken out of their complacency partly as a result of Steffens's stinging rebuke, but mainly because of Durham's April 1905 proposal to lease the municipal gas works to his friend Thomas Dolan's United Gas Improvement Company on a long-term basis and at generous terms to the private corporation.[92] The so-called "gas steal" provoked such an outburst of public indignation against the Organization that it sparked a decade of insurgent reform activity in the city.[93]

This popular protest was also reflected in the substantial increase in the number of voters who went to the polls. For example, the turnout of voters for the mayoral elections of 1907, 1911, 1915, and 1919 was 84.4 percent, 71.6 percent, 86.7 percent, and 79.5 percent, respectively.[94] Yet the reformers had little to show for the increased activity at the polls. Their only victories were in November 1905, when the City Party managed to elect its entire ticket in the election for county offices, and in November 1911, when as a result of a temporary split within the Organization, Keystone party candidate Rudolph Blankenburg was elected mayor by the narrow majority of 3,333 votes.[95]

The reformers' lack of electoral success, it appears, was due to a more formidable problem than public indifference: the local strength of Republican partisanship. That obstacle provided opponents of the Organization with their greatest difficulty. The reformers themselves, even though they claimed to be nonpartisan, had problems shaking off their Republican identity. For example, such third parties as the City Party (1905–7), the Keystone party (1910–15), the Washington party (1912–16), and the Franklin party (1915–16) were all Republican in orientation, at least in national politics.[96] Moreover, although Thomas R. White claimed that nonpartisanship was the key to the City Party's victory in 1905, he also noted that many City Party members had argued "that the candidates ought not to be named as City Party candidates but as Republican candidates, nominated by an independent wing of the party."[97] Lincoln Steffens also described the Philadelphia reformers as loyal Republicans. He told Teddy Roosevelt: "They are Republicans and they are friends of yours and their plan is to make the City or Lincoln [Party] Republicans the real Republicans of Philadelphia."[98]

Similarly in 1911, Blankenburg's election as mayor, at the head of the Keystone party ticket, was hailed as a victory for Republicanism as well as for reform. The *Public Ledger*, an anti-Organization journal that supported Blankenburg, argued that the success of the reformers

> indicates the unalterable devotion of Philadelphia to the genuine principles of the national Republican party. It shows that the voters recognized in Mr. Blankenburg a better Republican . . . than his opponent . . . and that they have finally reached the conclusion that the principles of Republicanism . . . are far safer in the hands of a Blankenburg than in those of a candidate named by the McNichol machine.[99]

Again in 1915, the *Evening Ledger*, supporting the Franklin party ticket, declared that George Porter's election as mayor would "be a triumph for Philadelphia Republicanism of the best type and an inspiration to Republicanism throughout the nation."[100]

This recurring display of Republican partisanship on the part of the local press and third parties rankled many anti-Organization Democrats who were potential supporters of reform groups. The Democratic *Record* complained that the prevailing view among Philadelphia reformers in regard to local politics was:

> If the city is to be saved from the contractors, it must only be by Republicans. . . . Evidently no help in municipal reform is desired from persons who do not care what happens to the Grand Old Party, and from those who are perfectly satisfied to have it indefinitely out of power.[101]

The short-lived Franklin party was the last third party to claim that it was nonpartisan in local affairs. By the 1920s, all reform activity remained within party ranks. Independent Republicans in suburban wards battled with the Organization only at party primaries and not in general elections. When a disagreeable candidate obtained the Republican nomination and was opposed by a Democrat in the general election, the Independents either maintained their party regularity by voting for the candidate named in the primary or did not participate in the contest at all. And yet potentially, in combination with the estimated 30,000 "anti-Organization" Democrats in the city, Independent Republicans in the ring wards could have provided William Vare with formidable opposition. But such an alliance never materialized. The Independents stubbornly refused to leave the Republican party, even if it meant the continuation of the Organization's ascendancy.[102]

Indeed, from 1919 on they actually fought against the Democrats in general elections when minority positions were at stake. Thus, rather than seeking to fuse with the Democrats in opposition to the Organization (as they had done in the past, in 1911, 1913, and 1917), the Independent Republicans forced the Democratic party into a position of dependence on the Republican machine.[103] By refusing to bolt party ranks and by attempting to secure minority representation, the Independent Republicans aided the Organization in the sense that their actions prevented a substantial united opposition to machine rule from forming. The behavior of the Independent Republicans in the 1920s indicates that they were more Republican than Independent, and this did not escape the notice of the *Record*. In September 1923 the *Record* printed a lengthy editorial entitled "What's the Matter with Philadelphia?" in which it asked why Philadelphians had continued to vote for the "same group of unscrupulous political bosses who had robbed them for so many years." "The answer," it suggested, "is to be found in the childish unreasoning belief that obsesses the average Philadelphian, that all governmental virtue reposes in the Republican party." The *Record* continued:

This belief is fostered from childhood, handed down from generation to generation, and unquestionably accepted as an article of faith in most households. Men who apply their well-developed reasoning faculties to all other problems of life blindly refuse to consider the truth or falsity of the creed that permeates the Philadelphia atmosphere.

In Philadelphia you must be a Republican, just as you must eat, sleep, keep your body clean, and be courteous to women. It matters not that the precepts of the Republican and Democratic parties have no more to do with municipal government than have the tenets of Buddhism, and that a Democrat is fully as capable of satisfactorily filling a municipal office as a Republican without prejudice to the application of Republican policies in the execution of the nation's business; the belief is fixed in the typical Philadelphian mind that the election of a Democrat to any important city office . . . would be reactionary, ruinous and in effect equivalent to a municipal disaster.

We diagnose the case as almost hopeless addiction to Republicanism; habitual overdosing with partisanship. . . . The strength of the Republican party in Philadelphia is the cause that blights our city, imposes upon it unnecessary burdens of taxation, hampers its development and enables venal politicians to fritter away its substance to their own personal enrichment. That's what's the matter with Philadelphia. [104]

"Hopeless addiction to Republicanism," then, was a key feature, though not the only one, of the Organization's success in controlling votes.

In sum, the Organization's ability to overwhelm its electoral opponents rested on a number of factors: public apathy, the demise of the Democratic party, the control the party exercised over the election machinery, its astute methods of campaigning, and the "personal service" it rendered to the individual voter, in addition to the local strength of Republican partisanship. Taken together, they account for the remarkable degree of electoral success the Organization enjoyed during the period of its "institutionalization."

This ability to control the electorate was a necessary prerequisite for the establishment of a reliable system of discipline within the Organization. But what still remains to be considered is who benefited from, and supported, the creation of such a centralized political structure, and who opposed it.

7

The Utility Monopolists

One of the main beneficiaries and supporters of the creation of a centralized political structure in Philadelphia seems to have been a major segment of the local business community, for the emergence of a full-fledged political machine at the turn of the century coincided with the consolidation of the public utilities industry in the city. Just as power was consolidated in the local polity, the Philadelphia Rapid Transit Company and the Philadelphia Electric Company both managed to establish monopoly control over the city's street railway and electricity supply systems respectively.[1] In addition, the United Gas Improvement Company established virtual control over the local gas supply system when it successfully managed to obtain a long-term lease of the municipal gas works in 1897.[2]

Although the relationship between consolidation in the local economy and consolidation in the urban polity was apparently coincidental, the centralization of political power and the consolidation of the public utilities industry were to the mutual benefit of utility entrepreneurs and the party boss. For instance, it was to the benefit of utility entrepreneurs to have political power highly centralized, because their particular industry was heavily dependent on, and vulnerable to, government action. As long as the polity remained fragmented, utilities companies, which had substantial fixed assets, were subject to, and vulnerable to, extortionate demands from legislators. The creation of a system of discipline over public officials was therefore very much in the interest of utility companies, since dealing with a single party leader who could control the flow of legislation they were vitally interested in was preferable to the chronic discord and legislative blackmail that prevailed under a system of rampant factionalism.[3]

Consolidation of the public utilities industry was also in the interests of a prospective party boss. As long as the industry remained fragmented, entrepreneurs, in competing with one another for favors from government, would be driven to offer bribes to secure legislative privileges. Bribery may or may not have provided the desired result as far as these entrepreneurs were concerned, but what it invariably did was subvert the ability of the party boss to discipline his subordinates. Therefore, if an arrangement could be struck between utility entrepreneurs and the political boss, the interests of both would be served.

The "New" Men of Substance

Just such an arrangement between the two was apparently reached in Philadelphia in the late nineteenth century, for the state government under Quay, and the city government under Martin and Durham, displayed considerable favoritism toward the utility companies controlled by such entrepreneurs as Peter A. B. Widener, William L. Elkins, William H. Kemble, and Thomas Dolan,[4] "the last of the great nineteenth century business Titans in Philadelphia."[5] This group of capitalists also had several other things in common. For example, nearly all of them were born in the 1830s in poor circumstances, educated to the high-school level, and went to work in their teens in retail establishments: Widener in his elder brother's butcher's shop, Dolan and Kemble in general dry-goods stores, and Elkins as a grocery clerk. None of them, despite their eligibility, served in the Union Army during the Civil War. Instead, they proceeded to pile up considerable fortunes in commerce, industry, and banking.[6]

Peter Widener (1834–1915), for example, quickly acquired his own meat shop and during the Civil War received a lucrative contract, courtesy of

Simon Cameron's War Department, to supply mutton to all troops within ten miles of Philadelphia. With the $50,000 profit from this contract, he opened a chain of meat stores throughout the city, bought several strategically located streetcar lines, and began to invest in suburban real estate. Also actively involved in local politics as a member of the Republican twentieth ward executive committee, Widener was elected to several minor offices before being appointed city treasurer in 1873. Failing to secure successive party nominations for state treasury and mayor of Philadelphia in 1877, however, Widener forsook his political ambitions in favor of his business interests.[7]

With Elkins and Kemble he worked out a strategy for combining, consolidating, and mechanizing all the streetcar lines in Philadelphia. After their Philadelphia Rapid Transit Company secured a local monopoly, the trio, in partnership with William C. Whitney and Thomas Fortune Ryan, proceeded to use the same strategy to monopolize control of street railway systems in New York, Baltimore, Pittsburgh, Chicago, and more than a hundred other cities across the nation.[8] In addition to his traction interests, Peter Widener helped organize both the United States Steel Company and the American Tobacco Company. He was also a large investor in the Pennsylvania Railroad, Standard Oil, and the United Gas Improvement Company. When he died in 1915, Widener left an estate of approximately $100 million, the largest single fortune in the city.[9]

Widener's closest friend and associate, William L. Elkins (1832–1903), also enjoyed similar initial success in retailing, though as a grocer rather than as a butcher. However, after ten years running his own produce business in New York and Philadelphia, he like many others was struck by the "oil fever" that broke out following the discovery of oil in western Pennsylvania in 1859. Over the next twenty years, Elkins acquired many prosperous wells and pioneered the refining of crude oil for illumination purposes and for gasoline. In 1880 he sold his business to the Standard Oil Company and thereafter, in partnership with Widener, concentrated on building up his interests in street railways, gas, electric lighting, and suburban real estate. At the time of his death in 1903, he was director of twenty-four companies and his personal fortune was estimated to be $25 million.[10]

The oldest member of the group, William Kemble (1824–1891), "accumulated a large fortune" by successfully combining a career in business with one in politics.[11] Kemble, like Widener, was an activist in local politics as a Republican committeeman. He served as an agent for federal revenue stamps during the Civil War and was subsequently elected state treasurer for the first of three successive terms in 1865. Kemble, in fact, pioneered the "treasury system" that became such an important component of Quay's state organization. [12] He also ensured that the largest recipient of state money was the "pet" institution he founded: the People's Bank of Philadelphia. Kemble's manipulation of public funds was such that he acquired immortality in the annals of Pennsylvania history as the author of the famous political maxim "Addition, division, and silence." [13] Pocketing his share of the spoils, Kemble was also active in the Philadelphia street railway industry. He served as secretary of the Union Passenger Railway Company, for instance, one of the largest streetcar lines in the city, before joining up with Widener and Elkins to consolidate Philadelphia's street railway system. A close associate of both Quay and Cameron, Kemble acted as the "connecting link" between the utility financiers and the state Republican organization. [14]

The final member of the group, Thomas Dolan (1834–1914), was like the others a self-made man, a sales assistant who became "one of Philadelphia's greatest nineteenth century business tycoons." [15] Dolan made his fortune as a manufacturer of menswear, fancy-knit goods, and hosiery. He began the manufacture of "Germantown Goods" in 1861 and speedily built up a prosperous trade until, at the close of the Civil War, although still only thirty years old, he was the eleventh wealthiest man in the city. [16] By 1871 his Keystone Knitting Mills was doing $1 million worth of business a year, which established Dolan as one of the largest producers of menswear in America and paved the way for his election as president of the National Association of Manufacturers.

Dolan also played a major role in organizing and directing gas and electric companies and became a national figure in the utility field when the company he organized with Widener and Elkins in 1882, the United Gas Improvement Company (UGI), grew within a decade to be America's largest public utility concern. It was also under Dolan's leadership that UGI leased the city's gas works in 1897. [17] Dolan, like Kemble, also had close links with Quay's state Republican machine. In 1882, for instance, supported by Quay, he was elected chairman of the state Republican party. Again, backed by Quay, he served as an adviser to the Republican National Committee in the 1890s. When he eventually died in 1914, Dolan's personal wealth in the city was exceeded only by that of Widener. [18]

As a group, Dolan, Widener, Elkins, and Kemble were "men of America's first plutocratic generation," the great organizers who were creators of and products of the general "organizational revolution" taking place in late nineteenth-century America. [19] Mutually bound together by a maze of interlocking business interests, this "federation of capital" acquired and developed utility companies to such an extent that one-eighth of the American population was dependent on these men for such daily needs as electric transit and gas and electric lighting.[20] They were essentially financiers, though their financial activities were not great speculative ventures, such as those of Jim Fiske and Jay Gould, but rather carefully orchestrated moves involving limited risk and yet yielding enormous return, as in the case of the phenomenal growth of UGI.

These utility financiers, who founded newer and fabulously wealthy family lines, were different from the families of earlier wealth in Philadelphia, not just in terms of their poor origins—limited education and the manner in which they accumulated their wealth—but also in the way they behaved and the place where they chose to live. The city's "first families" of the Revolutionary period, and the banking, business, and industrial elite of the mid-nineteenth century, tended to reside in the fashionable downtown neighborhoods, such as Independence Square and Rittenhouse Square, or in suburbs along the Main Line and in Chestnut Hill, to the west of the city. The new plutocrats, in defiance of Proper Philadelphia's popular convention that "nobody lives north of Market" (the main east-west thoroughfare connecting the Delaware and Schuylkill rivers), built tremendous Victorian mansions at the corner of Broad Street and Girard Avenue, a full twelve blocks north of Market Street.[21]

Aesthetic differences between the plutocrats and the aristocrats further compounded the geographic split between the two. Whereas mansions in Rittenhouse Square, for instance, tended to be simple, restrained, and conservative in their design, the ones Widener and Elkins built were "an overwhelming confection" that gave "an architectural definition to Thorstein Veblen's famous phrase 'conspicuous consumption,' "[22] a "pecuniary canon of taste" that made these newly rich Philadelphians "typical of America's Renaissance Princes of the 'Gilded Age.' "[23]

A final difference, and from our viewpoint perhaps the most important one, between the plutocrats and the aristocrats was their attitude toward local affairs and politics. The utility financiers were simply not interested in governance. Instead, they were primarily concerned with power as a means to personal wealth, and if that meant Pennsylvania and Philadelphia were ruled by the likes of Quay, Martin, Durham, McNichol, and the Vare brothers, then so be it. They were prepared to accept and support machine rule in Pennsylvania and Philadelphia because, like party workers, they reaped material rewards under such a system.[24]

The Consolidation of Street Railways

In what ways were these utility entrepreneurs favored by the various party bosses? How did they benefit from the centralized political structure in Philadelphia and, given that local affairs were subject to state interference, also Pennsylvania?

The way the companies these men controlled were able to establish monopoly control over the city's street railway, gas, and electricity supply systems demonstrates that the utility entrepreneurs received legislative favors from the state government under Quay and from the city government under Martin and Durham.

In the case of street railways, Kemble, Widener, and Elkins united, streamlined, and mechanized Philadelphia's streetcar lines into an electric-powered system that eventually monopolized local transit.[25] This accomplishment can be attributed to their skill, vision, and ability as entrepreneurs, but also the alliance they forged with the state and city Republican machines.

Kemble, as one of the original incorporators of the Union Passenger Railway Company in 1864, had been the first member of the group to get involved in street railways. Headed by State Treasurer William McGrath, and numbering politicians Jacob Ridgway and William Leeds among its directors, the Union quickly became one of the city's successful roads. With valuable north-south and east-west lines, it connected northern suburbs with the developing central business district and the Delaware riverfront.

While serving as secretary of the Union Company, Kemble began to develop a strategy for combining the city's twenty-odd competing horsecar lines into one, basing his strategy on the model provided by the Pennsylvania Railroad. As a lobbyist for "The Pennsy" in the early 1870s, Kemble had observed how the railroad's managers had assembled a self-sufficient regional system by creating a trunk and branch network through merging other roads and then leasing them to its main line. He also noted how they had divided the railroads into divisions and developed a line and staff structure to administer them.[26]

Kemble sought to apply the same techniques to the city's street railway system. He envisaged that the Union would become the trunk line for a system that would run through the heart of the business district and branch into the northern and western suburbs of the city. When his associates on the Union board balked at his scheme, Kemble teamed up with Widener and Elkins and formed a rival company (Continental), intending to capture control of the Union and then implementing his strategy of combination.[27]

However, in order to protect themselves from political raids by their opponents, and to ensure passage of appropriate legislation, the trio also needed to recruit the necessary political expertise. It was for this reason that Quay was added to the group. Together these four men formed "a combine that became the most powerful single force in the city's street railway industry."[28]

At the time the "Combine" entered the transit field in 1873, twenty-seven separate passenger railway companies had been granted charter rights by the state legislature to operate horsecar lines in Philadelphia (in the absence of a general law for the incorporation of street railways, and in the belief that competition was the best regulator of the public interest).[29] In practice, the uncoordinated and unsystematic development of street railways aroused considerable public opposition and hostility. Public criticism focused not just on the failure of company owners to cooperate on the provision of routes, schedules, and new technology, but also on the process by which they secured charters in the first place. For example, Philadelphians were indignant that, because local affairs were subject to state interference, they had no control over and were not consulted about the conferring of charters that made a gift of the use of their city's streets for private profit.[30] The passage of the so-called "Railway Boss Act" of 1868, which prohibited the city from regulating street railroads without specific authorization from the assembly, only added to their sense of injustice.[31] Such resentment was aggravated even further by the discovery that prospective companies often secured their charters through bribes, stock options, and other favors and that greedy legislators had willingly sacrificed the city's interests for such inducements.[32]

Concerted public protest over inadequate local control and special influence in charter grants brought about limited reform. The new state constitution of 1874 attempted to reduce legislative corruption by prohibiting, among other things, special charters for railways. It also provided that any further street railway construction was to be subject to municipal approval.[33]

This initiative to promote local regulation counted for little in practice, however, because reformers enacted no general law to permit the incorporation of additional lines. Indeed, because the constitution did not affect existing companies, it did not take long for the traction magnates to realize that by preventing passage of such a law they could consolidate their positions without having to worry about additional competitors appearing.[34] In fact, because of their close relationship with Quay they were able to delay passage of a general incorporation law for fifteen years, by which time, as Harold E. Cox and John F. Meyers pointed out, "it was too late to preserve competition—if indeed that was a purpose of the Act of 1889."[35] Cox and Meyers suggest: "The rapidity with which [they] succeeded in . . . consolidating their positions in Philadelphia, while at the same time exploiting their favored position within the state legislature, . . . commands even a cynic's respect."[36] And the way the Combine turned "the new Constitution to their advantage," Cox and Meyers conclude, amounted to "prostitution of an ideal."[37]

Cox and Meyers formed this opinion on the basis of how the Combine established its traction monopoly: through "legislative manipulation."[38] By way of the state legislature, under Quay's influence and direction, the Combine regularly "delivered" (or did not deliver) legislation that permitted the group to monopolize the city's street railway system.[39] In 1883, for instance, the Combine was in a dilemma. It had established a powerful system by capturing control of the Union Company in 1880 and control of the West Philadelphia railway in 1881. But because companies under their respective charters were restricted to horse traction and had limited capitalization, the group could not meet the growing demand for transportation by substituting cable technology and mechanical power for horse power without a general incorporation law and the risk of additional competition. In order to "get around [this] very obvious impasse," the state legislature "obligingly legalized the creation of a corporation that might in future be easily converted into a monopoly."[40] It enacted a motive power law that permitted an entirely new category of company: the traction motor company.

This law had "obvious advantages" for the Combine. It permitted the group to construct a cable line, and it did not interfere with the existing restriction against establishing new passenger railway companies in Philadelphia.[41] Because the Combine, at the time the act was passed, was the only group in Philadelphia financially able to construct a cable line, "the law was made to order for this organization."

> And it was no accident that the first company under the Act was the Philadelphia Traction Company, controlled by the syndicate. Using this new company as a base of operations, the syndicate unified the Union, West Philadelphia and Continental Companies into a single system. . . . Syndicate control was exercised through nine hundred and ninety-nine year leases—in effect, perpetual leases—under which the majority of the more lucrative and strategically located properties in Philadelphia were consolidated.[42]

By the time a general incorporation law was finally passed in 1889, "it was too late to preserve competition" or "significantly affect the march . . .

toward total monopoly," because by then virtually all the main thoroughfares in downtown Philadelphia were occupied by rail lines, so "constructing new lines was neither feasible nor necessary."[43] In the mid-1890s, only three important companies—the Philadelphia Traction Company (with 203 miles of track), the Electric Traction Company (with 130 miles), and People's Traction Company (73 miles), in addition to one small independent line, the Hestonville, Mantua & Fairmount Railway Company (24 miles)—had survived the city's traction wars (see Table 20).[44]

Following the conversion from cable to electric traction, renewed rivalry threatened to ruin all three companies, so "the state legislature was once again called upon; and once again it delivered."[45] In 1895 the state assembly passed the legislation necessary to allow a consolidation to take place. The company heads quickly chartered a new organization, the Union Traction Company, which assumed complete control of the assets and liabilities of the three competing traction companies. This merger virtually completed the combination of Philadelphia's street railways. Within two years, the Combine assumed direction of the new company, and, soon after, the Union Company absorbed the remaining independent line, the Hestonville Company, thus uniting the city's street railways into a powerful monopoly (see Table 20).[46]

The Triumph of Political Man

One might conclude—as indeed contemporary observers, such as Lincoln Steffens and Moisei Ostrogorski, and more recent scholars, such as Matthew Josephson, Richard Hofstadter, Robert Merton, E. Digby Baltzell, Edward Banfield, and James Q. Wilson, have argued—that the utility entrepreneurs were able to secure legislative favors from the state assembly because they themselves controlled the legislature, that the party boss and his machine were in fact mere functionaries of the new plutocrats.[47] But an examination of the infamous "franchise grab" of 1901, when the Combine had already consolidated its economic position, suggests that this would be an erroneous conclusion.[48] The "franchise grab" was a direct consequence of the deterioration in the political (rather than economic) position of the "Combine" following Kemble's death. With the loss of the "chief connection" between the traction syndicate and the Republican machine, relations between Quay and the remainder of the group—Peter Widener, his son George, William El-

Table 20. The Philadelphia Rapid Transit Company and Its Subsidiaries, 1857–1902

Philadelphia Rapid Transit Co. (1902)
- Union Traction Co. (1895)
  - Electric Traction Co. (1893)
    - Citizens' North End (1894)
      - Citizens' (1858)
      - 2nd & 3rd Sts. (1858)
      - Lombard & South St. (1861)
    - Frankford & Southwark (1854)
    - Citizens' East End (1894)
    - Brown & Parrish Sts. (1894)
    - Clearfield & Cambria St. (1894)
  - Hestonville, Mantua & Fairmount Co. (1859)
    - Fairmount & Arch St. (1858)
    - Fairmount (1858)
    - Fairmount Park & Haddington (1892)
  - People's Traction Co. (1893)
    - People's (1873)
      - Aramingo Ave. (1894)
      - East Aramingo Ave. (1894)
      - Green & Coates Sts. (1858)
      - Germantown (1858)
      - Northern (1890)
      - Centennial (1889)
      - Girard Ave. (1894)
      - Cheltenham & J'kintn (1892)
      - Hillcrest Ave. (1896)

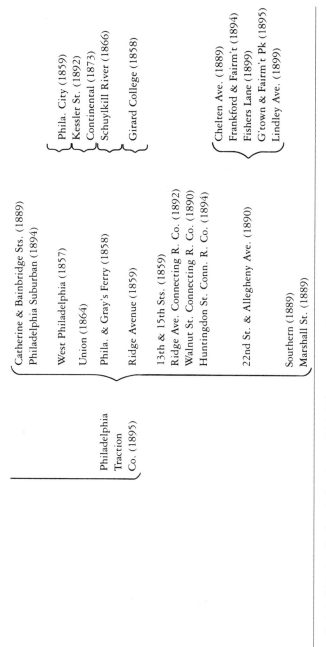

Philadelphia Traction Co. (1895)

Catherine & Bainbridge Sts. (1889)
Philadelphia Suburban (1894)

West Philadelphia (1857)

Union (1864)

Phila. & Gray's Ferry (1858)

Ridge Avenue (1859)

13th & 15th Sts. (1859)
Ridge Ave. Connecting R. Co. (1892)
Walnut St. Connecting R. Co. (1890)
Huntingdon St. Conn. R. Co. (1894)

22nd St. & Allegheny Ave. (1890)

Southern (1889)
Marshall St. (1889)

Phila. City (1859)
Kessler St. (1892)
Continental (1873)
Schuylkill River (1866)

Girard College (1858)

Chelten Ave. (1889)
Frankford & Fairm't (1894)
Fishers Lane (1899)
G'town & Fairm't Pk (1895)
Lindley Ave. (1899)

SOURCES: Frederic W. Speirs, *The Street Railway System of Philadelphia: Its History and Present Condition* (Philadelphia, 1897); Clinton R. Woodruff, "Philadelphia's Street Railway Franchises," *American Journal of Sociology* 7 (1901–2), 216–33; Edmund Stirling, "Inside Transit Facts," *Public Ledger*, February 10–March 13, 1930; Harold Cox and John F. Meyers, "The Philadelphia Traction Monopoly and the Pennsylvania Constitution of 1874: The Prostitution of an Ideal," *Pennsylvania History* 35 (October 1968), 406–23.

NOTES: The subsidiaries listed were all passenger railway companies.
The year in parentheses is the year the company was incorporated.

kins, and Thomas Dolan—declined sharply and temporarily ruptured when the elder Widener refused to support the state boss during a period of political crisis at the turn of the century.[49]

Following his reelection to the U.S. Senate and his acquittal on charges of misappropriating state funds, Quay determined to exact revenge on the ungrateful Widener by entering a marriage of convenience with paving contractor John Mack and supervising the passage of legislation that would destroy the Combine's monopoly of the street railway business in Philadelphia.[50] Capitalizing on public demands for rapid transit, and on Widener's and Elkin's absence on a European holiday, Quay, in May 1901, sponsored two bills in the state legislature that provided for yet another category of street railway company. The rapid transit companies created under the provisions of the Focht-Emery bills were also granted the right to enter upon street railway lines already built and to have unlimited power to borrow money on bonds. In addition, their franchises were to be exclusive and perpetual.[51]

The bills, as Clinton R. Woodruff observed, "came like a bolt of thunder out of a clear sky" and were "literally jammed through" the state legislature and Philadelphia's City Council "with unprecedented and reckless speed."[52] The "whole process"—the passage of the bills and the issuing of charters for thirteen companies in Philadelphia, all controlled by Mack—took just sixteen days, even though the legislation had far-reaching implications for every thoroughfare in the city and threatened the security of every existing transit franchise.[53] Wanamaker argued that these "ripper bills" were "little short of public plunder,"[54] while Woodruff claimed that they constituted "a new and hitherto unparalleled record of franchise looting and defiance of public opinion." He continued:

> I doubt if ever in the history of a state or a city, public opinion has been more openly or impudently defied; if ever the machinery of government has been more brazenly prostituted to private ends and profit; if ever there has been a more conscienceless betrayal of public trust.[55]

The Mack group had little capital and no plan for construction, so local reformers were outraged by the "ripper bills," not so much because they sympathized with the Combine's Union Traction Company—which, as Woodruff acknowledged, "was getting a dose of its own medicine"—but because "the public interest" was being sacrificed for the sake of "macing" (blackmailing) Widener, Elkins, and Dolan.[56] Given the threat that the Mack group could sell its franchises to a potential rival, the Combine was forced, and at considerable expense, to compromise with Quay's new associate.[57]

What the "franchise grab" of 1901 demonstrates, then, in my view, is not just a betrayal of "the public interest" or the ability of the boss to control the behavior of his subordinates in public office. It also indicates that the Republican political machines at both the state level and the city level were *independent of* and *not subservient to* utility interests, that legislative concessions were the prerogative of the party boss, for him to confer or withhold as he deemed appropriate.[58]

Apart from occasional differences, such as the one that precipitated the "franchise grab," relations between the utility entrepreneurs and Republican party bosses were generally smooth. The preferential treatment their gas and electric companies received at the hands of city government also suggests that the utility monopolists were favored beneficiaries of Republican machine rule.

In 1897, for instance, the Combine's United Gas Improvement Company ("UGI") managed to secure, "in the face of great public hostility" and "at a time when the tide of American public opinion" was "setting strongly toward enlarging municipal activity," a thirty-year lease of the municipal gas works, due to the efforts of Boss Dave Martin, a close friend of Dolan's.[59] Reform groups and local newspapers argued against the proposed lease on the grounds that it constituted "a bad financial bargain" because it was "estimated upon a depreciated value [of the works] based upon the earning capacity of a plant that has been inefficiently managed."[60] In addition, given the length of the lease and the fact that the gas works was a profitable $30 million public asset, reformers claimed that local citizens would receive "inadequate compensation," whether in the form of annual rental payments to the city treasury or in lower gas prices to the consumer.[61]

Reformers were also concerned about "the far-reaching principles" the issue raised, not just the "material aspects" of the lease.[62] For example, they argued that the city's gas works should be run "for the benefit, not of the few stockholders of a private corporation, but of the citizens who live within its bounds."[63] They were also worried that creating "a great private monopoly in gas supply" would increase the risk of "political corruption."[64]

Finally, and most damaging of all, according to Henry C. Lea, passage of the proposed lease would constitute, "an open admission that we are not competent to govern ourselves. . . . We shall have renounced our right to self government and shall have placed ourselves under the tutelage of a syndicate of capitalists."[65] But none of these arguments persuaded enough councilmen to sacrifice the city's short-term gains for long-term interests, and the lease was duly passed in November 1897.[66]

In 1905, Durham and Dolan negotiated a new agreement designed to benefit both the Organization and UGI. In return for canceling the existing lease in favor of a new seventy-five year one, UGI, instead of paying rentals, was to contribute $25 million to the city treasury over a period of three years. This arrangement suited both parties: it provided Durham with a "handsome kitty" with which to reward his faithful followers and allowed Dolan to secure long-term control of the gas works by "paying only a fraction of the real value of the lease."[67]

Durham's plan backfired, however, for he made a "serious blunder" in attempting to railroad the ordinance through City Council.[68] He "ignored the charged atmosphere"[69] in the city that followed Steffens's indictment of Philadelphia as "corrupt" and "contented," and by acting "in such a high-handed manner, provoked public sentiment in opposition."[70] "As the nature of the Gas Steal became evident, a wave of indignation swept throughout the city" and "caught the Organization by complete surprise."[71] Mayor John Weaver vetoed the new proposed gas lease, broke with Durham, and temporarily joined the ranks of the new independent party in the city.[72] Reform fever and popular indignation was so strong that Durham was ultimately forced to concede defeat in the "gas war."[73]

The "gas steal" is significant because it is usually regarded as the incident that ignited "a decade of insurgent reform activity in both city and state,"[74] but it also indicates something that has generally been overlooked: the depth of the mutual interdependent interest that bound the Organization and the utility entrepreneurs together.

The political favoritism displayed by the party boss toward the Combine's electric companies is a third example of collusion between the Organization and the utility monopolists. For instance, when Dolan's Brush Electric Light Company (1881) consolidated with Widener, Kemble, Quay, and Elkins's United States (originally Maxim) Electric Lighting Company (1881) to form an "Electric Trust" in 1886,[75] in order "to minimize competition, standardize rates and increase their earning power,"[76] these companies also entered into "a secret combination"[77] with electric light companies controlled by David Martin and Charles Porter, so they could farm out among themselves the work of lighting the city's streets with electricity.

At the same time, the city's Edison Electric Light Company was effectively "frozen out of competition for city lighting because its ordinance prohibited the company from furnishing current for arc lights."[78] Consequently, with the Edison company unable to compete, and the other "nine ostensibly separate companies furnishing arc lights" under the control of either the Electric Trust or Martin and Porter, the cost of public lighting was allegedly "twice as much" as it should have been.[79] This was because the nine companies formed "a public electric light monopoly" since they had "a tacit understanding and agreement not to compete in each other's territory"[80] and were therefore able to "maintain excessive profits by avoiding competition."[81]

In view of the growing unpopularity of the Electric Trust, however, and the increasing demands for a municipal electric lighting system, Martin Maloney, one of Dolan's closest associates, reasoned that a fresh initiative was needed to overcome both public agitation and the other problems that faced the city's electric light companies, notably their diverse systems of light and power distribution, ruinous competition, and the confusion and waste of duplication of service.[82]

Maloney established a new corporation, the Pennsylvania Heat, Light & Power Company (1895), which he envisaged would use culm (waste coal) in a revolutionary way to generate cheap electricity. Martin and Porter, as a favor to Dolan, provided Maloney's company with the necessary franchise to allow it to compete in the city. The party bosses then sold off their companies to "Penn. Heat," which also acquired control of the Edison company.[83] Maloney also reached agreement with the Electric Trust and in a few years established a monopoly of the city's electricity supply system under "The Philadelphia Electric Company" (1902), a Pennsylvania corporation that included Dolan, Widener, Elkins, and Mack on its board of directors (see Table 21).[84]

While acknowledging that the monopolization of the city's electricity supply system, like the street railway system before it, was in large measure due to the skill, enterprise, and foresight of such entrepreneurs as Maloney, Dolan, Widener, and Elkins, and that the process of consolidation required a high degree of technical, financial, and administrative expertise, it could not have been achieved without the necessary political support. Quay, Martin, and Durham appear to have played the role of political midwife in the consolidation of the public utilities industry.

The relationship between consolidation in the economy and consolidation in the polity was not one of coincidence. The politicos and the plutocrats were allies because it was in their mutual interest. Moreover, the former were not subservient to the latter. Not everyone welcomed this development in Philadelphia political affairs. Indeed, such an alliance prompted widespread opposition.

Table 21. The Philadelphia Electric Company of New Jersey and Its Subsidiaries, 1881–1909

Philadelphia Electric Co. (N.J. 1899)

- Pennsylvania Light & Power Co. (N.J. 1898)
  - Pennsylvania Heat, Light & Power Co. (Pa. 1895)
    - Edison (1886)
    - Brush (1881)
    - U.S. (1881)
    - Phila. (1882)
    - Columbia (1892)
    - Northern (1885)
    - Pa. West End (1887)
  - Hamilton Electric Co. (1896)
    - Powelton (1890)
    - Manufacturers' (1890)
    - Suburban (1890)
    - Diamond (1890)
    - Wissahickon (1893)
  - Germantown (1884)
  - Keystone (1886)
  - Bala & Merion (1891)
- National Electric Co. (1899)
  - Southern (1890)
  - Beacon (1896)
  - Overbrook (1893)
  - Cheltenham (1890)
- Kensington Electric Co. (1893)
- Delaware County Electric Co. (1909)
  - Philadelphia Suburban
  - Faraday
  - Citizen's
  - Media
- The Philadelphia Electric Co. (Pa. 1902)

SOURCES: Nicholas B. Wainwright, *History of the Philadelphia Electric Company, 1881–1961* (Philadelphia, 1961); E. M. Patterson, *A Financial History of the Philadelphia Electric Company*, Appendix to the Annual Report of the Director of Public Works (Philadelphia, 1914).

NOTES: All the subsidiaries listed were either electric light or heat and power companies. The year in parentheses is the year the company was incorporated.

8

The Nonpartisan Reform Movement

Between the introduction of the Bullitt City Charter in 1887 and the reemergence of a competitive two-party system in 1933, the most serious threat to the Organization's hegemony in Philadelphia politics was the nonpartisan reform movement. On the government level, the Organization was challenged by successive public watchdog committees, such as the Citizens' Municipal Association (CMA, 1886–1906) and the Committee of Seventy (1904 to the present), while in the electoral arena its supremacy was contested by a series of committees and third parties sponsored by nonpartisan reformers.[1] These included the Citizens' Committee of Fifty for a New Philadelphia (1890–92), the Citizens' Committee of Ninety-Five for Good City Government (1895), the Anti-Combine Committee (1895), the Municipal League (1891–1904), the Union party (1901), the City Party (1905–7), and the Keystone party (1910–15).[2]

These reform groups differed from their predecessors, such as the Citizens' Municipal Reform Association and the Committee of One Hundred, in organizational breadth, depth, coherence, and duration. That is, they tended

to be larger in size, far better organized, and more representative and durable
in that they usually persisted over several elections and legislative sessions.
They also differed from earlier reform organizations in composition, objectives, and their solutions to municipal problems.

These reform organizations of the late nineteenth century represented a
new kind of elite activism, one in which the participants, more interested in
political issues than social activities, strove to overcome the shortcomings of
their predecesssors by founding clubs and leagues of a permanent rather than
ad hoc character.[3] For example, conscious that "the trouble in the past has
been that reform movements have been too sporadic and too spasmodic,"[4] the
Municipal League deliberately set out to imitate the Republican machine's
organizational structure and to build up "a municipal party governed upon
the same general principles as national parties."[5] As the League's board of
managers reasoned,

> When we realize how thoroughly the regular politicians are en-
> trenched; how completely they are organized; how well they are
> supplied with the "sinews of war," those interested in developing the
> city along the highest possible lines and evolving a higher standard
> must leave no stone unturned to advance their cause, and must be as
> compactly organized as the "regulars." Organization then must be
> the "keynote" of the League and as this progresses the prospects of its
> ultimate success will grow brighter.[6]

In short, the Organization was to "be overcome by organization."[7] Indeed,
organization became the League's watchword[8] to the extent that "at its tenth
anniversary [in 1901] it recognized that to accomplish permanent results it
must adopt as its guiding policy 'All at it and always at it.' "[9]

The Municipal League's organization, like that of the Republican party,
paralleled the city's government structure. It included bodies representing
the electoral division, the ward, and the city at large. Overall authority
rested in a Central Board of Managers composed of twenty-five members
elected at large and one delegate elected from each of the city's wards.[10]
Within five years, the League built up a membership in excess of 5,000, a
considerable feat given that, unlike the Republican machine, "we have nothing to offer our workers except the satisfaction that comes from laboring in a
cause based upon fundamentally right principles."[11] In its thirteen-year life
span, the League participated in twenty local elections with varying degrees
of success.[12] "The best and most fruitful of all its work," however, as the

board of managers pointed out at the League's tenth anniversary celebration, was "not the mere election of candidates" but rather that it "has organized the city for reform."

> It has made visible and effective a reform vote that, without its aid, would have eddied hither and thither. . . . [Unlike] the Committee of One Hundred, . . . which should have been a permanent force for good [but instead] dissolved and left no organization behind, the Municipal League in this city has struck its roots deep.[13]

The Committee of Seventy, the City Party, and the Keystone party were the heirs and beneficiaries of the "local reform tradition" established by the Municipal League. For instance, in November 1904 the Committee of Seventy "took up the League's work under a fresh name and with fresh blood, and along somewhat broader and more general lines."[14] Like the League, the committee was committed to the view that "the machine cannot be destroyed by one victory at the polls. . . . Its influence can be held in check only by organized effort conducted on intelligent business principles."[15] Accordingly, committee members contributed enough funds not only to finance election campaigns but also to establish a Bureau of Information that would "provide the information the public needs to promote fair and efficient governance in Philadelphia."[16] In "keeping watch and ward over public interests"[17] with regard to election and municipal laws and to the conduct of public officials, the Committee of Seventy, over the last eighty years, has faithfully fulfilled the aims of its founders, who in January 1905 had planned to establish "an organization of a permanent character whose purpose shall be to aid in securing good government in Philadelphia."[18]

In its early days, the Committee of Seventy, by organizing the City Party, played a major role in directing the wave of reform insurgency that swept the city in May 1905 following Durham's proposal to lease the city's gas works to UGI.[19] The City Party itself inherited the Municipal League's organization in the wards and divisions throughout the city and managed to defeat the regular Organization ticket in the county elections in November 1905.[20] Six years later, the nonpartisans celebrated an even more stunning victory over the Organization when their Keystone party candidate Rudolph Blankenburg defeated George H. Earle in the mayoral election.[21] In both the 1905 and 1911 campaigns, more than 40,000 citizens participated in the primary elections for these two third parties, a level of support that easily outweighed the 24,000 "genuine" votes the Democratic party could barely muster even in a general election.[22]

In terms of electoral strength and political organization, then, party politics in Philadelphia at the turn of the century was dominated by an overriding cleavage between well-organized machine and reform forces. We have already accounted for the centralization of the Republican Organization in Philadelphia, but now we need to see how the founders of the nonpartisan reform movement were able to seize the initiative among those who opposed the machine and gain a substantial following. Or, put another way, how can we account for the emergence of the nonpartisan reformers as the main opposition to the Republican machine?

The Formation of a Reform Coalition

In the first instance, this development can be attributed to the institutionalization of the Organization under Durham's leadership. The establishment of a strict system of discipline within the Republican machine, combined with the Organization's ability to control the electorate, enabled party leaders to have a virtual monopoly over the recruitment of candidates for public office. Alongside the Organization's emergence as the central force in the government and politics of Philadelphia, this internal consolidation of power had important consequences for the city's men of substance as well. They were not only driven out of the Republican party organization, but were also (given that the Democrats were a "kept minority") forced to abandon the alternative major party as well, and thereby compelled to seek reform outside traditional party lines. These men of substance did not, as one might infer from the received wisdom, withdraw of their own accord.[23] In his reflections on the City Party's campaign of 1905, for instance, Franklin S. Edmonds, chairman of the City Committee and himself a young lawyer and college professor, suggested:

> The most serious error of the Organization in its political history was [its] absolute neglect of . . . the young men of independence and spirit whose ideals of political life have been formed largely upon the models suggested by Theodore Roosevelt and Joseph W. Folk. [This] large group of young men [have] found all the doors to political activity closed by the Organization and its agents. . . .

Indeed for many years in Philadelphia at the primary election only the officeholders have voted: the party machinery in divisions has been controlled by the officeholders; the nominating conventions have been attended by the officeholders and the independent has been told he must either "go along" or be impotent as a political factor.[24]

The consolidation of Quay and Durham's regime had another consequence that was shocking to men of substance in Philadelphia. The creation of a centralized and dominant party organization served the interests of some important elements of the city's business community, but if such a structure was a collective "good" for the utility monopolists and local contractors allied to it, it was a collective "bad"—a menace—for those who were not. In its report "to formulate a plan of Organization for the Promotion of Good Government in Philadelphia," for instance, the Committee of Seven appointed by the citizens' meeting of December 19, 1904, identified precisely the consequences of "machine rule" and "the evil condition which it is sought to remedy":

> The evil from which the city is suffering is not so much lack of ability in its employees as the existence, separate and apart from its government, of an unofficial organization, sometimes called "The Machine," established ostensibly for political purposes, but really for private profit, and which depends for its power and influence on:
>
> First. —Its absolute control of the appointment of all municipal officers and employees, and the fixing of their salaries.
>
> Second. —Its control of the police, so that it may, in return for votes and money, protect criminals and allow citizens to evade the law in special instances.
>
> Third. —Its control of election, so that its candidates may be elected at the polls.
>
> Fourth. —Its control of contracts and of grants of public franchises.
>
> This organization tends to demoralize to a greater or less extent every branch of municipal work. It decreases the efficiency of every department, because in the case of conflict between the interest of the city and the interest of "The Machine," the latter must prevail. It multiplies offices. It makes loyalty and service to "The Machine," rather than ability and honesty, the test of fitness. It enormously increases the cost of carrying on the business of the city, and it decreases the returns to the citizens from such cost.

It lowers the standards of public and private morality by bringing all classes of citizens into constant and familiar contact with "graft" as a mode of conducting business affairs.

Its effect upon the finances of the city is already becoming apparent. The annual tax on property, when the rate and the method of valuation are considered together, is high and there is every indication that it will be higher. Rents will of necessity advance and in the end the burden will fall most heavily on that large class of the community who are dependent upon their daily labor for their support, and whose comfort depends upon the relation between wages and the cost of living.[25]

"Conditions" were "fast becoming intolerable," particularly for a segment of the business community that was becoming increasingly significant in the early twentieth century[26]—that is, the dynamic elements of the new professional communities (such as scientific management, public health, public administration, and political science) that had newly emerged in turn-of-the-century America and that Samuel Hays has identified as being in the vanguard of the municipal reform movement.[27] More recently, Kenneth Fox has unraveled the intricate tangle of changes in legal, governmental, and political thought and practice that helped produce a new national model of urban government in the early twentieth century.[28] Fox identifies a national coalition of elite reform activists made up of experts in municipal law, political scientists, progressive city officials, and statisticians at the federal Bureau of the Census as being responsible for producing a new "functional mode" of government—a national social-scientific approach to the theory and practice of urban government.[29]

But in an examination of the early twentieth-century nonpartisan reform movement in Philadelphia, Bonnie Fox concludes that "the so-called 'Philadelphia progressives' resembled Richard Hofstadter's Mugwumps of the 1880s, conducting Samuel P. Hays's dispassionate type of campaign for municipal efficiency."[30] This conclusion is based on her analysis of Blankenburg's mayoral election campaign committee, the composition of which suggests to her that "the Philadelphia reformers of 1911, in fact, were the civic leaders of an earlier era. They had previously participated in movements for municipal improvement."[31]

This assessment, however, needs qualification. Bonnie Fox overstates the degree to which the Philadelphia progressives had been "civic leaders in an earlier era" and that it was "the younger members of the Committee of One

Hundred" who became "the leaders of the [reform] groups that followed."[32] A comparison of the membership register of the Committee of One Hundred with the membership rolls of the various reform "groups that followed," for instance, reveals that 60 percent of the committee's members (ninety-one) were not affiliated with any future reform organization, and the commitment of an additional twenty-seven members to the nonpartisan cause stretched only as far as enlisting to join the "public watchdog" committee, the CMA (see Appendix 2). As far as can be ascertained, it is possible to identify only 12 (8 percent) of the 153 members as being active participants in future nonpartisan reform groups.[33]

"Hofstadter's Mugwumps of the 1880s," then, apparently constituted only one element of the nonpartisan reform movement in turn-of-the-century Philadelphia. The problem with Bonnie Fox's study of the Philadelphia progressives is that it does not reveal the full range and depth of those committed to nonpartisan reform. There were, in fact, two cosmopolitan "elites" simultaneously interacting and competing for power and prestige at this time: one comprising Mugwumps and their descendants, the other largely young middle-class professional men.

Franklin S. Edmonds and "young [professional] men of independence and spirit" like himself were in the forefront of the City Party's struggle against the Organization in 1905.[34] Clinton R. Woodruff also observed: "The leaders of the opposition to the recent [1905] proposed extension of the Gas Lease were mainly young men who had been actively identified with the Municipal League and who had received their training in public works while identified with it."[35] Woodruff suggested this was because the League had been "a persistent and not an intermittent factor in the fight for good government," unlike the Committee of One Hundred.[36] Indeed, the League was not only better organized but also differed "essentially from the [self-constituted] Committee of One Hundred in being thoroughly representative."[37] "That element of representation in the American and republican sense" was reflected in the membership of the League's central board of managers.[38] The list of those who sat on the League's board between 1891 and 1904 reveals the true diversity of the Philadelphia nonpartisan reform movement. The League's managers included Mugwumps, such as retired Quaker businessman Charles Richardson, insurance broker Robert R. Corson, and publisher Robert R. Dearden; descendants of Mugwumps, such as locomotive manufacturer George Burnham Jr., lawyer R. Francis Wood, and reform pamphleteer Herbert Welsh; University of Pennsylvania academics, such as political scientists Walter J. Branson, Edmund J. James, and Leo S. Rowe, and the dean of the law school, William Draper Lewis; young lawyers, such as Clinton R. Woodruff, Samuel B. Scott, George D. Porter, and Walter S. McInnes; and engineers, such as James Christie and James Mapes Dodge, as well as newspaper editor George E. Mapes and a sprinkling of financiers, physicians, clergymen, and small businessmen (see Table 22).

The Committee of Seventy was similarly eclectic in its composition, as its founders deliberately intended it to be.[39] Its members included trade unionist Alfred D. Calvert, mechanical engineer Morris L. Cooke, dry-goods merchant Frederic H. Strawbridge, soap manufacturer Samuel Fels, physician George Woodward, book publisher John C. Winston, banker George Norris, and dye manufacturer J. Henry Scattergood, as well as former Mugwumps Joshua L. Bailey, William W. Justice, William H. Jenks, Lewis Madeira, Walter Wood, and Francis B. Reeves, and descendants of Mugwumps, like Francis R. Cope Jr., T. Morris Perot Jr., James Bateman Jr., and Coleman Sellers Jr. (see Table 23).

Representatives of the various elements that made up the local nonpartisan reform movement in Philadelphia were also conspicuous in the national coalition of elite reform activists that Kenneth Fox identifies as being responsible for devising a new systematic approach to the problems of urban government. Philadelphia lawyer Clinton R. Woodruff, for example, acted as the secretary, treasurer, and counsel for the local Municipal League, but he also served as the first secretary (1894–1920) of the national organization.[40] Similarly, Mugwump descendant and locomotive manufacturer George Burnham Jr. was simultaneously president of the Philadelphia Municipal League and treasurer (1894–1919) of the National Municipal League. In addition, both Woodruff and Burnham, along with university professor Leo S. Rowe and Mugwump businessman Charles Richardson, sat on the committee that drafted the National Municipal League's first model city charter, published in 1899.[41]

Philadelphia engineer Morris L. Cooke also provides an excellent example of a progressive city official who was so important in generating "innovations" in urban government. A close friend, neighbor, and professional disciple of Frederick W. Taylor, Cooke, in his capacity as Mayor Blankenburg's director of public works (1912–16), "brought scientific management into the mainstream of municipal progressivism."[42]

But what drew these disparate elements into a reform coalition aligned against the Organization? What did Mugwumps, their descendants, and dynamic elements of the urban business and professional communities have in common? One factor that pulled these various groups into a reform

Table 22. The Board of Management of the Municipal League of Philadelphia, 1891–1904

Name	Occupation	Other Political Affiliations[a]	Residence (Ward)
Finley Acker	Grocer	CMA, C50, ACC	22
John S. Adams	Lawyer	CMA	
Charles C. Binney	Lawyer	CSRA	29
Walter J. Branson	University professor		
Franklin N. Brewer	Retail manager, John Wanamaker's	C70, CP	22
Charles A. Brinley	Manufacturer	CMA, C95, CSRA	
George D. Bromley	Carpet manufacturer	CMA, C50	
George Burnham Jr.	Locomotive manufacturer	CSRA, CMA, C70	
James Christie	Engineer	CP	21
Frank B. Clapp	Lawyer	CMA, C70	
Robert R. Corson	Tailor	CMRA, C100, CSRA, CMA, C50	25
John P. Croasdale	Lawyer	CMA, C95	
Robert R. Dearden	Publisher	UP, CP	32
James A. Develin	Law professor	C70, CP	34
Horace A. Doan	Traction entrepreneur		9
D. Webster Dougherty	Lawyer		8
Charles W. Dulles	Physician	CMA, ACC	27
Theodore M. Etting	Unitarian minister	CSRA, C95	
Lincoln L. Eyre	Lawyer	CSRA, CMA	
George S. Fisher	Lawyer	CMA	28
Cyrus D. Foss Jr.	Lawyer	CP	10
J. Roberts Foulke	Financier	CMA	

Table 22. (cont'd.)

Name	Occupation	Other Political Affiliations[a]	Residence (Ward)
Harry B. French	Druggist	CMA	27
Ezra P. Gould	Clergyman	ACC	22
William H. Haines	Hardware manufacturer	CSRA, CMA, C70	
Alexander Henry	Clergyman		23
T. Comly Hunter	Iron manufacturer		
Edmund J. James	University professor		
Joseph R. Keim	Wool manufacturer	CMA	
Joseph W. Kenworthy	Wool manufacturer	UP	24
Charles A. Lagen	Lawyer	C50	26
Louis J. Lautenbach	Physician	CMA, ACC	8
William D. Lewis	Law professor	C95, C70	22
S.D. McConnell	Episcopal clergyman	ACC	8
H. Gordon McCouch	Lawyer		
Walter S. McInnes	Lawyer	CP	15
George E. Mapes	Editor, *The Record*	UP	32
Thomas Martindale	Grocer	CMA	
Joseph May	Clergyman	ACC	8
George C. Mercer	Lawyer	CSRA, CMA, C50, C95	
N. DuBois Miller	Lawyer, banker	CSRA, C50, C95	22
Samuel Morris	Banker		
Joseph P. Mumford	Banker	C95	
William I. Nichols	Clergyman	C95	
John E. Oughton	Textile manufacturer	UP, CP	28
Henry L. Phillips	Banker		
George D. Porter	Insurance broker, real-estate agent	CP	22
Frank P. Prichard	Lawyer	CSRA, C70	

E. Clinton Rhoads	Lawyer	C50, ACC	10
Charles Richardson	Retired businessman	C100, CSRA, CMA, C50, C95	
Craig D. Ritchie	Lawyer	CSRA, CMA	
John B. Roberts	Physician	CMA, C95	8
Leo S. Rowe	University professor		24
Samuel B. Scott	Lawyer	CP	22
W.S. Stewart	Physician	C95	10
William H. Tenbrook	Manufacturer		15
David Wallerstein	Lawyer	C70	22
Herbert Welsh	Pamphleteer	CSRA, CMA, C50, C95, ACC	22
Theodore Wernwag	Importer	CMA, C50, ACC	22
William White Jr.	Lawyer		
R. Francis Wood	Lawyer	CSRA, CMA	7
Clinton R. Woodruff	Lawyer	CSRA, C95	

SOURCES: *Committee of One Hundred* (undated leaflet listing members of the Committee and their residence); George Vickers, *The Fall of Bossism: A History of the Committee of One Hundred and the Reform Movement in Philadelphia and Pennsylvania*. vol. 1 (Philadelphia, 1883); Citizens' Municipal Reform Association, *Committee and Membership. 1871–1872*; Civil Service Reform Association, *Annual Report of the Executive Committee. 1882–1888*; Citizens' Municipal Association, *Constitution. By-Laws, and List of Members*, 1886, 1891, 1895; Citizens' Committee of Fifty, *First Annual Report*, 1892; *The Citizens' Committee of 95 for Good City Government. 1895* (Herbert Welsh Papers); Municipal League, *Annual Report of the Board of Managers* (1891–92 to 1902–3); Anti-Combine Committee, *For Good Government* (1895), 1; *North American*. August 31, 1901; *Record*. September 21, 1901, Israel Durham Scrapbook (for details of the Union Party); Committee of Seventy, *Sixth Report of the Executive Board* (May 8, 1906), 20–23; City Party, *Hand-Book*, 1905, 8–19; Keystone Party, *City Committee*. October 24, 1912; *Gopsill's Philadelphia City Directory*. 1882–1911; "The North American," *Philadelphia and Popular Philadelphians* (Philadelphia, 1891). All the pamphlets listed were published in Philadelphia and are held at the Historical Society of Pennsylvania.

[a]ACC = Anti-Combine Committee; C50 = Citizens' Committee of Fifty for a New Philadelphia; C95 = Citizens' Committee of 95 for Good City Government; CMA = Citizens' Municipal Association; CMRA = Citizens' Municipal Reform Association; CP = City Party; CSRA = Civil Service Reform Association; C100 = Committee of One Hundred; C70 = Committee of Seventy; UP = Union Party.

Table 23. The Committee of Seventy, Philadelphia, 1905–1906

Name	Occupation	Other Political Affiliations[a]	Residence (Ward)
Joshua L. Baily	Dry-goods merchant	C100, CSRA, CMA, C50	9
John E. Baird	Marble manufacturer	CMA, UP	
James Bateman Jr.	Wool merchant		22
J. Claude Bedford	Lawyer	UP, CP	34
George I. Bodine	Banker	CMA	22
Franklin N. Brewer	Retail manager, John Wanamaker's	ML, CP	
Thomas Bromley Jr.	Carpet manufacturer	CMA	Palmyra
John D. Brown	Lawyer	CMA	
Reynolds D. Brown	Lawyer	CSRA	22
William C. Bullitt	Lawyer	UP	8
George Burnham Jr.	Locomotive manufacturer	CSRA, ML, CMA	Berwyn, Pa.
Alfred D. Calvert	Pres. of Typographical Union, No. 2	CP	34
Samuel Christian	Shoe manufacturer		
Solis J. Cohen	Physician	CSRA, CP	22
Henry H. Collins	Cardboard manufacturer		Bryn Mawr
Morris L. Cooke	Engineer		22
Francis R. Cope Jr.	Shipping merchant		22
Neville B. Craig	Retired businessman		
Frank M. Day	Merchant		22

Name	Occupation		Number
Henry T. Dechert	Lawyer	CP	27
James A. Develin	Law professor	ML, CP	34
Louis DiBerardino	Banker	CP	3
James M. Dodge	Engineer	ML	22
Russell Duane	Lawyer	CP	7
Franklin S. Edmonds	Law professor	CP	22
Frederick G. Elliott			10
Samuel S. Fels	Soap manufacturer		
Simon B. Fleischer	Yarn manufacturer	C50	10
Cyrus D. Foss Jr.	Lawyer	ML, CP	22
Alfred C. Gibson	Gas-fixture manufacturer		33
George R. Goodman	Printer	CP	29
Emil Guenther	Coal & lumber dealer	CP	22
William H. Haines	Hardware manufacturer	CSRA, ML, CMA	
Walter P. Hall	Catering supplier		
Clarence L. Harper	Insurance broker	CP	15
Joseph S. Harris	Railway company director		22
H. La Barre Jayne	Lawyer	CSRA	
Charles F. Jenkins	Water company director		22
Robert D. Jenks	Lawyer		
William H. Jenks	Cotton manufacturer	CMRA, C100, CSRA, CMA	9
William W. Justice	Wool merchant	C100, CSRA, CMA, CP	22
J. Percy Keating	Lawyer, banker	CSRA, CP	7
Mahlon N. Kline	Drug wholesaler	CMA, CP	22

Table 23. (cont'd.)

Name	Occupation	Other Political Affiliations[a]	Residence (Ward)
C. Hartman Kuhn	Banker	CMA	
E. Frank Leake	Physician	CMA, ACC	
Max Levy	Photo engravers' supplier		22
Theodore J. Lewis	Steel manufacturer	CSRA, CMA	22
William D. Lewis	Law professor	ML, C95	22
Thomas McCaffrey	Coal dealer	CP	36
Francis S. McIlhenny	Lawyer	CP	22
J. Gibson McIlvaine	Lumber dealer		East Downington
Lewis C. Madeira	Insurance broker	C100, CSRA	7
Henry F. Mitchell	Grocer, banker		
George W. Norris	Investment banker		
Harlan Page	Cement manufacturer	CP	22
T. Morris Perot	Drug wholesaler	CMRA, CMA, CSRA, C100, C50	8
William H. Pfahler	Heating manufacturer	CP	
Frank P. Prichard	Lawyer	ML, CSRA, UP	
Francis B. Reeves	Pres., Girard National Bank	CMA, CSRA, C100, C50, C95, ACC, CP	22
Charles Richardson	Retired businessman	CMA, CSRA, C100, ML, C50, C95, ACC	10
James S. Rogers	Lawyer		24
J. Henry Scattergood	Dye manufacturer	CP	24
William H. Scott	Printer	CMA	22
Coleman Sellers Jr.	Machine manufacturer		
Theodore B. Stork	Lawyer		22
Frederic H. Strawbridge	Dry-goods merchant	CMA	22

Allen Sutherland	Chairman, Erie National Bank	CP	38
Ellerslie Wallace	Retired businessman		
David Wallerstein	Lawyer	ML	22
Thomas R. White	Lawyer		22
Asa S. Wing	Financier	CSRA, CP	27
John C. Winston	Book publisher	CP	22
Stuart Wood	Iron manufacturer	CSRA, CMA, C50, ACC, CP	10
Walter Wood	Iron manufacturer	C100, CSRA, CMA, ACC, UP	10
George Woodward	Physician	CP	22

SOURCES: *Committee of One Hundred* (undated leaflet listing members of the Committee and their residence); George Vickers, *The Fall of Bossism: A History of the Committee of One Hundred and the Reform Movement in Philadelphia and Pennsylvania*. vol. 1 (Philadelphia, 1883); Citizens' Municipal Reform Association, *Committee and Membership. 1871–1872*: Civil Service Reform Association, *Annual Report of the Executive Committee. 1882–1888*: Citizens' Municipal Association. *Constitution. By-Laws, and List of Members*. 1886, 1891, 1895; Citizens' Committee of Fifty, *First Annual Report*. 1892: *The Citizens' Committee of 95 for Good City Government*. 1895 (Herbert Welsh Papers); Municipal League, *Annual Report of the Board of Managers* (1891–92 to 1902–3); Anti-Combine Committee, *For Good Government* (1895), 1; *North American*. August 31, 1901; *Record*. September 21, 1901, Israel Durham Scrapbook (for details of the Union Party); Committee of Seventy, *Sixth Report of the Executive Board* (May 8, 1906), 20–23; City Party, *Hand-Book*. 1905. 8–19; Keystone Party, *City Committee*. October 24, 1912; *Gopsill's Philadelphia City Directory*. 1882–1911; "The North American," *Philadelphia and Popular Philadelphians* (Philadelphia, 1891). *Boyd's Co-Partnership and Residence Business Directory of Philadelphia* (Philadelphia, 1906). All the pamphlets listed were published in Philadelphia and are held at the Historical Society of Pennsylvania.

[a]ACC = Anti-Combine Committee; C50 = Citizens' Committee of Fifty for a New Philadelphia; C95 = Citizens' Committee of 95 for Good City Government; CMA = Citizens' Municipal Association; CMRA = Citizens' Municipal Reform Association; CP = City Party; CSRA = Civil Service Reform Association; C100 = Committee of One Hundred; C70 = Committee of Seventy; ML = Municipal League; UP = Union Party.

coalition was the traditional and conventional factor: the political "outs" combining in an attempt to replace the "ins."[43] Another factor seems to have been a common aversion to urban democracy as expressed in party government, and, conversely, a strong commitment to purge local government of party politics and transform it into an institution run according to the social values of the middle and upper classes.[44]

The pursuit of efficiency in government as a mutual objective was also an important area of cooperation among the various reform elements.[45] Mugwump reformers in Philadelphia were mainly motivated not by status anxieties, as defined by Hofstadter and Mowry, but by the threat that political corruption posed to the security of their private and business wealth.[46] In contrast, young middle-class professional men were drawn to the reform cause through the "inherent dynamics" of their occupations rather than because of their class connections.[47] But whatever the motivation, government efficiency was the common goal that pulled them together. Both elites wanted to apply the same principles (and hence the rule of the same forces) in the political world as those that were reshaping the economic order.

In tracing the changing meaning of "efficiency," Martin J. Schiesl showed that, by the turn of the century, this concept no longer meant purifying local government by replacing "bad" officials with "good" ones, but instead encompassed three key objectives: the "business-like" management of municipal affairs (or nonpartisanship), provision for a strong executive, and the separation of politics from administration.[48] These key objectives also formed the basis of the recurring demands of Philadelphia reformers at this time, in their various platforms, declarations of principles, and programs, which were designed to thwart machine government. For example, all the reform groups sought "the separation of municipal affairs from state and national politics," "honest and fair elections," "the honest, open, economical and efficient administration of our municipal affairs by enlightened methods and upon business principles," "the sincere and impartial enforcement of civil service provisions of the City Charter," "the absolute divorce of officeholders from political control," "the granting of franchises for limited periods only and after proper compensation," "the impartial award of contracts after due publicity and open competition," and "a comprehensive system of public improvements."[49] Some reform agencies were dedicated entirely to improving the technical rather than political aspects of city administration. The Philadelphia Housing Commission and the Bureau of Municipal Research, for instance, were both committed to promoting the efficient and scientific management of municipal business.[50] Prominent reformers and efficiency-minded businessmen, such as Samuel Fels, George Burnham Jr., George W. Norris, and Dr. George Woodward, sat on the board of directors of both organizations.[51]

The pursuit of and demand for government efficiency not only drew young professionals and old Mugwumps and their descendants together, but also mobilized against the machine additional elements of the city's business community and of its native middle class, because such an objective served the interests of these groups well. And the municipal reform movement was able to extend its appeal still further because it developed an ideology of compelling force. The nonpartisan reformers argued that the cleavages of national politics (on such issues as the tariff) were irrelevant to the concerns of municipal government and should not be permitted to cloud the enormous commonality of interests among the propertied classes in urban politics. Philadelphia progressive and political satirist Edmund Sage, for example, in his novel *Masters of the City* (1909), remonstrated with those who were taken in by the cry of "party regularity":

> Because the Machine here is called Republican—the same as in New York it is called Democratic—if you are not with the Machine, you are not with your party. That is the answer of the Machine to every demand for civic betterment. You demand reform and the answer is: "Vote for Smith, Jones, Brown, and the whole Republican ticket! Hurrah!" Thousands of men do not take time to analyse this statement. Can high or low tariffs clean our streets: can silver or gold standards give us improved pavements; or transit; or schools; or poor little kids good playgrounds? What has Taft or Bryan or Debs to do with public bath houses or with well-lighted streets; the suppression of gambling; the proper regulation of recognized dangerous amusements? "Nothing," you say. Yet as soon as you start to talk that way, the whip is cracked and the cry goes out: "Vote for THE REPUBLICAN PARTY!"[52]

The Municipal League also saw its main role as "educational"—that is, "to demonstrate to the public the advantages to be derived from the absolute separation of national and state politics from municipal politics."[53] It sought to achieve this objective by publishing a series of tracts and addresses on municipal affairs arguing that the business corporation should be used as a model for reorganizing local government but also that the city itself was a corporation, "a joint-stock affair in which the taxpayers are the stockholders."[54]

Reform efforts to persuade upright citizens that they had a common interest in local politics were not restricted only to political arguments about the relevance of partisanship to city affairs. There was also a moral dimension to the reformers' campaign.[55] Woodruff, for instance, insisted that the question of municipal government was as much a moral as a political or economic one; the Committee of Seventy stated that the Organization maintained "its control" over the city "through a combination of the police, the criminal classes, and the election officers."[56] In a more sensational reform effort, the city's Law and Order Society, at the turn of the century, exposed the "corrupt alliance" between the Organization and the White Slave syndicate in Philadelphia. The society's agents discovered that, in return for bribes and illegally registered votes, the police, "unscrupulous officials," and "corrupt politicians" furnished aid and protection to white slave dens, gambling houses, and speakeasies in the city's "Tenderloin District" (wards 11, 12, and 13).[57]

By publicizing the links between the Organization and the city's criminal classes, reformers such as Rudolph Blankenburg and newspaper editor Louis Seaber attempted to warn (and at the same time recruit into the reform coalition) members of the native middle class about the threat the city's "idle and vicious classes" posed to the city's moral and political community.[58] Such propaganda seems to have worked, for D. Clarence Gibboney, secretary of the Law and Order Society and "the terror of Philadelphia's evil-doers," was narrowly defeated by only four hundred votes in the Republican primary election for district attorney in 1909.[59] Again, two years later, Gibboney was to present the only serious challenge to Blankenburg in the Keystone party's primary election for the mayoralty.[60]

In Philadelphia, as in other cities, moral and political reform converged and intertwined to produce, in electoral terms, a substantial class-based core of opposition to the Organization, a fitting tribute to the efforts of the nonpartisans in convincing the propertied classes of their commonality of interest in local politics.[61] Having mobilized the city's wealthy native-born white population into a reform coalition, the nonpartisans sought to challenge the Organization's hegemony in local politics. How successful were they?

"Corrupt and Contented?"

They were not very successful at all. In the elections to city and county office, reformers had only two successes between 1887 and 1933, and even then it can be argued that the so-called "victories" of 1905 and 1911 were due more to errors of judgment by the city boss, and to divisions within the Organization, than they were to a genuine commitment to reform on the part of the electorate.[62]

In his analysis of reform insurgency in 1905, Lloyd Abernethy suggests that the City Party's victory was a direct consequence of a "serious blunder" by the Organization. If Durham had not "selected this time" to implement his plan to lease the city's gas works to UGI, "it is quite probable," Abernethy speculates, "that the movement, like many in the past, would have gradually subsided."[63] Abernethy bases his opinion partly on the fact that the City Party owed much of its victory to "Mayor Weaver's laudable, if not altruistic, decision to bolt the machine leadership [by vetoing the gas bill] at the crucial moment," for the mayor's betrayal "gave the movement not only more color and respectability but the support of the vast city administration as well."[64]

The election returns in 1911 for the Republican mayoral nominee George Earle Jr. also suggest that Blankenburg's victory was due as much to a temporary split within the Organization as it was to a popular upsurge in reform sentiment. For example, in the November general election, which Blankenburg won by the slender majority of 3,333 votes, Earle polled only 131,123 votes—almost 60,000 votes less than the total number of registered Republican voters who had participated in the party's primary election the previous month.[65] In that particular election, Earle, the Penrose-backed nominee, had narrowly outpolled William Vare by 105,455 votes to 82,256 in a bitterly fought contest.[66]

Earle's subsequent poor performance in the contest against Blankenburg, it seems, was due to the fact that the Vare brothers were unable to bury their differences with Penrose (contrary to William Vare's later claims), and therefore "cut" the Republican ticket in the general election.[67] The brothers' lack of enthusiasm for Earle's candidacy is reflected in the ward returns made by their home base (South Philadelphia) in the two elections. For example, in the Republican primary election, Vare managed to secure 88.5 percent, 83.9 percent, and 92.6 percent of the vote in the first, twenty-sixth, and thirty-ninth wards, respectively, yet in the general election these three wards furnished Earle with only 60.6 percent, 50.9 percent, and 55.8 percent of their respective total votes—a reduction of more than one-third for the Republican nominee.[68] Overall, Earle received just 60.8 percent of the total vote in South Philadelphia, which was 10 percent less than Reyburn (70.9 percent) had achieved in 1907, and almost 20 percent less than Weaver (81.9 percent) and Smith (79.0 percent) managed in the 1903 and 1916 mayoral elections.[69] Earle's reduced majority in South Philadelphia, combined with the increased pluralities Blankenburg enjoyed in North and West Philadelphia, resulted in "the Old Dutch Cleanser" being elected by the narrowest of margins.[70]

It can also be argued that the gains the reform "victories" of 1905 and 1911 secured were not as great as contemporary reformers believed them to be. For instance, the most significant and "permanent result of the Philadelphia upheaval of 1905–6," from a reform viewpoint, resulted from the special session of the state legislature held in spring 1906, which enacted a series of reforms that progressives had considered long overdue.[71] In the wake of electoral defeats for the Republican party in November 1905, not only in Philadelphia but also statewide, party leader Boies Penrose had responded promptly to reform pressure for a special session of the legislature, in the hope he would be able to woo the insurgents back to the G.O.P. The major measures passed by the thirty-day special session provided for personal registration of voters, a stricter civil service code to prohibit political activity by city employees (the Shern Law), a civil service bill (the Gable Bill) to establish a bona fide merit system in Philadelphia, a corrupt-practices act requiring candidates to file reports of campaign receipts and expenditures, and a uniform system of primary elections for all candidates for city and county offices.[72]

This list of reforms, although impressive, did not result in a "revolution in Philadelphia politics," as Clinton R. Woodruff hoped, or bring about "the end of the oligarchy," as George Woodward predicted—because, unfortunately for the reformers, these new laws were not administered as they intended them to be.[73] Under the Personal Registration Act of 1906, for instance, lists of qualified voters in each of the city's election divisions were to be drawn up by four registrars (two each from the majority and minority parties), selected by a Registration Commission, which was in turn appointed by the state governor. By replacing the existing voter registration system conducted by "assessors" elected at party primary elections, this measure was designed to curb the Organization's extralegal practice of registration fraud.[74] Organization control over the system did not wane, however, for 90 percent of the people recommended by the Republican machine to act as registrars were appointed by the commission, and with the eclipse of the Democratic party the Organization soon exercised influence over minority registrars as well. Consequently, registration abuse continued to flourish in the city.[75]

The attempt to establish a bona fide merit system in Philadelphia by placing the power of appointment to public office in the hands of a three-member commission selected by the mayor was also unsuccessful—because the chief executive (with the exception of Weaver between 1905 and 1907) invariably remained loyal to the Organization.[76] That the good intentions behind the Gable civil service reform bill of 1906 were not fulfilled is suggested by the report published in 1919 by the Women's League for Good Government (WLGG) during its campaign for a new city charter. In its *Facts About Philadelphia,* the WLGG argued in favor of transferring the power of appointment from the mayor to City Council, since under the existing system "the Mayor appoints the Civil Service Commission and can therefore control it politically." The report continued: "A Civil Service Commission to examine the Mayor's appointees which is itself appointed by the Mayor is a laughable absurdity and is merely a fiction to appease the public."[77]

The effort to prohibit political activity by city employees by forbidding them to solicit political assessments or to take "an active part in politics" proved to be an abject failure in practice, because under the new civil service code enforcement of the Shern Law was the responsibility of the employee's superior officer—that is, the head of each of the city's departments. In practice, these Organization stalwarts simply either ignored the Shern Law or refused to enforce it.[78] The Committee of Seventy, for instance, was frequently inundated with complaints about the political activity of officeholders, in particular the actions of police officers. In one election campaign alone, that of 1911, the committee investigated more than 1,500 alleged violations of the Shern Law and filed complaints against police officers and other city employees with the appropriate head of department, "but no action was ever taken against the offenders."[79]

Morris L. Cooke, Blankenburg's director of public works, also discovered on taking office that approximately 94 percent of the city's employees paid political assessments to the Republican Organization even though "it was, and is, against the law to solicit these subscriptions."[80] Given that the Shern Law had "remained a dead letter until you [Blankenburg] came into office," Cooke and the other departmental heads of government set about eliminating solicitation of "voluntary contributions" from city employees and disciplining any officeholder found guilty of "taking an active part in politics."[81] Once Blankenburg left office, however, political activity by public officeholders[82] and the practice of levying political assessments from city employees[83] gradually resumed.

Finally, the Corrupt Practices Act, like the Shern Law, was also ignored or poorly enforced, while the Uniform Primary Act, which in theory made selection of party candidates for public office fairer and more competitive, did not in practice affect the ability of the city boss to control Republican party nominations.[84]

These various reforms, then, although welcomed by Woodruff as "representing a very substantial measure of progress in the direction of protecting the fundamental liberties of the people and advancing the cause of decent and effective government," subsequently failed to "end the Oligarchy" because they were not effectively implemented.[85] Moreover, local interest in reform following the special session noticeably and characteristically waned, as Penrose and Durham had hoped. Mayor Weaver defected back to the Organization in November 1906, and the City Party itself dissolved quickly thereafter.[86] Charles E. Carpenter, chairman of the City Party's campaign committee when it won the election of November 1905, even endorsed Republican candidate John E. Reyburn for mayor in February 1907, along with the rest of the Organization ticket.[87]

With regard to the reform "victory" of 1911, Blankenburg's term of office was not the roaring success contemporary reformers suggested it would be.[88] The fact that Blankenburg kept his promise that his administration would be nonpartisan and committed to putting city operations on a business basis alienated his supporters as much as it did the Organization.[89] Most reform advocates were pleased to see in the mayor's cabinet such able and dedicated professional men as Morris L. Cooke (Public Works), George D. Porter (Public Safety), George W. Norris (Wharves, Docks, and Ferries), Herman Loeb (Supplies), and A. Merrit Taylor (Transit), particularly since they were all committed to developing an efficient program of public services.[90]

Cooke, for instance, finding that there was only one trained engineer among 1,000 employees in the Highways Bureau, replaced inept political appointees with technical experts. He also modernized office routine and initiated on-the-job training, paid vacations, loan schemes, and other benefits designed to meet the needs of the department's 4,000 workers and their families.[91] Indeed, Cooke confided to the mayor (and Blankenburg subsequently agreed with him) that "without a doubt the biggest single change brought about in this department during your administration will be in the status of the individual employee."[92] Cooke also ended collusion between public officials and contractors (as did all Blankenburg's departmental heads), drew up standard specifications, and awarded city contracts to the "lowest and best" bidder only after open bidding for public work.[93] He also insisted that municipal complaint books be available in various locations throughout the city and that all grievances be promptly investigated.[94]

Cooke's cabinet colleagues matched his enthusiasm for efficiency in their respective departments. For example, George D. Porter was determined to insulate the police and fire departments from machine influence, to set up a training school for recruits, and to abolish the political assessment of employees in both departments.[95] The Blankenburg administration saved the city an estimated $5 million.[96] Yet in spite of such public economy and improvements in city services as increased expenditures on local schools, the reconstruction of Philadelphia General Hospital, an increase in municipal wharves for ocean trade, the abolition of hazardous grade crossings, and a blueprint for the construction of the Broad Street subway, Blankenburg's administration failed to satisfy both the electorate (which rejected the mayor's protégé George D. Porter when he ran for mayor in 1916) and its supporters.[97] Why?

First, and ironically, it seems that Blankenburg's decision to honor his campaign pledge to respect the civil service system and to prohibit political activity by municipal employees alienated the Keystone party workers who had helped to elect him. Dismissing him as a "Benedict Arnold, an ingrate," these job-hungry Keystoners deserted Blankenburg, thereby depriving his administration of the support of what had initially been his most committed followers.[98] Blankenburg's reluctance to provide the Bull Moosers (or Washington party, as the Roosevelt progressives were known in Pennsylvania) with patronage positions after 1912 also increased dissension within local reform ranks and diffused the support for his administration still further.[99]

Second, and conversely, Blankenburg's failure to keep a campaign promise to lower gas prices disappointed consumers and disillusioned some of his staunchest supporters, such as the reform newspaper *North American*.[100] Third, Blankenburg's ability to win public support was constrained by the actions of the Organization-controlled city council, which thwarted mayoral proposals that required legislative action.[101] For example, a new housing code was crippled by City Council's refusal to vote adequate funds to ensure enforcement.[102] Similarly, during the economic recession of 1914–15, City Council also refused to fund Blankenburg's modest public works program to help the unemployed. An attempt to lower food costs by initiating a system of trolley freights to bring cheaper Delaware Valley produce into the city was also blocked by City Council.[103] A final example of legislative obstruction is provided by Blankenburg's continual failure to persuade the Councils' Finance Committee to raise additional public revenues (and thereby permit a reduction in gas prices) through a combination of tax reform, new levies, and an increase in the size of the city's debt limit.[104]

If such measures had been implemented rather than blocked, Porter's hopes for election as Blankenburg's successor would have been more realistic. As it turned out, the essentially administrative achievements of Blankenburg's term of office did not have sufficient appeal to the city's voters to justify their electing the former director of public safety to the mayoralty in November 1915. Moreover, some of Blankenburg's reforms were only short-term achievements. Open bidding for city contracts, for example, did not prevent the Vare and McNichol firms from continuing to get most of the city's business during Blankenburg's term of office, and under his successor, Mayor Thomas B. Smith, there was a return to "business as usual"—that is, collusion between city officials and contractors—for the "contractor bosses."[105] Similarly, the "emancipation" of the individual employee "from the galling yoke of the political gangster,"[106] which Blankenburg regarded as "the greatest single change effected by my administration," was a reality only for the length of his term.

Porter's defeat in the mayoralty contest of 1915 precipitated the disbanding of the nonpartisan (Franklin) party he and his supporters had formed during the campaign and the defection of the insurgents back to the Republican fold.[107] The Franklin party was the last of the independent reform parties to challenge the Organization's hegemony in local politics. Thereafter, all reform activity remained within party ranks, even though this meant the continued ascendancy of the Organization in Philadelphia political life.[108] The major advances toward political reform in the post-Blankenburg era— the introduction of a new city charter in 1919, and Bill Vare's downfall as city boss in June 1934—were not the achievements of reformers but more the result of internal dissension within the Organization.

The new city charter for Philadelphia approved by the state legislature in 1919 was essentially a product of the occasional party factional warfare that broke out between the Vare brothers and state Republican leader Boies Penrose. Penrose supported the charter proposal in the hope that, by establishing more accountability and responsibility in Philadelphia's system of government, and not least in the creation of a unicameral legislature, it would also threaten the Vares' power base in the "Neck" of the city.[109] Reformer Clinton R. Woodruff identified "U.S. Senator Boies Penrose" as "the greatest single factor in securing the passage of the bill."[110] In a recent review of Philadelphia city government, the Committee of Seventy has also suggested that "the 1919 charter was more a victory of Penrose over Vare than of reformers over corruption."[111]

Similarly, although contemporary political scientist John T. Salter identified a number of factors—personal ill-health, errors of judgment, the onset of the Great Depression, and the reemergence of a two-party system in local politics in 1933—as responsible for the downfall of William Vare as city boss in June 1934, he concluded that the "final destruction of Vare over the Republican Central Campaign Committee was brought about by a palace intrigue rather than a revolt from the people."[112] The questions now are: Why were "the people" so supine in the face of the Organization's hegemony in local politics? Why were the nonpartisan reformers not more successful in their efforts? Was Philadelphia as "corrupt and contented" as Steffens claimed?

Leading reformer and contemporary political scientist Frank Goodnow certainly seemed to believe it was, for—he suggested after reviewing Steffens's writings—Philadelphia appeared to be the prominent exception to the rule that bad city government resulted from undesirable social and economic conditions rather than from failings of human nature.[113] Other local contemporary reformers, such as Rudolph Blankenburg, Theophilus Baker, Herbert Welsh, and Clinton R. Woodruff, would also have agreed with Goodnow's assessment that in Philadelphia "something in the moral character of the people militated against good city government."[114] And yet, public apathy and indifference was not only a short-lived phenomenon in the city but also merely one of a number of factors—which included the demise of the Democratic party, the local strength of Republican partisanship, the Organization's control of the election machinery, its astute campaign methods, and its provision of a "personal service" to the individual voter—that accounted for the Republican machine's electoral supremacy in Philadelphia between 1887 and 1933.[115]

Another factor that contributed to the Organization's electoral success should be added to the above list: the reformers were themselves unfaithful to the principle of nonpartisanship. Although in theory the nonpartisans were committed to separating municipal affairs from state and national politics, their behavior in practice indicates that they were not all fully convinced of their own propaganda. The reformers seem to have been persistently divided over whether to pursue reform within the Republican party or outside traditional party lines—a weakness the Organization exploited. The Committee of Fifty and the Citizens' Committee of Ninety-Five, for example, both split up during the mayoral election campaigns of 1891 and 1895, respectively, because they were "hopelessly divided" over which candidate to support.[116] In the 1895 election campaign, in fact, a splinter group from the Citizens' Committee formed "The Business Men's Republican Association" to endorse Martin and Porter's candidate for the mayoralty, rather than support the anti-Combine's nominee, distinguished Democrat and former governor Robert E. Pattison.[117]

Many City Party members also seem to have been insincere in their commitment to nonpartisan reform, for once the measures guaranteeing "reform within the party" had been passed by the special session of the state legislature in 1906, the reform party virtually collapsed as the bulk of its members followed the example of the chairman of its campaign committee and defected back to the Republican party.[118]

In 1911, the reformers were again divided between those who participated in the Keystone primary and who were genuinely committed to the principle of nonpartisanship in local affairs, and those who took "advantage of the [1906] primary act" and supported Dimner Beeber, "the only Republican candidate and Platform of Absolute Independence" in the Republican primary election.[119] More than one-third (thirty-five) of the one hundred members of the Republican Nomination League that endorsed Beeber had been conspicuous nonpartisan reformers before the 1911 campaign, in such groups as the Municipal League, the City Party, and the Committee of Seventy. They included such familiar reform figures as George Burnham Jr., Dr. George Woodward, John C. Winston, Frederic H. Strawbridge, Thomas Raeburn White, and Franklin S. Edmonds (see Table 24).

This recurring division within the reform movement over the issue of partisanship in local affairs suggests that many reform activists found it as difficult as the "average Philadelphian" to overcome, as John C. Winston put it, the "political trance" induced "by the purring cry of party regularity"— that is, to resist their "natural" inclination to vote Republican, even when it came to municipal elections.[120] Indeed, in the post-Blankenburg era all reform activity remained within party ranks. Independent Republicans tended to be more Republican than independent, in that they battled with the Organization only at party primaries and not in general elections.[121]

So "good city government" was elusive in turn-of-the-century Philadelphia not because of "sinful contentment"[122] or failings of human nature, or because of undesirable social and economic conditions in the "City of Homes," but because of the city's "hopeless addiction to Republicanism," an affliction that affected reformers as much as the "average Philadelphian."[123] Ironically,

Table 24.   Nonpartisan Reformers Who Joined the Republican Nomination League,
Philadelphia, 1911

Name	Previous Nonpartisan Affiliation		
	Municipal League	City Party	Committee of Seventy
Richard L. Austin			x
Reynolds D. Brown		x	
Samuel J. Buck		x	
George Burnham Jr.	x		x
William Burnham		x	
B. Frank Clapp	x		
James M. Dodge	x		x
Franklin S. Edmonds		x	x
V. Frank Gable		x	
Francis Goodhue		x	
Emil Guenther		x	x
William H. Haines	x		x
Clarence L. Harper		x	x
Alexander Henry	x		
E.C. Irwin		x	
Arthur H. Lea			x
Max Levy			x
Francis A. Lewis			x
William M. Longstreth		x	
J. Gibson McIlvaine			x
Walter S. McInnes	x	x	
John H. Musser Jr.		x	
William R. Nicholson		x	
David C. Nimlet		x	
Horace T. Potts		x	
Owen J. Roberts			x
William H. Scott			x
Haseltine Smith		x	
Frederic H. Strawbridge			x
Albert E. Turner		x	
Thomas R. White			x
Asa S. Wing		x	x
John C. Winston		x	x
Stuart Wood	x	x	x
George Woodward		x	x

SOURCES: Republican Nomination League, *Advantage of the Primary Act* (Philadelphia, 1911); Municipal League, *Annual Report of the Board of Managers* (1891–92 to 1902–3); Committee of Seventy, *Sixth Report of the Executive Board* (Philadelphia: May 8, 1906), 20–23; idem, *Report of the Executive Board* (Philadelphia: March 20, 1912), 30–34; City Party, *Hand-Book* (Philadelphia, 1905), 8–19.

therefore, it was the partisanship of the nonpartisans that underpinned the Organization's hegemony in local politics and was responsible, as much as any factor listed above, for Philadelphia being what Steffens regarded as "the worst governed city in the country."[124]

Conclusion

With the Republican organization in Philadelphia as the model for inquiry, we have examined certain issues concerning the urban political machine that have not been satisfactorily resolved in the existing literature, such fundamental questions as: How can we account for the emergence of the urban political machine? Can we draw valid distinctions between so-called "bosses"? Which sections of the urban population supported the machine, and why? What functions has the machine fulfilled in the American city? What conclusions can be drawn from this analysis of machine politics in Philadelphia?

First, it is clear that theories of the political machine that are based solely on a "social analysis" of urban politics fail to provide us with an adequate explanation for the emergence of this form of party organization in Philadelphia. It cannot be explained simply by the predominance of certain social groups in the city's population. On the contrary, this development came about not so much because of the influence of (external) large-scale social forces like mass immigration, but because of the changes, orchestrated by the

Republican party leadership, in the (internal) structure and organization of this system of politics in the city.

Second, and contrary to received wisdom, genuine boss rule did not become a reality in Philadelphia until the late nineteenth century, when David Martin assumed leadership of the Republican party organization.

Third, the Republican organization in Philadelphia exercised the hegemony over political affairs that political machines, as portrayed by conventional wisdom, were supposed to have enjoyed. Its domination of the local polity was such that its leaders were able to exercise control not only within the Republican party but also in Philadelphia city government from the turn of the century until the early 1930s.

Last, even though the Organization managed to secure the support of the overwhelming majority of Philadelphia's new immigrant, poor, and black population in return for the "personal service" it rendered, it exploited these social groups as much as it helped them. In other words, its role in Philadelphia was dysfunctional: it effectively prevented political parties and government from responding to the real needs of the city's poor inhabitants, and also thwarted the emergence of *alternative* structures that could have met those needs—namely, structures grounded in the effective mobilization of mass political power at the grass-roots level and committed to "giving people what they [really] wanted" rather than what the Organization perceived they wanted.

But this study has significant implications for the historical study of the urban political machine in general, not just for the development of a party organization in a single city. It confirms that if we are to achieve a clearer understanding of the emergence of political machines, scholars must broaden the scope of their inquiries to examine forces that precipitated change from the "inside," not just the forces, such as immigration, urbanization, and industrialization, that shaped them from the "outside." In the future, analysts of the political machine should consider reverting to a method similar to that which characterized the study of urban political history before the "revolution" in the subject, which Samuel Hays's work set in motion in the mid-1960s. This means an approach that focuses on the "formal aspects" of the political machine—its structure, organization, and most important, its operation—in short, one that views the machine as a political entity in its own right and not merely as a product of a particular social environment.[1]

Such an approach would provide a more accurate explanation for the emergence of the urban political machine. It also would help us identify the degree of clout exercised by particular party bosses and thereby enable us to avoid distorting historical reality, which is inherent in the traditional accounts of machine politics.

This case analysis raises a question about the role the political machine allegedly played in American cities. The consensus on this issue—based on sociologist Robert Merton's theoretical model of machine politics—is that, in the absence of official alternative structures, the political machine served as the natural functional substitute for government for the various subgroups (notably immigrants and the poor, but also businessmen) that made up its constituency. This contention, however, rests on the implicit assumption (among others) that the relationship between the machine and its clients was more or less equal,[2] but this was not always the case. In Philadelphia, the relationship between the Organization and its clients was a profoundly unequal one in which the boss had the upper hand. The received wisdom on the machine's role, and with it the "good guy" reputation the boss currently enjoys in the literature for his part in helping it perform such a role, may need to be revised. Whether or not it should be can be determined only by further critical examination of the effects machine rule had on the clients and communities they allegedly served. It is clear, however, that the premise on which our current understanding of this issue now rests—an untested theory based on a number of dubious assumptions—is not sound.

The final implication of this case analysis, then, is for the historical study of urban politics in general. Scholarly research in this area has recently been aimed at generating alternative ways of viewing American municipal development—that is, other than through the inadequate framework of the boss-reformer dichotomy.[3] Desirable and long overdue though such initiatives may be, these efforts to "rewrite the history of urban politics and government along new lines" are bound to be incomplete, and will remain so, as long as the outstanding issues concerning the emergence, role, and sphere of influence of the political machine in the American city are unresolved.[4]

APPENDIX 1

The Citizens' Municipal Reform Association: Membership, Residence, Occupation, and Other Affiliations, Philadelphia, 1870–1875

Name[a]	Occupation	CMRA[b]	Reform Club	Union League[c]	Board of Trade	Residence (Ward)
William B. Adamson	Glue mfr.	CC				22
Lehman P. Ashmead	Mfr.	CC	O			
Matthew Baird (2nd)	Locomotive mfr.	CC	M	63	M	2
Clement Biddle (39th)	Lawyer	M	M	63		39
T. A. Boyd	China mfr.	CC				
Matthew J. Brady	Mfr.	WR				18
Henry Budd	Lawyer	CC				
George Bull	Lawyer	Sec.				
George L. Buzby	Merchant	WR	M	63	Sec.	7
Archibald Campbell	Mfr.	CC		M		
		FC				
Joseph Chapman	Painter	WR				14
George W. Childs	Newspaper publisher	M	M	63	M	8
George M. Coates	Wool mfr.	M	M	63	M	
Lemuel Coffin	Dry-goods merchant	FC				
Benj. B. Comegys	Banker	M	M	63	M	27
Edwin R. Cope	Paper mfr.	CC				
Francis R. Cope	Shipping merchant	CC				22
John C. Copper	Publisher	WR				13

Appendix 1 *(cont'd.)*

Name[a]	Occupation	CMRA[b]	Reform Club	Union League[c]	Board of Trade	Residence (Ward)
Robert R. Corson	Tailor	Sec., FC				25
Theo. de W. Cuyler	Lawyer	M	M			8
James Devereux	Shipping merchant	WR				5
Samuel Dickson	Lawyer	CC				
James Dougherty	Mfr.	M	M	63	O	
Anthony J. Drexel (6th)	Investment banker	FC	VP	63	M	27
J. Hughes Edwards	Lawyer	EC, CC				
John Farnum	Dry-goods merchant	FC				
Joseph C. Ferguson	Lawyer	WR				19
Samuel F. Flood	Lawyer	CC				
Richard Garsed	Yarn mfr.	EC, CC				23
J.J. Gumpper	Hotel proprietor	WR				11
Henry Hagert	Lawyer	M	M			
Edward S. Handy	Hardware mfr.	CC	M			
Edward Hoopes	Metal mfr.	FC				
John Hulme	Notary public	FC				
Barton Jenks	Textile mfr.	M	M	63	M	9
William H. Jenks	Cotton mfr.	M	M	63	O	9
Henry C. Lea (27th)	Publisher, scholar	VP, EC	Pr.	63	M	24
Henry C. Lewis	Goods haulager	M	O	63		8
Joshua B. Lippincott (18th)	Publisher	CC	VP	63	O	8
Amos R. Little	Dry-goods merchant	M	M	63	M	22

Name	Occupation					
Charles McIlvaine	Dye mfr.	EC, CC	O	75	O	
William Massey	Brewer	M	O			21
William Matthews	Mfr.	M	M			22
J. Vaughan Merrick	Iron mfr.	CC	M			
William H. Merrick	Mfr.	M	M			
E. Spencer Miller	Lawyer	M		63		
Israel W. Morris	Coal owner	M	M	63	M	
E. Morwitz	Publisher	WR	M			6
Caleb H. Needles	Druggist	EC, CC				
John S. Newbold Jr.	Banker	M	M	63	M	
Col. James Page	Lawyer	EC, CC	M			8
Joseph E. Patterson	Banker	CC	o	63	O	
T. Morris Perot	Maltster	M	M			27
Thomas Potter Jr.	Oilcloth mfr.	M	M	63		
William S. Price	Merchant	M	M			
William H. Rawle	Lawyer	EC, CC	M	63	M	
John J. Ridgway	Lawyer	EC	M	64		8
Edward Robins	Stockbroker	CC		65	O	
Coleman Sellers	Mfr.	WR		74		24
Nathan P. Shortridge	Railroad executive	M	M	63		
R. Rundle Smith	Lawyer	Pr.	VP			
Thomas Sparks	Lead mfr.	CC, FC				
Thomas H. Speakman	Lawyer	CC				
James Starr	Lawyer	M	M	64		10
William B. Stephens	Cotton-goods merchant	WR				21
Henry B. Tatham	Lead pipe mfr.	CC, FC	o			

Appendix 1 *(cont'd.)*

Name[a]	Occupation	CMRA[b]	Reform Club	Union League[c]	Board of Trade	Residence (Ward)
Joseph H. Trotter	Broker	FC				
Ellerslie Wallace	Physician	CC				
Samuel Walsh	Physician	WR				3
Thomas Webster	Cigar-maker	EC				
		CC				
John Welsh	Merchant	M	O		O	
George D. Wetherill	Drug wholesaler	WR				8
John P. Wetherill	Merchant importer	M		63	O	8
Charles Wheeler (5th)	Iron mfr.	Tr.	O	63	O	8
Henry Winsor	Shipping merchant	FC		69	O	8

SOURCES: Citizens' Municipal Reform Association, *Committee and Membership, 1871–1872* (Philadelphia, 1872); *Gopsill's Philadelphia City Directory for 1872* (Philadelphia, 1871); E. Digby Baltzell, *An American Business Aristocracy* (New York, 1958), chaps. 5–7; "The North American," *Philadelphia and Popular Philadelphians* (Philadelphia, 1891); Howard F. Gillette, "Corrupt and Contented: Philadelphia's Political Machine, 1865–1887" (Ph.D. diss., Yale University, 1970), 53–54.

[a] The figure in parentheses following a name indicates the position of the member in the table of the wealthiest individuals in the city in 1864.

[b] The list of members of the CMRA has been restricted to individuals who can be identified as having been prominent activists within the group—that is, generally, the men of substance who served as ward representatives or officers of the association.

[c] The figure in this column refers to the year the particular individual became a member of the Union League.

CC = Central Council (elected at large); EC = Executive Committee; FC = Finance Committee; M = Member; Mfr. = Manufacturer; O = Officer; Pr. = President; Sec. = Secretary; Tr. = Treasurer; VP = Vice-president; WR = Ward representative.

The Committee of One Hundred: Membership, Residence, Occupation, and Other Affiliations, Philadelphia, 1880–1912

Name	Occupation	CMRA	CSRA	CMA	Nonpartisan Groups	Residence (Ward)
Charles B. Adamson*	Glue mfr.		M	M	C50, C95	22
George N. Allen*	Dry-goods merchant					8
William Allen*	Clothing mfr.		M			28
William Arrott*	Insurance broker		M			15
John T. Audenreid*	Coal owner		M			8
John T Bailey*	Bagging mfr.		M	O	C50, ACC	20
Joshua L. Bailey*	Dry-goods merchant		M	O	C50, C70	9
Joel J. Baily*	Hosiery merchant		M	O	C50, ACC	9
Robert V. Barber	Druggist					
Thomas W. Barlow	Lawyer		M		C95	28
Henry W. Bartol*	Sugar refiner					8
William B. Bement*	Mfr. of machinery				C95	27
Henry Bettle	Wool merchant		M			6
Charles H. Biles*	Banker		M			23
Rudolph Blankenburg*	Yarn mfr.		M	M	C50, UPKP	9
James Bonbright*	Dry-goods wholesaler		M	M		10
Peter Boyd	Lawyer					
William Brockie*	Shipping merchant		M	O		22
Alexander Brown*	Banker		M			
George Burnham	Locomotive mfr.			O	C50, C95	15
Henry S. Butcher	Oil company president			M		
George L. Buzby*	Merchant	WR		M		7

Appendix 2 (*cont'd.*)

Name	Occupation	CMRA	CSRA	CMA	Nonpartisan Groups	Residence (Ward)
Morris Carpenter						
J. Hays Carson	Conveyancer			M		27
William H. Castle	Leather mfr.			M		13
Samuel Castner Jr.	Coal merchant					
Adam A. Catanacht*	Builder		M			30
Thomas Child*	Jeweller			M		6
Edward W. Clark	Banker		M			22
Edward H. Coates	Cotton mfr.		M	M		22
Lemuel Coffin*	Dry-goods merchant	FC	M			
Charles Cohen*	Wholesale stationer					8
Benj. B. Comegys*	Banker	M				27
Edwin R. Cope*	Paper mfr.	CC	M			
Robert R. Corson*	Tailor	Sec. / FC	M	O	C50, ML	25
John F. Craig*	Merchandise broker			M		24
Matthew H. Crawford*	Retired gentleman		M			28
George V. Cresson*	Mfr. of machinery					8
Samuel Croft*	Confectioner					24
James Dobson*	Carpet mfr.	FC				
Anthony J. Drexel*	Investment banker		M			27
William Dunlap						
George H. Earle Sr.*	Lawyer		M	M		8
George H. Earle Jr.	Lawyer					15
William Ellison*	Clothing wholesaler					7
Henry O. Evans*	Retired merchant					8
William Exley	Flour merchant					16
George Farr Jr.*	Jeweller		M			8
John Field*	Wholesaler		M	M	C95	3
W. W. Frazier Jr.*	Sugar refiner		O	M		8

Name	Occupation				
Clayton French	Dry-goods wholesaler		M		8
Philip C. Garrett *	Retired mfr.		O	C50	22
David Garrison *	Lumber merchant		M		29
Jabez Gates *	Grocer		M		22
Henry C. Gibson *	Liquor wholesaler		M		8
John E. Graeff *	Coal owner		M		8
James H. Graham *	Coffee jobber				27
R.H. Griffith *	Farmer				
Fredr. Gutekunst *	Photographer		M		22
Job Hambleton					
William Harkness Jr.	Builder		O	C50, CP	26
Charles Harrah	Steel mfr.		O		14
Thomas S. Harrison *	Lead mfr.		M	C50	8
Thomas Hart Jr.			M		
Eli Hartley					
R. Edgar Hastings *	Gold leaf mfr.		O		8
Samuel Hecht *	Wholesaler		M		12
F. Oden Horstmann *	Trimmings mfr.		M		27
William Hunt Jr.	Lawyer		M		8
John A. Hunter	Physician				3
Nathaniel E. Janney *	Real-estate broker	M	M	C95, ACC	29
Eben C. Jayne *	Wholesale druggist		M	C70	29
William H. Jenks *	Cotton mfr.		M		9
Joseph de F. Junker	Lawyer		M		27
Theodore Justice *	Wool merchant		M	C95	22
William W. Justice	Wool merchant		M	CP, C70	22
Godfrey Keebler	Baker		M		10
Charles C. Knight *	Iron mfr.		M		15
J.K. Knorr	Physician		VP		
Henry C. Lea *	Publisher, scholar	VP	O		24
Thomas Leaming	Lawyer		M		8
Edmund Lewis	Wool merchant		M		8
Henry Lewis *	Dry-goods merchant		M		8
Amos R. Little *	Dry-goods merchant	M	M		22

Appendix 2 (cont'd.)

Name	Occupation	CMRA	CSRA	CMA	Nonpartisan Groups	Residence (Ward)
Edward D. Lockwood*	Envelope mfr.		M			15
J. Fredr. Loeble*	Mfr. of mincemeat					1
Edward Longstreth*	Locomotive mfr.		M	M		15
George D. McCreary*	Coal operator					8
George McKelway	Druggist					10
John McLaughlin*	Gun dealer		M			15
Lewis C. Madeira*	Insurance broker		M		C70	7
James A. Main						
James Mason*	Blacking mfr.		M	M		20
Theodore Megargee*	Paper mfr.		M			28
William Mencke	Clothing mfr.			M	C50	10
Merle Middleton	Manager			M		13
John T. Monroe	Shoe mfr.			M		22
Thomas G. Morton*	Physician					8
Aquila Nebeker*	Druggist					2
Morris Newberger*	Clothier		M	M	C50, CP	12
H.M. Oliver*	Shoe mfr.		M			15
Joseph Parrish*	Lawyer		O			8
T. Morris Perot*	Maltster	M	M		C50	8
James Peters*	Hardware merchant		M	O	C50	28
Horace W. Pitkin*	Mfr. of govt goods	M	M	O		8
Thomas Potter Jr.*	Oilcloth mfr.		M			27
William Potter	Oilcloth mfr.		M			22
Robert Purvis				M	CP	15
Francis B. Reeves*	Wholesale grocer		O	O	C50	22
Charles Richardson	Capitalist		M	O	C50, ACC, C70, CP, KP	10
Charles Roberts*	Glass mfr.		O		C50, ACC, C95, ML, C70	9

Name	Occupation					No.
Charles H. Rogers*	Banker		M			22
Seville Schofield*	Wool mfr.		M			21
Henry Scott	Lawyer					4
Samuel Scott*	Dry-goods merchant		M			27
David Scull Jr.*	Wool mfr.		M	M	C50	
Thomas M. Seeds	Hat merchant		M			6
Oswald Seidensticker*	Univ. professor		M			10
William Sellers*	Steel mfr.		M		C95	15
Fredr. Shelton*	Banker		M			8
Benj. H. Showmaker*	Glass importer		M			22
Alexander Simpson	Lawyer					
John A. Siner						
Clermont Smith						
Fredr. W. Snyder	Conveyancer		M	O	C50, UP	12
Edward A. Souder	Shipping merchant		M			27
James Spear*	Stove mfr.		M	M	C50	8
Charles Spencer*	Hosiery mfr.					22
William G. Steel	Clothier					24
John S. Stevens	Builder					14
Justus Strawbridge	Dry-goods merchant		M	O	C50	22
Alfred C. Thomas*	Importer of gems		M			28
Henry C. Thompson	Lawyer					7
Constantine Thorne		Tr.				
William H. Trotter*	Importer of metals		M			8
John P. Veree*	Iron & steel mfr.					8
John Wanamaker*	Dry-goods merchant		M			8
George Watson*	Builder					13
John C. Watt*	Cotton goods mfr.		M			24
Chris. Wetherill*	Drug importer		O			8
Charles Wheeler*	Ironmaster, banker		M			8
Edward Whelen	Retired		M	M		29
Alexander Whilldin*	Wool merchant		M			
George Whitney						
Ellis Williams*	Lawyer		M	M	ACC	13

Appendix 2. (cont'd.)

Name	Occupation	CMRA	CSRA	CMA	Nonpartisan Groups	Residence (Ward)
Thomas Williams	Physician					
Henry Winsor*	Shipping merchant	FC	M			8
Edward R. Wood*	Iron mfr.		M			8
Walter Wood	Iron mfr.		O	O	ACC, UP, C70, KP	10
William Wood*	Textile mfr.		M			15
James A. Wright	Shipping merchant		M	M	C50	22

SOURCES: *Committee of One Hundred* (undated leaflet listing members of the Committee and their residence); George Vickers, *The Fall of Bossism: A History of the Committee of One Hundred and the Reform Movement in Philadelphia and Pennsylvania*, vol. 1 (Philadelphia, 1883); Citizens' Municipal Reform Association, *Committee and Membership, 1871–1872*; Civil Service Reform Association, *Annual Report of the Executive Committee, 1882–88*; Citizens' Municipal Association, *Constitution, By-Laws, and List of Members*, 1886, 1891, 1895; Citizens' Committee of Fifty, *First Annual Report, 1892*; *The Citizens' Committee of 95 for Good City Government, 1895* (Herbert Welsh Papers); Municipal League, *Annual Report of the Board of Managers* (1891–92 to 1902–3); Anti-Combine Committee, *For Good Government* (1895), 1; *North American*. August 31, 1901; *Record*, September 21, 1901, Israel Durham Scrapbook (for details of the Union Party); Committee of Seventy, *Sixth Report of the Executive Board* (May 8, 1906), 20–23; City Party, *Hand-Book*, 1905, 8–19; Keystone Party, *City Committee*, October 24, 1912; *Gopsill's Philadelphia City Directory, 1882–1911*; "The North American," *Philadelphia and Popular Philadelphians* (Philadelphia, 1891). All the pamphlets listed were published in Philadelphia and are held at the Historical Society of Pennsylvania.

NOTE: Biographical details about some members of the Committee of One Hundred are unavailable but their names are included anyway.

*Members of the original committee, set up in November 1880.

REFORM GROUPS: ACC = Anti-Combine Committee; C95 = Citizens' Committee of 95 for Good City Government; CMA = Citizens' Municipal Association; CMRA = Citizens' Municipal Reform Association; CP = City Party; CSRA = Civil Service Reform Association; C50 = Committee of Fifty for a New Philadelphia; C70 = Committee of Seventy; KP = Keystone Party; ML = Municipal League; UP = Union Party.

POSITION: CC = Central Council; EC = Executive Committee; FC = Finance Committee; M = Member; O = Officer; Pr. = President; Sec. = Secretary; Tr. = Treasurer; VP = Vice-president; WR = Ward representative.

NOTES

Introduction

1. Lincoln Steffens, *The Autobiography of Lincoln Steffens*, vol. 1 (New York, 1931), 422; idem, *The Shame of the Cities* (New York, 1904), 193.

2. Steffens, *Shame of the Cities*, 15.

3. Ibid., 195.

4. Ibid., 4–5.

5. Ibid., 16. See also Bruce Stave, John M. Allswang, Terrence J. McDonald, and Jon C. Teaford, "A Reassessment of the Urban Political Boss: An Exchange of Views," *History Teacher* 21 (May 1988), 300–301; David C. Hammack, *Power and Society: Greater New York at the Turn of the Century* (New York, 1982), 7–19.

6. Arthur P. Dudden, "Lincoln Steffens's Philadelphia," *Pennsylvania History* 31 (October 1964), 449–58; John M. Allswang, *Bosses, Machines, and Urban Voters: An American Symbiosis* (Port Washington, N.Y., 1977), 15–19.

7. Stave et al., "Reassessment of the Urban Political Boss," 300–303; Robert Merton, *Social Theory and Social Structure: Toward the Codification of Theory and Research* (Glencoe, Ill., 1949), 71–81; Oscar Handlin, *The Uprooted* (New York, 1951); Richard Hofstadter, *The Age of Reform: From Bryan to FDR* (New York, 1955).

8. Only recently, for example, has there been an attempt to provide a broad aggregate profile of the emergence and evolution of political machines in American cities. See M. Craig Brown and Charles N. Halaby, "Machine Politics in America, 1870–1945," *Journal of Interdisciplinary History* 17 (Winter 1987), 587–612; Steven P. Erie, *Rainbow's End: Irish-Americans and the Dilemmas of Urban Machine Politics, 1840–1985* (Berkeley, Calif., 1988) for details.

9. Hofstadter, *The Age of Reform*, 9; Edward Banfield and James Q. Wilson, *City Politics* (Cambridge, Mass., 1963), 40–41, 234–40; Nathan Glazer and Daniel P. Moynihan, *Beyond the Melting Pot* (Cambridge, Mass., 1970), 221–29; Merton, *Social Theory and Social Structure*, 71–81; Richard Wade, "Urbanization," in C. Vann Woodward (ed.), *The Comparative Approach to American History* (New York, 1968), 195–205; Handlin, *The Uprooted*, 201–26; William F. Whyte, *Street Corner Society* (Chicago, 1943). Exceptions to this mode of investigation can be found, most notably, in Martin Shefter, "The Emergence of the Political Machine: An Alternative View," in Willis Hawley et al. (eds.), *Theoretical Perspectives on Urban Politics* (Englewood Cliffs, N.J., 1976), 14–44; and in Amy Bridges, *A City in the Republic: Antebellum New York and the Origins of Machine Politics* (Cambridge, Mass., 1984).

10. Shefter, "Emergence of the Political Machine," 18–21.

11. Moreover, empirical tests conducted to date on party organizations in New York City and Memphis have demonstrated that the ability of these political machines to attract the overwhelming support of the immigrant population within their jurisdiction cannot be accounted for by any of the conventional theories. See, for details, Martin Shefter, "The Electoral Foundations of the Political Machine: New York City, 1884–1897," in Joel H. Silbey, Allan

G. Bogue, and William H. Flanigan (eds.), *The History of American Electoral Behavior* (Princeton, N.J., 1978), 263–98; and Kenneth D. Wald, "The Electoral Base of Political Machines: A Deviant Case Analysis," *Urban Affairs Quarterly* 16 (Summer 1980), 2–29.

12. Steffens, *Shame of the Cities*, 142–43; John T. Salter, *The People's Choice: Philadelphia's William S. Vare* (New York, 1971), 9; Harold Zink, *City Bosses in the United States* (Durham, N.C., 1930), 194–229; Sam Bass Warner Jr., *The Private City: Philadelphia in Three Periods of Its Growth* (Philadelphia, 1968), 86–91, 215–19.

13. Insights into the nature of the Republican "Organization" have been provided (from a reform perspective) by contemporary observers, such as Steffens, *Shame of the Cities*, 193–229; Louis Seaber, "Philadelphia's Machine in Action," *Independent* 58 (1905), 584–87; Clinton R. Woodruff, "Philadelphia's Revolution," *Yale Review* 30 (May 1906), 8–23; Austin F. MacDonald, "Philadelphia's Political Machine in Action," *National Municipal Review* 15 (January 1926), 28–35; Thomas R. White, "The Philadelphia System," *Forum* 77 (1927), 678–88. However, there is still no account of the machine during the period of its ascendancy over the city's polity (1887–1933). Indeed, except for Howard F. Gillette's "Corrupt and Contented: Philadelphia's Political Machine, 1865–1887" (Ph.D. diss., Yale University, 1970), which provides a detailed analysis of the various formations that fought for political power in the city before enactment of the Bullitt Bill as the new city charter in 1887, and two "participant-observer" studies (John T. Salter, *Boss Rule: Portraits in City Politics* [New York, 1935], and David H. Kurtzman, "Methods of Controlling Votes in Philadelphia" [Ph.D. diss., University of Pennsylvania, 1935]) conducted at the very time the Organization lost control of the city (1933), scholars have ignored the "institutionalization" of machine politics in what was, then, the third largest city in the country.

14. Merton, *Social Theory and Social Structure*, 71.

15. Handlin, *The Uprooted*, 210–13, 221; Hofstadter, *The Age of Reform*, 4–22; Eric L. McKitrick, "The Study of Corruption," *Political Science Quarterly* 72 (December 1957), 502–14; Elmer Cornwell Jr., "Bosses, Machines, and Ethnic Groups," *Annals of the American Academy of Political and Social Sciences* 353 (May 1964), 27–39; Alexander B. Callow Jr. (ed.), *The City Boss in America: An Interpretive Reader* (New York, 1976), 6; Seymour J. Mandelbaum, *Boss Tweed's New York* (New York, 1965), 58; Zane L. Miller, *Boss Cox's Cincinnati: Urban Politics in the Progressive Era* (New York, 1968); Allswang, *Bosses, Machines, and Urban Voters*.

16. Terrence J. McDonald and Sally K. Ward (eds.), *The Politics of Urban Fiscal Policy* (Beverly Hills, Calif., 1984), 20–21; Terrence J. McDonald, *The Parameters of Urban Fiscal Policy: Socioeconomic Change and Political Culture in San Francisco, 1860–1906* (Berkeley, Calif., 1986), 1–3.

17. A notable exception here is Roger Lotchin's analysis "Power and Policy: American City Politics Between the Two World Wars," in Scott Greer (ed.), *Ethnics, Machines, and the American Urban Future* (Cambridge, 1981), 1–50.

18. Terrence J. McDonald, "The Problem of the Political in Recent American Urban History: Liberal Pluralism and the Rise of Functionalism," *Social History* 10 (October 1985), 328–36; Bruce Stave et al., "Reassessment of the Urban Political Boss," 302–4; Hammack, *Power and Society*, 12–13.

19. James C. Scott, *Comparative Political Corruption* (Englewood Cliffs, N.J., 1972), 114–18; Banfield and Wilson, *City Politics*, 117–27; Edward C. Banfield, *Political Influence* (New York, 1961), 307–23; Raymond Wolfinger, *The Politics of Progress* (Englewood Cliffs, N.J., 1974), 99–106; Shefter, "The Electoral Foundations of the Political Machine," 266–69.

20. Scott, *Comparative Political Corruption*, 107.

21. Christopher Lasch, *The New Radicalism in America, 1889–1963: The Intellectual as a Social Type* (New York, 1965), 251–87.

Chapter 1.   Local Politics in Antebellum Philadelphia

1. Warner, *Private City,* 10–16, 79–82; Edgar P. Richardson, "The Athens of America, 1800–1825," in Russell F. Weigley (ed.), *Philadelphia: A 300-Year History* (New York, 1982), 208–23, 234–45; E. Digby Baltzell, *Philadelphia Gentlemen: The Making of a National Upper Class* (Glencoe, Ill., 1958), 87–88.

2. Warner, *Private City,* 80, 102–6, 111–17; Richardson, "The Athens of America," 226–30; Nicholas B. Wainwright, "The Age of Nicholas Biddle, 1825–1841," in Weigley (ed.), *Philadelphia: A 300-Year History,* 297.

3. Warner, *Private City,* 82, 86–90, 98–102.

4. Maxwell Whiteman, *Gentlemen in Crisis: The First Century of the Union League of Philadelphia* (Philadelphia, 1975), 1, 5–6; *Inquirer,* October 11, 1865. There were only three non-Republican administrations—Daniel Fox (Democrat, 1868–71), Samuel King (Democrat, 1881–84), Rudolph Blankenburg (Keystone, 1912–16)—between McMichael's election to the mayoralty in 1865 and that of Joseph S. Clark Jr. in 1952, and even then Blankenburg, a self-confessed Republican in national politics, was victorious only because of a temporary split in the ranks of the ruling Republican organization. See below, Chapter 8.
A similar pattern of Republican domination also characterized the state polity. More specifically, Simon Cameron's election as U.S. senator for Pennsylvania in 1867 marked the emergence of a Republican dynasty of party bosses—which included Cameron's son Donald, Matthew S. Quay, and Boies Penrose and which was to rule the state until the latter's death in 1921. See Philip S. Klein and Ari Hoogenboom, *A History of Pennsylvania* (New York, 1973), 317–33, for details.

5. Amy Bridges, *A City in the Republic: Ante-Bellum New York and the Origins of Machine Politics* (New York, 1984), 1–17, 61–82; Ronald P. Formisano, "Boston, 1800–1840: From Deferential-Participant to Party Politics," in Ronald P. Formisano and Constance K. Burns (eds.), *Boston, 1700–1980: The Evolution of Urban Politics* (Westport, Conn., 1984), 29–57.

6. Bridges, *A City in the Republic,* Warner, *Private City,* 85–91.

7. Bruce Laurie and Mark Schmitz, "Manufacture and Productivity: The Making of an Industrial Base, Philadelphia, 1850–1880," in Theodore Hershberg (ed.), *Philadelphia: Work, Space, Family, and Group Experience* (New York, 1981), 44–45.

8. Hershberg (ed.), *Philadelphia: Work, Space, Family, and Group Experience,* 465; Dennis Clark, *The Irish in Philadelphia* (Philadelphia, 1973), 17, 24.

9. Howard Gillette Jr., "The Emergence of the Modern Metropolis: Philadelphia in the Age of Its Consolidation," in William Cutler III and Howard Gillette Jr. (eds.), *The Divided Metropolis: Social and Spatial Dimensions of Philadelphia, 1800–1975* (Westport, Conn., 1980), 4–7.

10. Gillette, "Emergence of the Modern Metropolis," 7; Michael Feldberg, *The Philadelphia Riots of 1844: A Study of Ethnic Conflict* (Westport, Conn., 1975), 41–50; Clark, *The Irish in Philadelphia,* 20–22; E. Digby Baltzell, *The Protestant Establishment* (New York, 1964), 73.

11. Formisano and Burns (eds.), *Boston, 1700–1980,* 47–52, 262–63; Bridges, *A City in the Republic,* 61; Warner, *Private City,* 86–102.

12. Warner, *Private City,* 85.

13. Gillette, "Corrupt and Contented," 45–48.

14. George Vickers, *The Fall of Bossism: A History of the Committee of One Hundred and the Reform Movement in Philadelphia and Pennsylvania* (Philadelphia, 1883), 1:5. See also *North American,* January 9, 1868; Whiteman, *Gentlemen in Crisis,* 106–7.

15. Warner, *Private City,* 85.

16. *Inquirer,* November 18, 1874. For details of councilmen who were jobbers and contrac-

tors and who abused their public office for personal profit, see Gillette, "Corrupt and Contented," 46, and Whiteman, *Gentlemen in Crisis,* 106–7.

17. James Bryce, *The American Commonwealth* (New York, 1914), 2:406–7. Bryce's analysis was based on information he received from Philadelphia publisher, historian, and civic reformer Henry Charles Lea; see Edward S. Bradley, *Henry Charles Lea: A Biography* (Philadelphia, 1931), 179–80.

18. Vickers, *Fall of Bossism,* 1:64–66.

19. William Dusinberre, *Civil War Issues in Philadelphia, 1856–1865* (Philadelphia, 1965), 12–13, 183–84; Russell F. Weigley, "The Border City in Civil War, 1854–1865," in Weigley (ed.), *Philadelphia: A 300-Year History,* 384–88, 390, 392–93; Whiteman, *Gentlemen in Crisis,* 1, 5–6; Theodore Hershberg, "Free Blacks in Antebellum Philadelphia: A Study of Ex-Slaves, Freeborn, and Socioeconomic Decline," in Hershberg (ed.), *Philadelphia: Work, Space, Family, and Group Experience,* 368, 370.

20. Bruce Collins, "The Democrats' Loss of Pennsylvania in 1858," *Pennsylvania Magazine of History and Biography* (PMHB) 109 (October 1985), 499, 520–26, 535. Also James L. Huston, "The Demise of the Pennsylvania American Party, 1854–1858," *PMHB* 109 (October 1985), 478–81, 490–91.

21. Weigley, "The Border City," 389–92, 405, 411; Dusinberre, *Civil War Issues,* 77–78; Whiteman, *Gentlemen in Crisis,* 63.

22. Bridges, *A City in the Republic,* 155; Gillette, "Corrupt and Contented," 16–17, 26.

23. Bruce Laurie, *Working People of Philadelphia, 1800–1850* (Philadelphia, 1980), chaps. 2–5, 7–9; Philip Scranton, *Proprietary Capitalism: The Textile Manufacture at Philadelphia, 1800–1885* (Cambridge, 1983), chap. 9; Laurie and Schmitz, "Manufacture and Productivity," 43–92.

24. As exhibited, for example, in the cooperative ventures that underpinned the organization of the Pennsylvania Railroad in 1846 and the political consolidation of Philadelphia City and County in 1854. See Jeffrey P. Roberts, "Railroads and the Downtown: Philadelphia, 1830–1900," in Cutler and Gillette, *Divided Metropolis,* 28–33; Gillette, "The Emergence of the Modern Metropolis," 9–14.

25. Bridges, *A City in the Republic,* 28–29, 67; Richardson, "The Athens of America," 248.

26. For further details of the party's electoral base, see Chapter 6.

27. Whiteman, *Gentlemen in Crisis,* 15–18, 29–35, 56; Weigley, "The Border City," 407, 412–13; Gillette, "Corrupt and Contented," 18. For a detailed breakdown of the new business, industrial, and banking elite that displaced the old colonial gentry at the top of the city's social structure by the end of the Civil War, see E. Digby Baltzell, *An American Business Aristocracy* (New York, 1958), 129–30. See also Table 6 and Appendix 1 of this book.

28. Warner, *Private City,* 80–82, 86–91; Baltzell, *An American Business Aristocracy* (New York, 1958), 114; Bruce Laurie, "Fire Companies and Gangs in Southwark: The 1840s," in Allen F. Davis and Mark H. Haller (eds.), *The Peoples of Philadelphia: A History of Ethnic Groups and Lower Class Life, 1790–1940* (Philadelphia, 1973), 73–76; David R. Johnson, "Crime Patterns in Philadelphia, 1840–1870," 99, in Davis and Haller (eds.), *The Peoples of Philadelphia.*

29. Bridges, *A City in the Republic,* 74; Banfield and Wilson, *City Politics,* 115. See also above, Introduction, note 19.

30. Merton, *Social Theory and Social Structure,* 71–72.

31. Edward P. Allinson and Boies Penrose, *The City Government of Philadelphia* (Baltimore, 1887), 37–38. This fragmentation, the result of City Council's policy of creating independent committees as and when it extended the range of services provided by government, was itself a legacy of the local fear of strong executives inherited from the Revolution and Jackson. So

acute was this fear in Philadelphia that by 1854 the mayor had been "relegated . . . to being simply chief of police and the figure-head of the corporation, not holding even the check of the veto-power," an executive condition that remained unaltered until the adoption of the Bullitt Bill as the new city charter in 1887 (ibid., 47). For further details of the fragmentation characteristic of Philadelphia's government under its (second) charter of 1789, see also ibid., 33–48, and Warner, *Private City,* 9–16, 99–123.

32. Michael P. McCarthy, "The Philadelphia Consolidation of 1854: A Reappraisal," *PMHB* 110 (October 1986), 533; Weigley, "The Border City," 368–69.

33. Formisano, "Boston, 1800–1840," 40–43, 50–52; Warner, *Private City,* 86–88, 91, 93, 96, 98.

34. William L. Riordan, *Plunkitt of Tammany Hall* (New York, 1905), 55.

35. Frank Willing Leach, "Twenty Years with Quay," *North American,* May 28, 1905. Subsequent to Quay's death in May 1904, the *North American* asked Leach to submit a personal review of the state party leader's political career for publication. Readers showed such interest in Leach's article that the paper commissioned him to write a more detailed account of his time as Quay's secretary.

Leach's reminiscences, spread over forty-two highly descriptive and extensive articles, were published in the Sunday editions of the *North American* between July 3, 1904, and June 25, 1905. Given his intimate relationship with Quay, Leach was well qualified to comment not only on state and national politics but also on city affairs, particularly because he had begun his political career as a Republican party divisional worker in the eighth ward in downtown Philadelphia in the 1870s. Leach subsequently dabbled with Independent Republicanism and served as secretary of the Independent Republican State Committee in the early 1880s, before finally accepting Quay's offer of employment as his personal secretary in 1884. Also serving as chief clerk in the city controller's office (1881–84) and as real estate deputy for the Sheriff's Department (1891–95), Leach was as well in a good position to comment on public office and city government in Philadelphia. Leach's work was based on his personal files and recollections, and contemporary newspapers and correspondence he had with both party politicians and reformers between the 1870s and the turn of the century. Where appropriate, his claims have been checked for accuracy with other sources, generally the *Times* and the *Public Ledger.* The *Public Ledger* was an orthodox conservative Republican newspaper that represented the views of downtown business interests, while Alexander McClure's *Times* was strongly committed to reform within the Republican party and considered itself the main "opposition" journal in the city.

36. Laurie, "Fire Companies and Gangs," 71, 75, 77; Clark, *The Irish in Philadelphia,* 116.

37. Laurie, "Fire Companies and Gangs," 75, 78, 80, 82; Clark, *The Irish in Philadelphia,* 109, 116.

38. Johnson, "Crime Patterns," 99–100.

39. Laurie, "Fire Companies and Gangs," 77–78.

40. Johnson, "Crime Patterns," 101–2; Clark, *The Irish in Philadelphia,* 116; Stewart, "The Deal for Philadelphia," 44; "The North American," *Philadelphia and Popular Philadelphians* (Philadelphia, 1891), 27–28.

41. Laurie, "Fire Companies and Gangs," 78; Johnson, "Crime Patterns," 97.

42. Johnson, "Crime Patterns," 98; Clark, *The Irish in Philadelphia,* 114.

43. Laurie, "Fire Companies and Gangs," 78–80.

44. See above, note 10 of this chapter.

45. Riordan, *Plunkitt of Tammany Hall,* 14. The nature of party politics in the state at this time also bore a striking resemblance to the character of political life that prevailed in Philadelphia. Before Simon Cameron's emergence as the undisputed leader of the state Republican party in 1873, party politics in Pennsylvania, as in the urban polity, was not dominated by an overriding cleavage between well-organized machine and reform forces.

William Gienapp and James Huston's analysis of the breakup of the Jacksonian-Whig party system in Pennsylvania, for example, reveals that personal rivalries were responsible—as much as disputes over policy or different orientations to politics—for the cleavages between the individual political actors and formations who contended for power within the main parties. See William E. Gienapp, "Nebraska, Nativism, and Rum: The Failure of Fusion in Pennsylvania, 1854," *PMHB* 109 (October 1985), 426–27, 450–51, 469–70; Huston, "The Demise of the Pennsylvania American Party," 482–83. The same can be said of the factionalism that married the ascendancy of the Republican party in Pennsylvania. For details of the power struggle between former protectionist Democrat, Simon Cameron and former Whig Andrew Gregg Curtin for control of the state Republican party organization, a battle for leadership that dogged the party for almost the first twenty years of its existence and one in which the protagonists found it necessary to bribe their nominal followers (with favors and cash payments) in order to secure and maintain their cooperation, see Brooks M. Kelly, "Simon Cameron and the Senatorial Nomination of 1867," *PMHB* 88 (1963), 375–92; John D. Stewart, "The Deal for Philadelphia: Simon Cameron and the Genesis of a Political Machine, 1867–1872," *Journal of Lancaster County Historical Society* 77 (1973), 41–52; Klein and Hoogenboom, *A History of Pennsylvania,* 254–62, 317–21; James A. Kehl, *Boss Rule in the Gilded Age: Matt Quay of Pennsylvania* (Pittsburgh, 1981), 21; Rudolph Blankenburg, "Forty Years in the Wilderness; or, Masters and Rulers of the Freemen of Pennsylvania," *Arena* 33 (January 1905), 4–5, 8; Herbert Welsh, "The Degradation of Pennsylvania Politics," *Forum* (November 1891), 3–4.

46. The fourth ward covered the same geographical area throughout this period—that is, from the Delaware River to Broad Street and from South Street to Fitzwater Street. Comprised largely of working-class and immigrant neighborhoods, it traversed Southwark and Moyamensing on the southern edge of the old city. See Figures 1 and 4 and John Daly and Allen Weinberg, *Genealogy of Philadelphia County Subdivisions,* 2nd ed. (Philadelphia, 1966), 64, 83; and U.S. Department of the Interior, Census Office, *Vital Statistics of Boston and Philadelphia Covering a Period of Six Years Ending May 31, 1890* (Washington, D.C., 1894), 90.

47. Johnson, "Crime Patterns," 104–5; Harry C. Silcox, "William McMullen, Nineteenth-Century Political Boss," *PMHB* 110 (July 1986), 390–95.

48. Silcox, "William McMullen," 409.

49. Ibid., 389.

50. Ibid., 403, 408.

51. Warner, *Private City,* 93; Clark, *The Irish in Philadelphia,* 118–19.

52. Warner, *Private City,* 95–96.

53. Silcox, "William McMullen," 394; Johnson, "Crime Patterns," 106.

54. *Popular Philadelphians,* 13; Leach, "Twenty Years with Quay," May 28, 1905.

55. Allinson and Penrose, *City Government,* 56; Bryce, *American Commonwealth,* 2:107–9; George Morgan, *The City of Firsts: A Complete History of the City of Philadelphia* (Philadelphia, 1926), 279; Citizens Municipal Reform Association (CMRA), *Facts for the People* (Philadelphia, October 1873). The district attorneyship was one of five county offices left outside city authority following political consolidation in 1854. Located on State House Row—aptly named, since these officials were responsible solely to the state—the district attorney along with the city treasurer, the recorder of deeds, the register of wills, and the sheriff, were compensated by commissions rather than a fixed salary. So lucrative were the "pecuniary prizes" attached to these "Row" offices that reformers believed them to be "the most potent source of corruption in our local politics, stimulating unprincipled men to obtain nominations by all the disgraceful arts known to Ring politicians and moreover furnishing the means through which every fibre of our local political system is vitiated." CMRA, *Address,*

May 1872, 6–7; see also Thomas H. Speakman, *The People v. the Politicians: Where and How the People's Money Goes, and How Political Morals are Corrupted* (Philadelphia, 1878).

56. CMRA, *Facts for the People,* October 1873; Leach, "Twenty Years with Quay." May 28, 1905.

Chapter 2. Ring Rule

1. Zink, *City Bosses,* 196–99; see also McManes's obituary in the *North American* and the *Public Ledger,* November 24, 1899.

2. Bryce, *American Commonwealth,* 2:409. See also Zink, *City Bosses,* 195–96, 198.

3. Bryce, *American Commonwealth,* 2:407. See also Bradley, *Lea,* 180.

4. Bryce, *American Commonwealth,* 2:408; Zink, *City Bosses,* 194–95; CMRA, *The Gas Trust* (Philadelphia, April 20, 1874).

5. CMRA, *The Gas Trust,* 12–13.

6. Frederic W. Speirs, "The Philadelphia Gas Lease," *Municipal Affairs* 4 (1897), 719.

7. Bryce, *American Commonwealth,* 2:412.

8. Ibid., 407; Bradley, *Lea,* 180–81; Zink, *City Bosses,* 201; CMRA, *Third Report on the Philadelphia Gas Trust* (June 15, 1874), 2.

9. CMRA, *The Gas Trust,* 3–16.

10. Zink, *City Bosses,* 201; Henry C. Lea, "A Letter to the People of Philadelphia," *Forum* 2 (January 1887), 533–34.

11. CMRA, *The Gas Trust,* 2–3, 16.

12. *Public Ledger,* November 24, 1899.

13. Bryce, *American Commonwealth,* 2:409.

14. Vickers, *Fall of Bossism,* 69.

15. Ibid., 67, 156–57. See also Allinson and Penrose, *City Government,* 55–57.

16. Zink, *City Bosses,* 197–98.

17. *North American,* November 24, 1899.

18. *Popular Philadelphians,* 19; Howard O. Sprogle, *The Philadelphia Police: Past and Present* (Philadelphia, 1887), 150–54; *The Report of a Committee of One on the Official Life and Administrations of the Hon. William S. Stokley, Mayor of Philadelphia* (Philadelphia, 1880), 5–10.

19. Johnson, "Crime Patterns," 102–3; Weigley (ed.), *Philadelphia: A 300-Year History,* 346, 348, 375–76, 438, 440; *The Report of a Committee of One,* 6–7.

20. Howard F. Gillette, "Philadelphia's City Hall: Monument to a New Political Machine," *PMHB* 97 (April 1973), 233–34; see also Roger Butterfield, "The Cats on City Hall," *PMHB* 77 (October 1953), 439–48.

21. Gillette, "Philadelphia's City Hall," 235; Stewart, "The Deal for Philadelphia," 50.

22. Gillette, "Philadelphia's City Hall," 236–37.

23. Allinson and Penrose, *City Government,* 53–54.

24. CMRA, *Address* (Philadelphia, September 1871).

25. Vickers, *Fall of Bossism,* 59.

26. Gillette, "Philadelphia's City Hall," 237; Stewart, "The Deal for Philadelphia," 51.

27. Gillette, "Philadelphia's City Hall," 240–41; Stewart, "The Deal for Philadelphia," 51–52.

28. Gillette, "Philadelphia's City Hall," 240–41; Stewart, "The Deal for Philadelphia," 51–52.

29. *Manual of Councils, 1899–1900* (Philadelphia, 1899), 110–11.

30. Gillette, "Philadelphia's City Hall," 242–43; Dorothy G. Beers, "The Centennial City, 1865–1876," in Weigley (ed.), *Philadelphia: A 300-Year History,* 426.

31. Stewart, "The Deal for Philadelphia," 52; Gillette, "Philadelphia's City Hall," 243–48.

32. Plunkitt explained what he meant by "honest graft" or "boodle" by example: "My party's in power in the city, and it's goin' to undertake a lot of public improvements. Well, I'm tipped off, say, that they're going to lay out a new park at a certain place. I see my opportunity and I take it. I go to that place and I buy up all the land I can in the neighborhood. Then the board of this or that makes its plan public, and there is a rush to get my land, which no body cared particular for before. Ain't it perfectly honest to charge a good price and make a profit on my investment and foresight? Of course, it is. Well, that's honest graft." (Riordan, *Plunkitt of Tammany Hall,* 3.)

33. No longer the "walking city" of the mid-nineteenth century, Philadelphia's spatial area, like the size of its population, had doubled by the mid-1870s. This dramatic growth did not result in a duplication of the spatial arrangements that characterized the 1850 city, for the city did not merely expand; its basic spatial structure changed. It was turned inside out—that is, the significant changes in economic and social structure wrought by industrialization were expressed physically in the spatial form of the city. Indeed, spatial and socioeconomic differentiation complemented one another to such an extent that by 1880 the city "had begun to assume the unmistakable dimensions of the modern metropolis." See Hershberg (ed.), *Philadelphia: Work, Space, Family, and Group Experience,* 472–73, and 122 for the quotation.

34. Gillette, "Corrupt and Contented," 153, 158–60.

35. Ibid., 153.

36. *Philadelphia Times,* March 21, 1875, quoted in Gillette, "Corrupt and Contented," 162. (Unless otherwise noted, hereafter *"Times"* refers to the Philadelphia newspaper.)

37. Gillette, "Corrupt and Contented," 148; Whiteman, *Gentlemen in Crisis,* 113; Alexander K. McClure, *Old Time Notes of Pennsylvania,* vol. 2 (Philadelphia, 1905), 387.

38. Whiteman, *Gentlemen in Crisis,* 114–115.

39. Gustavus Myers, "The Most Corrupt City in the World," *Living Age* 22 (1904), 460.

40. Morgan, *City of Firsts,* 280; Zink, *City Bosses,* 197–98; Bradley, *Lea,* 180; Bryce, *American Commonwealth,* 2:407; Vickers, *Fall of Bossism,* 5; *North American,* November 24, 1899. Simon Cameron, once he had established himself as the undisputed leader of the state Republican party in 1873, was similarly depicted as "master of the state" and "the new Proprietor of Pennsylvania." See Daniel Dougherty, *"The Cameron Dynasty": Earnest Protest Against Its Continuance* (Lancaster, Pa.: October 21, 1878), 28; and *Public Ledger,* March 13, 1877.

41. Bryce, *American Commonwealth,* 2:412.

42. Ibid., 408.

43. Bradley, *Lea,* 180.

44. Philip C. Garrett, *Party Politics in Great Cities* (Philadelphia, 1882), 27.

45. Vickers, *Fall of Bossism,* 3–5.

46. *North American,* November 24, 1899; *City Bosses,* 202, 197–98.

47. Gillette, "Corrupt and Contented," 142; idem, "Philadelphia's City Hall," 233.

48. Vickers, *Fall of Bossism,* 5; *Popular Philadelphians,* 19; *The Report of a Committee of One,* 5–10; Gillette, "Corrupt and Contented," 165.

49. Gillette, "Corrupt and Contented," 141, 175.

50. Zink, *City Bosses,* 203; Kehl, *Boss Rule,* 44–45.

51. Rufus E. Shapley, *Solid for Mulhooly* (Philadelphia, 1881), 24–25, 137.

52. Gillette, "Corrupt and Contented," 246–48; *Times* and *Public Ledger,* February 16, 1881; Leach, "Twenty Years with Quay," February 19 and March 12, 1905.

53. Leach, "Twenty Years with Quay," February 26, 1905.

54. Zink, *City Bosses,* 204; Gillette, "Corrupt and Contented," 278; Leach, "Twenty Years with Quay," March 12 and April 2, 1905.

55. *The Republican Manual Containing Information in Relation to the Government of the Republican Party in the City of Philadelphia* (Philadelphia, 1857), 10–22; *Rules of the Union Republican Party of Philadelphia* (Philadelphia, 1868), 3–4; ibid. (Philadelphia, 1871), 3; ibid. (Philadelphia, 1877), 4–5.

56. CMRA, *Address of the Executive Committee,* Philadelphia, March 18, 1872; *Rules of the Union Republican Party, 1868,* 6.

57. *The New Rules of the Union Republican Party, 1877,* 14; Leach, "Twenty Years with Quay," March 19, 1905.

58. Leach, "Twenty Years with Quay," February 19, 1905; *Popular Philadelphians,* 24. See also Chapter 3, note 10.

59. For examples of rowdyism at conventions, which resulted in the suspension of proceedings and police intervention to restore order, see Leach, "Twenty Years with Quay," February 19, March 19, and May 7, 1905. See the *Inquirer* and *Public Ledger,* September 15, 1877, September 30, 1881, January 10, 1884, and September 23, 1886 for reports of the Republican party's efforts to nominate a district attorney and a coroner in 1877, two city commissioners in 1881, a receiver of taxes in 1884, and a judge for Common Pleas Court No. 3 in 1886.

60. Gillette, "Corrupt and Contented," 170; Leach, "Twenty Years with Quay," February 12, 1905; *Public Ledger,* November 8, 1876.

61. Gillette, "Corrupt and Contented," 246–47; Leach, "Twenty Years with Quay," February 19, 1905; *Public Ledger,* November 7, 1877; February 16, 1881; *Times,* February 16, 1881.

62. Leach, "Twenty Years with Quay," April 23, 1905. General Louis Wagner, a contestant for the Republican party nomination for recorder of deeds in 1881, also believed that a candidate needed to "have a silver mine at his back, a drinking capacity equal to the camel and be able to smoke like the stack of an iron furnace." Wagner subsequently withdrew from the contest on the grounds that "a personal canvass [of the wards and divisions] of the character indicated [was] absolutely needed," if one wanted to secure the party's nomination (*Public Ledger,* September 19, 1881).

63. Leach, "Twenty Years with Quay," February 12, 1905.

64. Ibid., March 19, 1905.

65. Ibid., March 19 and April 9, 1905; *Public Ledger,* September 30, 1881; September 21, 1882; January 4, 9, and 10, 1884.

66. Leach, "Twenty Years with Quay," March 19, 1905.

67. *The New Rules of the Union Republican Party, 1877,* 5.

68. Leach, "Twenty Years with Quay," February 12, 1905; *Public Ledger,* January 4 and February 16, 1876.

69. Leach, "Twenty Years with Quay," February 26, 1905; *Public Ledger,* January 15 and February 19, 1879.

70. Leach, "Twenty Years with Quay," February 26, 1905; *Public Ledger,* February 21, 1877, February 26, 1880.

71. Leach, "Twenty Years with Quay," March 12, 1905; *Public Ledger,* February 16 and 17, 1881; Zink, *City Bosses,* 207.

72. Leach, "Twenty Years with Quay," March 26, 1905; *Public Ledger,* February 22, 1882.

73. *Manual of Councils, 1879–1880,* 51–94; *Ring Rule: What Has the Republican Party Done for Philadelphia? Report of a Committee of 80,000* (Philadelphia, 1881), 21–22.

74. Patronage Appointment Book, Water Department, 1875, 1876, 1879 (Department of Records, City Hall, Philadelphia).

75. Sprogle, *Philadelphia Police,* 152–54; *The Report of a Committee of One,* 17.

76. *Rules for the Government of the Union Republican Party, 1871,* 3; Minutes Book, Nineteenth Ward Union Republican Executive Committee, 1875–80 (Department of Records, City Hall, Philadelphia).

77. *Sunday Times,* January 9, 1876, quoted in Leach, "Twenty Years with Quay," February 12, 1905.

78. For other examples of Stokley's inability to control the behavior of his followers, see Gillette, "Corrupt and Contented," 146, 148, 163, 169.

79. Zink's uncritical acceptance of the source materials he used for his chapter on McManes, for instance (that is, Vickers's *Fall of Bossism* and Bryce's *American Commonwealth;* Lea's investigation of the gas works, and the gas trust leader's obituary in the crusading reform journal *North American*) meant that his *City Bosses,* 194–205, reiterated the distorted views of contemporary reform observers and thereby perpetuated the notion of the all-powerful "boss," "King" James McManes. Neither, it should be noted, was Simon Cameron (contrary to received wisdom) the supreme nabob of the state Republican party. His power base in central government was "too vulnerable for effective boss rule" (Kehl, *Boss Rule,* 60), in the sense that federal patronage, even when it was readily available to him (which it sometimes was not, when he was faced with an uncooperative President like Rutherford B. Hayes or James Garfield) failed to provide him with the sufficient means necessary to establish a reliable system of discipline within his "organization." For details of Cameron's inability to control the state legislature, and the behavior of senior elected public officials (such as Governors Geary, 1867–73, and Hoyt, 1879–83) who owed their positions to him, see Kehl, *Boss Rule,* 36–37, 44–45, 54–55, 142–43, and Klein and Hoogenboom, *A History of Pennsylvania,* 260, 324.

80. In this respect, their power was similar in scope to that exercised by a fellow contemporary "boss" in New York; the infamous Bill Tweed of Tammany Hall. See Shefter, "Emergence of the Political Machine," 15–17, 21–25, for details of how Tweed's reputation belies the real limitations on the power he wielded both within the New York Democratic party and in the city as a whole.

81. *Times,* November 29, 1894; Leach, "Twenty Years with Quay," January 29, 1905; Walter Davenport, *Power and Glory: The Life of Boies Penrose* (New York, 1931), 68–69.

82. Harold E. Cox and John F. Meyers, "The Philadelphia Traction Monopoly and the Pennsylvania Constitution of 1874: The Prostitution of an Ideal," *Pennsylvania History* 35 (October 1968), 410.

83. Vickers, *Fall of Bossism,* x, 59; Allinson and Penrose, *City Government,* 53–54.

84. Henry C. Lea, *Constitutional Reforms* (Philadelphia: October 31, 1872), 4–5.

85. Gillette, "Corrupt and Contented," 37; *The Republican Manual, 1857,* 77–78. Details of public officials in Philadelphia who were appointed by the state governor can be found in the annual Council manual.

86. *The Republican Manual, 1857,* 75–77. Federal officers, like state officials in the city, were also listed in the annual Council manual; see, for example, *Manual of Councils, 1885–1886,* 122–24.

87. Gillette, "Corrupt and Contented," 30–31.

88. *New York Tribune,* n.d., cited in *Inquirer,* May 19, 1873.

Chapter 3.   The Politics of Protest and Reform

1. Baltzell, *An American Business Aristocracy,* 20, 131; Warner, *Private City,* 85–86, 98; Weigley, "The Border City," 372; Vickers, *Fall of Bossism;* McClure, *Old Time Notes,* 2:361; Bryce, *American Commonwealth,* 2:406–25; E. V. Smalley, "The Philadelphia Committee of One Hundred," *Century Magazine* 4 (1883), 395–99; Bradley, *Lea,* 183–200.

2. Kenneth Fox, *Better City Government: Innovation in American Urban Politics, 1850–1937* (Philadelphia, 1977), 22. Fox's assertion that the main significance of these early reform groups lay "in solidifying groups of gentlemen reformers" together "and elevating them to prominence" rather than in "the practical reform work [they] managed to accomplish" also provides an appropriate assessment of the contribution of the CMRA and the Committee of One Hundred to political reform in postbellum Philadelphia (ibid., 46). Another subscriber to this viewpoint is Martin J. Schiesl, *The Politics of Efficiency: Municipal Administration and Reform in America, 1880–1920* (Berkeley, Calif., 1977), 3.

3. Warner, *Private City*, 85–86. See also above, Chapter 1.

4. Bradley, *Lea*, 189–90; Vickers, *Fall of Bossism*, 60–64; Whiteman, *Gentlemen in Crisis*, 112.

5. Vickers, *Fall of Bossism*, 59. See also Allinson and Penrose, *City Government*, 61–62.

6. Baltzell, *An American Business Aristocracy*, 90–99, 124–26, 130–31, 133, 141, 169, 172, 211; *Popular Philadelphians*, 77; Bradley, *Lea*, 9–10.

7. Gillette, "Corrupt and Contented," 52–53; Vickers, *Fall of Bossism*, 73.

8. Cutler and Gillette, *Divided Metropolis*, 9–14, 32–33.

9. Gillette, "Corrupt and Contented," 57.

10. Ibid., 55–57. These businessmen were also alike in that they formed their companies in partnership or individually, and not through incorporation (which required a special act of the state legislature until 1874). Big business was not yet dominant or very much in evidence in Philadelphia in the immediate postbellum period. As late as 1880, for example, there were no corporations among the 849 textile firms in Philadelphia. See Philip Scranton, *Proprietary Capitalism: The Textile Manufacture at Philadelphia, 1800–1885* (Cambridge, 1983), 3. Firms such as Alfred Jenks's machine works; the Baldwin locomotive works; Henry Disston & Sons, the largest saw and tool manufacturer in the country; and the Cramp Shipyards, all with nearly 3,000 workers apiece, were exceptions to the usual scale of organization. See Laurie and Schmitz, "Manufacture and Productivity," 47–65.

11. *Inquirer*, November 18, 1874.

12. CMRA, *Address*, May 1872, 1. The reformers' pessimistic forecast was based on the analysis they conducted of the city's finances; their examination revealed that although levels of taxation had risen dramatically since the antebellum period, city income had failed to keep pace with public expenditure. Public revenue raised by taxation, for instance, had more than quadrupled, from $2,653,474 in 1860 to $11,640,571 in 1874, as a result of a 26 percent rise in the tax rate from $1.75 (on every $100 of taxable property) to $2.20 and the tripling of the assessed valuation of property from $155,697,669 to $548,243,585, while city expenditures had also exhibited a similar pattern of growth, rising from $4 million to $13 million over the same period. Put another way, in terms of per head of population, taxation revenue had increased from $4.79 in 1860 to $16.03 in 1874, while city expenditures had risen from $7.10 to $18.09 over this period.

As a result of this imbalance, the annual deficit on the city's budget the reformers noted had doubled from an average of $271,749 between 1854 and 1861, to $593,896 during the Civil War (1861–67). By the postwar decade, city expenditure was exceeding income by, on average, in excess of $1 million ($1,045,172) a year. These yearly deficiencies were reflected in the size of the city's floating debt, which by the early 1870s exceeded $4 million, having stood at under half a million dollars only a decade earlier. Even more disturbing, particularly from the reform viewpoint, had been the remorseless growth in the city's funded debt (money borrowed to provide "permanent improvements," such as schools, bridges, sewers, waterworks, and so forth) which rose from $20,913,505 in 1860 to $58,165,516 in 1874. See CMRA, *Reform Tracts No. 1: Municipal Taxation* (Philadelphia, December 1871); CMRA, *Facts for the People* (Philadelphia: March 4, 1874), 1–3; Allinson and Penrose, *City Government*, 44–46, 57–58.

It was, then, the city's increasing indebtedness, along with "the progress of taxation and expenditure ever onward at a rate far exceeding that of the increasing population and the value of property," which so alarmed the reformers and formed the basis of their gloomy prediction for the future (CMRA, *Address,* May 1872, 1).

13. Ibid., 2.

14. Ibid., 1.

15. CMRA, *Address,* September 1873, 3; CMRA, *Facts for the People,* March 1874, 1.

16. Lea, *Constitutional Reforms,* 2.

17. CMRA, *Memorial to the Constitutional Convention of Pennsylvania* (Philadelphia: January 13, 1873), 1–2.

18. CMRA, *Address,* May 1872, 2.

19. CMRA, *Report of the Executive Committee,* December 13, 1871, 1.

20. Bradley, *Lea,* 189–90; CMRA, *Address of the Executive Committee,* October 26, 1871, 4; Reform Club of Philadelphia, *Constitution* (Philadelphia, 1875), 1.

21. Bradley, *Lea,* 185; Whiteman, *Gentlemen in Crisis,* 108–9.

22. Bradley, *Lea,* 185; Whiteman, *Gentlemen in Crisis,* 108–9.

23. See, for example, CMRA, *Municipal Taxation, Reform Tracts No. 2: The Registry and Election Laws* (Philadelphia, [c 1872]) and *Facts for the People,* October 1873, March, 1874.

24. Bradley, *Lea,* 188–89. Lea's *Songs for the Politicians* (Philadelphia, 1872) were reproduced in full by Leach, "Twenty Years with Quay," January 29, 1905.

25. Gillette, "Corrupt and Contented," 63–66; Leach, "Twenty Years with Quay," January 29 and February 5, 1905.

26. Gillette, "Corrupt and Contented," 63–66; Leach, "Twenty Years with Quay," January 29 and February 5, 1905. For further details of the nature of the local problems that faced the reformers, see CMRA, *The Registry and Election Laws,* 4; CMRA, *Address,* October 1871, 2; Bradley, *Lea,* 183–84; Klein and Hoogenboom, *A History of Pennsylvania,* 318; Stewart, "The Deal for Philadelphia," 47.

27. For details of the corrupt practices and the campaign for constitutional reform, see Klein and Hoogenboom, *A History of Pennsylvania,* 261–62, 318–19; Stewart, "The Deal for Philadelphia," 47, 49.

28. CMRA, *Memorial to the Constitutional Convention;* Bradley, *Lea,* 190; Whiteman, *Gentlemen in Crisis,* 111–13.

29. Lea, *Justices' Courts in Philadelphia* (Philadelphia: September 1, 1873). For further details of the convention's deliberations and the provisions of the new state constitution, see Klein and Hoogenboom, *A History of Pennsylvania,* 319–21; Gillette, "Corrupt and Contented," 72–76, 103–9.

30. Gillette, "Corrupt and Contented," 228–29.

31. Vickers, *Fall of Bossism,* 72.

32. Gillette, "Corrupt and Contented," 238–39.

33. Ibid., 239.

34. Municipal League of Philadelphia, *Annual Report of the Board of Managers, 1897–1898* (Philadelphia, 1898), 26.

35. Vickers, *Fall of Bossism,* 74–76, 139–40.

36. Ibid., 111–12.

37. Ibid., 113–15; Smalley, "The Philadelphia Committee of One Hundred," 398; Leach, "Twenty Years with Quay," March 5, 1905.

38. See Appendix 2.

39. Vickers, *Fall of Bossism,* 230–33; Leach, "Twenty Years with Quay," February 19, 1905.

40. Vickers, *Fall of Bossism*, 112. See also Smalley, "The Philadelphia Committee of One Hundred," 398.

41. Vickers, *Fall of Bossism*, 99; Leach, "Twenty Years with Quay," March 5 and 12, 1905.

42. Vickers, *Fall of Bossism*, 99; Leach, "Twenty Years with Quay," March 5 and 12, 1905.

43. See the *Report of the Sub-Committee of the Committee of One Hundred on the Bullitt Bill* (Philadelphia, 1885).

44. Leach, "Twenty Years with Quay," April 30, 1905; Philip S. Benjamin, "Gentlemen Reformers in the Quaker City, 1870–1912," *Political Science Quarterly* 85 (March 1970), 67–68.

45. Gillette, "Corrupt and Contented," 50; CMRA, *Address*, May 1872, 1.

46. Vickers, *Fall of Bossism*, 59. See also CMRA, *Address*, September 1871, 2.

47. Lea to Joseph Caven, November 17, 1878 (Lea Papers, University of Pennsylvania), quoted in Gillette, "Corrupt and Contented," 224.

48. Smalley, "The Philadelphia Committee of One Hundred," 398.

49. Ibid.; *North American*, October 15, 1873.

50. Whiteman, *Gentlemen in Crisis*, 106–7.

51. Bradley, *Lea*, 195–97; Vickers, *Fall of Bossism*, 29–37, 60–61, 63, 65–66.

52. Bradley, *Lea*, 197–98.

53. Smalley, "The Philadelphia Committee of One Hundred," 396.

54. McClure, *Old Time Notes*, 2:361.

55. Vickers, *Fall of Bossism*. See Bryce, *American Commonwealth*, 2:415.

56. Vickers, *Fall of Bossism*, 73.

57. Bradley, *Lea*, 191–93.

58. Gillette, "Corrupt and Contented," 229.

59. Bradley, *Lea*, 195.

60. Leach, "Twenty Years with Quay," May 21, 1905.

61. Gillette, "Corrupt and Contented," 228–29; Beers, "The Centennial City," 459–70.

62. Whiteman, *Gentlemen in Crisis*, 132.

63. Reform Club, *Constitution*, 1.

64. Leach, "Twenty Years with Quay," February 19, 1905.

65. *The Court of Common Pleas for the County of Philadelphia, Sitting in Equity, Between J. Ingham, Plaintiff, and the Reform Club of Philadelphia* (Philadelphia, 1876), 4–6.

66. Leach, "Twenty Years with Quay," February 19, 1905; Gillette, "Corrupt and Contented," 229.

67. Whiteman, *Gentlemen in Crisis*, 114–15.

68. Ibid.; Leach, "Twenty Years with Quay," February 12, 1905.

69. Whiteman, *Gentlemen in Crisis*, 114–15; Leach, "Twenty Years with Quay," February 12, 1905.

70. *Public Ledger*, November 8, 1876; Gillette, "Corrupt and Contented," 172–73, 245; Leach, "Twenty Years with Quay," February 12, 1905. Rowan polled 2,530 votes in the twenty-ninth ward, 2,137 in the tenth ward, 1,153 in the ninth, and 2,861 in the nineteenth, compared with Southworth, who received 3,282 (twenty-ninth ward), 2,783 (tenth), 1,418 (ninth), and 3,378 (nineteenth) votes.

71. Quoted in Leach, "Twenty Years with Quay," February 12, 1905.

72. In the fifteenth and twenty-second wards, Rowan polled 3,618 and 2,247 votes, respectively, compared with Southworth, who received 4,881 and 3,050 votes (*Public Ledger*, November 8, 1876). At the ward level, the most consistent Republican majorities in mayoral elections between 1865 and 1884 were provided by wards 7, 8, 9, and 10, just west of the old downtown core, and wards 24 and 27, farther to the west across the Schuylkill River, as well as wards to the northwest of the old city (13, 14, 15, 20 [29], 21 [28], 22) (see Figure 4 and

Table 8)—that is, the new residential areas on the urban periphery to which those who benefited most from industrialization (managers, supervisors, and clerks) were relocating (Alan N. Burstein, "Immigrants and Residential Mobility: The Irish and Germans in Philadelphia, 1850–1880," in Hershberg [ed.], *Philadelphia: Work, Space, Family, and Group Experience,* 178–79).

73. *Public Ledger,* September 13, 1877.

74. Leach, "Twenty Years with Quay," February 19, 1905.

75. Unlike the elections of November 1876, when Rowan was the only Republican candidate to be defeated, all the Republican candidates for office in November 1877 were narrowly beaten by their Democratic opponents: James Sayre (52,626 votes) by Robert E. Pattison (majority, 1,620) in the city controller election; Russell Thayer (53,859) by Hagert (majority, 773) in the district attorney election; and Andrew J. Knorr (51,818) by Gilbert (majority, 1,024) in the coroner's election. For details of how party factionalism robbed these three Republican candidates of victory, see the *Public Ledger,* November 7, 1877; Gillette, "Corrupt and Contented," 246–47; Leach, "Twenty Years with Quay," February 19, 1905.

76. *Public Ledger,* November 1, 1880; Vickers, *Fall of Bossism,* 41–43, 46; Leach, "Twenty Years with Quay," February 26, 1905.

77. *Public Ledger,* November 1, 1880.

78. Ibid., November 3, 1880; Vickers, *Fall of Bossism,* 53.

79. Bradley, *Lea,* 196–97; Vickers, *Fall of Bossism,* 65–66.

80. *North American,* November 3, 1880.

81. The defeat of six "regular" Republican nominees by Independent candidates in ring wards 21, 22, 26, and 30 in council elections held on the same day as the mayoral contest also indicates that there was a repetition of the spontaneous bolt in suburban areas. See *Public Ledger,* February 16, 1881; Leach, "Twenty Years with Quay," March 12, 1905.

82. Vickers, *Fall of Bossism,* 219; *Times,* February 16, 1881.

83. Bradley, *Lea,* 196–97; Vickers, *Fall of Bossism,* 65–66, 212–13.

84. Vickers, *Fall of Bossism,* 184, 203.

85. Smalley, "The Philadelphia Committee of One Hundred," 398.

86. Vickers, *Fall of Bossism,* 73–74, 111.

87. Ibid., 76, 107–10.

88. Ibid., 111–13.

89. Ibid., 114.

90. Ibid., 115; Leach, "Twenty Years with Quay," March 5, 1905.

91. Ibid., 128, 131; *Times,* January 17, 1881.

92. Ibid., 138, 144–48.

93. Ibid., 141–44.

94. *Inquirer,* February 12, 1884.

95. Municipal League, *Annual Report, 1897–1898,* 26.

96. *Press,* November 27, 1881; Baltzell, *An American Business Aristocracy,* chap. 9.

97. Bradley, *Lea,* 196–97; Vickers, *Fall of Bossism,* 72–82.

98. *Times,* November 21, 1880.

99. Leach, "Twenty Years with Quay," May 21, 1905.

100. Smalley, "The Philadelphia Committee of One Hundred," 398–99; Vickers, *Fall of Bossism,* 99.

101. Leach, "Twenty Years with Quay," March 26 and April 23, 1905; *Public Ledger,* February 22 and 23, 1882, February 12, 1884; *Times* and *Inquirer,* February 12, 1884.

102. Leach, "Twenty Years with Quay," March 26, 1905; *North American, Public Ledger,* and *Times,* February 22 and 23, 1882. While listing the election returns for Select Council, for example, these newspapers point out that "Gas Trust nominees" Dan Blair (eighth ward),

Dave Mullen (ninth ward), James Miles (thirteenth), William S. Reyburn (fifteenth), James Dobson (twenty-eighth), and Frances Martin (thirty-first) were all defeated by Independent Republican candidates who had been endorsed by the Committee of One Hundred. This implies that the Committee played an integral role in the defeat of the gas trust faction.

While not contesting that the election results constituted a victory for Independent Republicanism or "reform" as such, these newspapers do give a misleading impression of the importance of the committee in the "reform victory" of February 1882. Indeed, by wrongly crediting the victory to the reform group, these newspaper accounts reinforced the claims of reform publicists, who argued that the Committee of One Hundred was responsible for bringing about "the fall of bossism."

103. Benjamin, "Gentlemen Reformers," 66.

104. Ibid., 61.

105. *Public Ledger*, January 9, 1884; Leach, "Twenty Years with Quay," April 23, 1905.

106. Benjamin, "Gentlemen Reformers," 67.

107. McClure, *Old Time Notes*, 2:362.

108. Steffens, *Shame of the Cities*, 203–4; Allinson and Penrose, *City Government*, 64; Zink, *City Bosses*, 204; Leach, "Twenty Years with Quay," May 14, 1905.

109. Kehl, *Boss Rule*, 74–75; Steffens, *The Autobiography*, 1:409.

110. Stewart, "The Deal for Philadelphia," 44–45, 49–50; Gillette, "Corrupt and Contented," 94–96, 99–100.

111. Klein and Hoogenboom, *A History of Pennsylvania*, 258–59, 262; Kelley, "Simon Cameron and the Senatorial Nomination of 1867," 375–78, 392; Stewart, "The Deal for Philadelphia," 50–51. During the period 1860–71, when Cameron and Curtin contested each election, Republican candidates had failed to attract Philadelphia's full electoral strength, usually securing pluralities of less than 5,000. But, following Cameron's accommodation with key political leaders, such as Mann and McManes, the state party could anticipate a 20,000 majority in the city and certain victory in the state. See Gillette, "Corrupt and Contented," 100–102.

112. See Kehl, *Boss Rule*, 38–39, 44, 50, 54–55, 75, and Gillette, "Corrupt and Contented," 68–69, 268–69, for details of how first Stokley in 1876 and then McManes in 1880 successfully led a bolt of Philadelphia representatives against Cameron's leadership at the Republican National Convention of those years. In the latter case, McManes, much to Cameron's chagrin, was credited by many newspapers as being the individual most responsible for Ulysses S. Grant's failure to be nominated for a third term of office.

113. Kehl, *Boss Rule*, 53.

114. *Times*, January 7, 1876; Leach, "Twenty Years with Quay," February 26, 1905.

115. *Public Ledger*, January 31, 1878. Highways expenditure, for example, fell from $1,515,929 in 1876 to $589,419 in 1878 and $326,798 in 1880, under William Baldwin, John Hill's successor as highways commissioner. Overall, the total expenditure by city departments fell by almost $4 million between 1875 and 1880, from $10,105,919 to $6,370,578. See *Ring Rule . . . Report of a Committee of 80,000*, 20–21; *Manual of Councils, 1885–1886*, 105; Allinson and Penrose, *City Government*, 58–59.

116. Gillette, "Corrupt and Contented," 262.

117. Vickers, *Fall of Bossism*, 72, 93–94; Gillette, "Corrupt and Contented," 271–72; Leach, "Twenty Years with Quay," March 12, 1905. Although embarrassed, for instance, by the Investigating Committee's report, which was very critical of the management of the Gas Works, McManes was able to fend off its recommendations due to the strength of his support in Select Council (Gillette, "Corrupt and Contented," 274–75; Leach, "Twenty Years with Quay," April 12, 1905). McManes's defeat for reelection to the gas trust in January 1883 was only a temporary setback, for he was again elected to the board the following year. He did,

however, face a hostile minority in the trust, since such opponents as David Lane, William H. Smith, Alfred Moore, James Work, and William W. Alcorn were all elected trustees between 1881 and 1883 (Leach, "Twenty Years with Quay," April 2 and 16, 1905; Zink, *City Bosses,* 204).

118. Leach, "Twenty Years with Quay," April 23, 1905. Put another way, the URA was formed to provide an alternative focus for those who had felt excluded from the party by those who contended for influence at the Central Union Republican Club at Eleventh and Chestnut streets, and at "Seventh Street," the "synonym for the Ring," which met at the offices of the gas trust (ibid.; see also Gillette, "Corrupt and Contented," 279).

119. Leach, "Twenty Years with Quay," April 23, 1905.

120. *North American,* May 15, 1883, quoted in Gillette, "Corrupt and Contented," 229.

121. Leach, "Twenty Years with Quay," April 23, 1905.

122. *Times,* February 24, 1884, quoted in Gillette, "Corrupt and Contented," 282.

123. Kehl, *Boss Rule,* 56; Steffens, *The Autobiography,* 1:409. Businessmen reformers supported structural changes in city government because they anticipated that the concentration of power and responsibility incorporated in the new charter would not only improve accountability but also promote the efficient management of city services and ultimately bring about lower taxes. For further details of the reasons reformers supported the passage of the Bullitt Bill, see *Report of the Sub-Committee of the Committee of One Hundred on the Bullitt Bill;* Civil Service Reform Association of Philadelphia, *Fourth Annual Report of the Executive Committee* (Philadelphia, 1885); *The Bullitt Bill: What the Reform Charter Is, and Why It Should Become a Law* (Philadelphia, [1885]); *The Bullitt Bill: Who Favor and Who Oppose Its Enactment* (Philadelphia, [1885]).

124. Davenport, *Power and Glory,* 44–45; Robert D. Bowden, *Boies Penrose: Symbol of an Era* (New York, 1937), 58–59.

125. *Times,* June 3, 1883, quoted in Leach, "Twenty Years with Quay," May 14, 1905.

126. *Times,* March 22, 1885.

127. Quoted in Leach, "Twenty Years with Quay," May 14, 1905.

128. *The Bullitt Bill: Who Favor and Who Oppose,* 22.

129. Allinson and Penrose, *City Government,* 7.

130. Bryce, *American Commonwealth,* 2:421.

131. Lucretia L. Blankenburg, *The Blankenburgs of Philadelphia* (Philadelphia, 1929), 15.

Chapter 4.   Centralization of the Republican Party Organization

1. Similar changes also took place in the organization and structure of state party politics in the late nineteenth century. For example, the Republican machine of Cameron's successor, Matthew S. Quay (1833–1904) emerged as the dominant institution in Pennsylvania's government and politics in the mid-1880s. Embracing 20,000 "regulars" and an annual payroll of $24 million, Quay's machine was indeed, in the opinion of the party leader's critics, "the most perfect and complete of all state [political] organizations" that emerged elsewhere throughout the nation in the last two decades of the nineteenth century (Jesse Macy, *Party Organization and Machinery* [New York, 1912], 111). For details of the rivalry between Quay's entrenched machine and the determined reform opposition led by Philadelphia's "merchant prince" John Wanamaker, see Kehl, *Boss Rule,* 138–44, 150, 157, 162, 177, 207–24; *The Speeches of Hon. John Wanamaker on Quayism and Boss Domination in Pennsylvania Politics* (Philadelphia, [1898]); Herbert A. Gibbons, *John Wanamaker,* vol. 1 (New York, 1926), 253–301, 347–67; Bradley, *Lea,* 202–4. See also Clifton K. Yearley, *The Money Machines: The Breakdown and Reform of Governmental and Party Finance in the North, 1860–1920* (Albany, N.Y., 1970), and Richard L.

McCormick, *From Realignment to Reform: Political Change in New York State, 1893–1910* (Ithaca, N.Y., 1981) for details of the emergence of party organizations in other states during this period.

2. Scott, *Comparative Political Corruption,* 101–3, 111–12; Banfield and Wilson, *City Politics,* 134–37.

3. Woodruff, "Philadelphia's Revolution," 13.

4. Kehl, *Boss Rule,* 57, 59–60.

5. Ibid., 60, 61–62, 66–67, 70–71, 82–83.

6. Ibid., 62.

7. Ibid., 63–64. Quay, in response to reform claims that the control of federal and state patronage (which provided him with an estimated annual payroll of $7,600,000, an amount sufficient to sustain 14,705 officeholders in 1898) had permitted him to become "the dictator of the State Republican party" (Bradley, *Lea,* 202), publicly asserted that it was "a positive disadvantage [because] everybody cannot be gratified. For every single appointment a dozen or more who have been disappointed become disgruntled and indifferent" (*Kansas City Star,* November 11, 1889, quoted in Kehl, *Boss Rule,* 123). The fact that no fewer than twenty men expected his support when a vacancy arose in the state Supreme Court in 1901 suggests that Quay, on this occasion, was not attempting to deceive the public and that the allocation of patronage did provide him with a genuinely difficult problem. See Kehl, *Boss Rule,* 122–23, 137, 144, 235–37; *Speeches of Wanamaker on Quayism,* 231–35.

8. Kehl, *Boss Rule,* 66–67. According to Quay's critics, in the late nineteenth century the treasury funds amounting to as much as $5 to $6 million a year were held on deposit in private ("pet") banks throughout the state while school districts, hospitals, and state charities languished because of unpaid public appropriations. These deposits yielded the Republican machine in excess of $150,000 a year in "substitute interest" and earned Quay the nickname of "Farmer General of the State Finance" (Isaac F. Marcosson, "The Fall of the House of Quay," *World's Work* 11 [1906], 7120; *Speeches of Wanamaker on Quayism,* 19–23, 158; Kehl, *Boss Rule,* 67). For details of other ways in which state funds were converted to political capital by Quay, and of the methods he used to disburse the money in the most effective manner to influence elections, see Kehl, *Boss Rule,* 63–67, 144, 214–15; Davenport, *Power and Glory,* 56, 58, 61; Marcosson, "Fall of the House of Quay," 7120–23; *Speeches of Wanamaker on Quayism,* 20, 41–42, 369.

9. Kehl, *Boss Rule,* 62–63, 83, 122–23, 137, 144, 237; *Speeches of Wanamaker on Quayism,* 195, 197, 231–35. Details of personal and political indiscretions committed by legislators were compiled by Quay's agents, who relied on private detectives, municipal policemen, subsidized journalists, and "shysters at law, medicine, banking and of the pulpit" to provide them with potentially damaging material (Davenport, *Power and Glory,* 70–71). They were recorded on card files (known as "Quay's coffins") which the state boss kept among his private papers (Kehl, *Boss Rule,* 63–64).

10. *Speeches of Wanamaker on Quayism,* 283. For an excellent illustration of the control Quay exercised over the state Republican party, see Kehl, *Boss Rule,* 241–42. See Blankenburg, "Forty Years in the Wilderness," March 1905, 237–38, and Edward J. Stackpole, *Behind the Scenes with a Newspaperman: Fifty Years in the Life of an Editor* (Philadelphia, 1927), 81–82, for details of how the state boss made a successful eleventh-hour switch in his choice of candidate for the gubernatorial nomination at the state Republican convention held in June 1902.

11. Steffens, *Shame of the Cities,* 204.

12. Ibid.; Kehl, *Boss Rule,* 62, 75–76; Zink, *City Bosses,* 204–5.

13. Kehl, *Boss Rule,* 76; Morgan, *City of Firsts,* 284; *Popular Philadelphians,* 27–28.

14. Kehl, *Boss Rule,* 76.

15. Ibid.; Morgan, *City of Firsts,* 284; *Popular Philadelphians,* 28.

16. *Times,* January 12, 1895.

17. *Press,* January 10, 1895; Steffens, *Shame of the Cities,* 213; Citizens' Municipal Association (CMA), *11th Annual Report* (Philadelphia, 1897), 2. (Hereafter, *"Press"* refers to the Philadelphia newspaper.)

18. Leach, "Twenty Years with Quay," June 25, 1905; Zink, *City Bosses,* 209; *North American,* June 29, 1909; Kehl, *Boss Rule,* 74–75; Municipal League, *Annual Report, 1896–1897,* 11–14; Clinton R. Woodruff, "The Municipal League of Philadelphia," *American Journal of Sociology* 11 (1905–6), 349.

19. Kehl, *Boss Rule,* 192–94; *Speeches of Wanamaker on Quayism,* 17, 150; Municipal League, *Annual Report, 1896–1897,* 26.

20. Kehl, *Boss Rule,* 191; *North American,* June 29, 1909. For details of how Quay eventually overcame the challenge of the "Hog Combine," see also Kehl, *Boss Rule,* 193–95, 209–13; Leach, "Twenty Years with Quay," November 27, 1904, June 25, 1905; Zink, *City Bosses,* 208–10. Charter revision, state investigating committees, federal and state patronage, and the advocacy of reform (when politically expedient) were also the "weapons" used by Quay's successor, Boies Penrose, to influence political affairs in Philadelphia for his own benefit. See Lloyd M. Abernethy, "Insurgency in Philadelphia, 1905," *PMHB* 87 (January 1963), 12; Committee of Seventy (C of 70), *Second Report of the Executive Board* (Philadelphia, 1905), 36–39; and below, Chapter 8, for example, for details of how Penrose used charter revision (that is, the passage of the 1905 "Ripper Bill" and the introduction of a new city charter in 1919), first, to support his loyal follower Iz Durham, who was experiencing difficulties during a period of reform insurgency (1905–7), and second, to punish the Vare brothers for their disobedience. See also Lloyd M. Abernethy, "Progressivism, 1905–1919," in Weigley (ed.), *Philadelphia: A 300-Year History,* 551; William S. Vare, *My Forty Years in Politics* (Philadelphia, 1933), 114–18; and "The Campaign in Philadelphia," *Outlook,* September 16, 1911, 97–98, for details of how Penrose managed to seal victory for his candidate George H. Earle in the Republican mayoral primary election of 1911, by establishing a state Committee of Inquiry (into allegations of corruption in the Reyburn mayoral administration), which dealt a mortal blow to the campaign of his opponent, William Vare. Penrose-inspired interventions in local affairs, it should be noted, tended to be of a punitive rather than supportive nature following Iz Durham's death in 1909. This was because the Vare brothers, Edwin and Bill, unlike Durham (and McNichol, who continued to serve as Penrose's able lieutenant until his death in 1917), were not always prepared to acquiesce to the wishes of the state party leader. Consequently, Penrose's relationship with the Vares was an uneasy one oscillating between compromise and harmony in certain campaigns, and violence and murder in others. See Davenport, *Power and Glory,* 138–45; Vare, *Forty Years,* 124–37; William A. McGarry, "Government by Murder," *Independent* (October 27, 1917), 178–80; Abernethy, "Progressivism," 561–62, for details.

21. Bowden, *Boies Penrose,* 182, 203–4. See also Kehl, *Boss Rule,* 76; Steffens, *Shame of the Cities,* 216; Zink, *City Bosses,* 206–21.

22. *North American,* June 29, 1909.

23. *The New Rules of the Union Republican Party,* 1877, 5.

24. Woodruff, "Philadelphia's Revolution," 13; *Public Ledger,* October 30, 1905; Kurtzman, "Methods of Controlling Votes," 12; John T. Salter, "Party Organization in Philadelphia: The Ward Committeeman," *American Political Science Review* 27 (August 1933), 626.

25. *Press,* June 27, 1905, Israel W. Durham Scrapbook, Historical Society of Pennsylvania (HSP).

26. Lists of party committeemen and ward leaders for this period no longer exist, though it has been possible to compile the membership of the Republican City Committee for 1895 and

1905 using the following: *Press,* January 12, 1895; *Public Ledger,* June 18, 1905; *North American,* June 19, 1905; *Record,* June 20, 1905.

27. *Press,* January 12, 1895; *Record,* June 20, 1905. *Public Ledger,* October 30, 1905, Durham Scrapbook.

28. Woodruff, "Philadelphia's Revolution," 13.

29. Kurtzman, "Methods of Controlling Votes," 19–21, 46; Salter, "Party Organization in Philadelphia," 625.

30. See above, Chapter 2, and Chapter 2, note 59.

31. See Chapter 2, note 59. *The New Rules of the Union Republican Party, 1877,* 21–22; Walter J. Branson, "The Philadelphia Nominating System," *Annals of the American Academy of Political and Social Science* 14 (1899), 20.

32. Branson, "The Philadelphia Nominating System," 23.

33. Ibid., 24; "Rules and Rulers," *Public Ledger,* March 15 and May 5, 1898.

34. Branson, "The Philadelphia Nominating System," 24.

35. Leach, "Twenty Years with Quay," March 19, 1905.

36. Ibid., February 12, 1905.

37. *Public Ledger* and *North American,* July 10, 1901, Durham Scrapbook.

38. Municipal League, *Annual Report, 1902–1903,* 4. For a good illustration of this "automationism," see *Public Ledger, North American* and *Inquirer,* July 10, 1901, Durham Scrapbook; William R. Stewart, "The Real John Weaver," *October Cosmopolitan,* 1905, 1–30; and *The True John Weaver* (Philadelphia, 1905), 1–19—all for details of how convention delegates, upon receiving last-minute instructions from Durham, adopted the relatively unknown John Weaver instead of the current incumbent Peter F. Rothermel as the party's nominee for district attorney in 1901.

39. See Chapter 5.

40. See Chapter 5.

41. *North American,* August 17, 1909, Durham Scrapbook.

42. Bardsley, as city treasurer, personally and legitimately received more than $200,000 in interest on the deposit of public funds. Failing to clear his debts by speculation with this money, however, led him to misappropriate a further $778,858.38 of public funds for his own ends. Bardsley's fraudulent manipulation of the city's money was uncovered following the failure of two banks that were key depositories for public funds: *Report of the Sub-Committee of the Finance Committee of Councils of Philadelphia upon the Investigation of the City's Deposits in the Keystone, National and Other Banks, and the Transactions of John Bardsley, late City Treasurer in the Management of Public Funds* (Philadelphia: March 13, 1892); CMA, *6th Annual Report, 1892,* 3, 11–14.

43. *The Political Assessment of Office Holders: A Report on the System as Practised by the Republican Organization in the City of Philadelphia, 1883–1913* (Philadelphia, 1913), 5. This investigation of the political assessment of public employees was carried out on behalf of Reform Mayor Blankenburg, by his director of public works, the gifted progressive engineer Morris Llewellyn Cooke. For further details of their reform efforts, see below, Chapter 8.

44. Ibid., 12; *Public Ledger,* February 6, 1895.

45. Ibid., 6, 9.

46. Ibid., 5; "Address of Rudolph Blankenburg," Academy of Music, September 27, 1917, 2–3, Blankenburg Papers, HSP.

47. Quoted in Charles F. Jenkins, "The Blankenburg Administration in Philadelphia," *National Municipal Review* 5 (April 1916), 213–14.

48. See Chapter 2.

49. Albert A. Bird, "The Mayor of Philadelphia," *The Citizen,* December 1895, 233–36;

Manual of Councils, 1887–1906. County offices, it should be noted, remained outside the civil service law until 1949, when Philadelphia's dual form of government was finally abolished. See C of 70, *The Charter: A History* (Philadelphia, 1980), chap. 1.

50. *Manual of Councils, 1889–1890*, 56; *1899–1900*, 44; *1905–1906*, 77; *Popular Philadelphians*, 12–13; *Public Ledger*, June 18, 1905; *Inquirer*, October 12, 1905.

51. *Manual of Councils, 1899–1900*, 44.

52. T. Everett Harry, "Philadelphia's Political Redemption," *International* (November 1912), 126. For further details of the reformers' inability to insulate public office from party influence, see Owen Wister, "The Case of the Quaker City," *Outlook*, May 25, 1912, 172; Frederick P. Gruenberg, "Philadelphia's Charter Victory," *Survey*, August 9, 1919, 701; Women's League for Good Government (WLGG), *Facts About Philadelphia* (Philadelphia, 1919), 47.

53. Kurtzman, "Methods of Controlling Votes," 47, 66; Salter, *Boss Rule*, 30. In 1900 there were 4,502 positions available in the city government, making up a total payroll of $4,535,450. By 1930 the number of jobs had almost tripled to 12,887, and the public payroll quadrupled to $18,840,900. See *Manual of Councils, 1899–1900, 1930*.

54. Morris L. Cooke, *Business Methods in Municipal Works: An Informal Record of the Operation of the Department of Public Works, of the City of Philadelphia, Under the Administration of Mayor Blankenburg* (Philadelphia, 1913), 28–29; Karl De Schweinitz, "Philadelphia Striking a Balance Between Boss and Business Rule," *Survey*, January 17, 1914, 460.

55. Kurtzman, "Methods of Controlling Votes," 40; Salter, "Party Organization in Philadelphia," 624–25.

56. John A. Smull, *Smull's Legislative Hand Book* (Harrisburg, 1920), 1101–18.

57. Ibid. (1890), 662–86.

58. For a definition of what in Plunkitt's view constituted "honest graft," see Chapter 2, note 32.

59. Marcosson, "The Awakening of Philadelphia," *World's Work* 10 (September 1905), 6646; Blankenburg, "Forty Years in the Wilderness," August 1905, 129.

60. *North American*, October 18, 1911, C of 70 Scrapbook, Urban Archives Center, Temple University.

61. Ibid.

62. *Bulletin*, October 18, 1911, C of 70 Scrapbook.

63. For details of John Mack and his relationship with Durham, see below, Chapters 5 and 7. With regard to Martin's reconciliation with Durham, see *North American*, October 20, 1909; *Times*, October 25, 1911; C of 70 Scrapbook.

64. *Times*, October 25, 1911; C of 70 Scrapbook.

65. Blankenburg, "Forty Years in the Wilderness," August 1905, 129.

66. Ibid., June 1905, 581.

67. Ward leader Thomas W. Cunningham, for example, served six successive terms (1904–28) as clerk of the Quarter Sessions Court. Similarly, "Boss" William Vare (1902–12) and James M. Hazlett (1912–32), president of the Republican City Committee, occupied the Recorder of Deeds Office for virtually the first third of the twentieth century. See *Manual of Councils; Inquirer*, October 12, 1905; *Philadelphia Bulletin*, October 25, 1911, C of 70 Scrapbook; Kurtzman, "Methods of Controlling Votes," 79.

68. Salter, *Boss Rule*, 36–37, 39.

Chapter 5. The Characteristics of Republican Boss Rule in Philadelphia

1. All the various party leaders, including McManes and Stokley, had something in common that has tended to be underrated or overlooked in the past: their ability and

competence as professional politicians. For details of just how capable and talented these "bosses" were in the business of politics (whatever else they may have been), see the character sketches of McManes, Vare, and Durham in Bryce, *American Commonwealth,* 2:407–9; John T. Salter, "The End of Vare," *Political Science Quarterly* 50 (June 1935), 216; Steffens, *Shame of the Cities,* 216; Zink, *City Bosses,* 212; and *Pittsburgh Dispatch,* May 19, 1902, Durham Scrapbook.

2. Bryce, *American Commonwealth,* 2:421. The party leaders at the state level, like their counterparts in Philadelphia, were also party professionals of the highest caliber. The only significant difference between the two groups seems to have been one of social background. Unlike the city "bosses," who were of humble origin, state leaders Quay and Penrose came from the upper echelons of society. Quay, for instance, was a classical scholar and son of a Presbyterian minister. He was also, in the opinion of Rudyard Kipling, the best literary critic in America (Kehl, *Boss Rule,* xii, 253, 283). Penrose (1860–1921), a Harvard law graduate, and descendant of prominent colonial shipbuilder Bartholomew Penrose, was "Proper Philadelphia's most interesting and gifted politician in the late nineteenth and early twentieth centuries" (Baltzell, *An American Business Aristocracy,* 163–64). For further details of Penrose's career, see the two biographies of this colorful political figure, who "certainly measured up to Ernest Hemingway's ideal of the gentleman" (ibid.); Walter Davenport, *Power and Glory: The Life of Boies Penrose* (New York, 1931); and Robert D. Bowden, *Boies Penrose: Symbol of an Era* (New York, 1937).

3. Steffens, *Shame of the Cities,* 203.

4. Ibid., 204.

5. *Philadelphia Record,* June 20, 1905, Durham Scrapbook. (Hereafter, unless otherwise noted, *"Record"* refers to the Philadelphia newspaper.)

6. Rudolph Blankenburg, "Forty Years in the Wilderness," July 1905, 15–16.

7. Salter, "Party Organization in Philadelphia," 626.

8. *Sunday Dispatch,* June 19, 1932, quoted in Kurtzman, "Methods of Controlling Votes in Philadelphia," 12.

9. Those occasions (such as the local elections of 1899, 1905, 1921, 1923, and 1927) when the Organization not only elected its own candidates but also deliberately transferred enough votes to the Democratic ticket (in order to ensure that minority party representation remained in the hands of its traditional partisan opponents rather than a reform third party) are also illustrative of the boss's ability to exercise control over his party subordinates. The successful outcome of these intricate, extralegal, ticket-splitting ventures was dependent on the full cooperation of party workers across the city. See below, Chapter 6.

10. MacDonald, "Philadelphia's Political Machine in Action," 33; White, "The Philadelphia System," 680.

11. From the 1890s onward, one-third to one-half of the members of Select Council also sat on the Republican party's City Committee, while the Common Council was packed with party workers who had served the Organization loyally in their respective wards. More specifically, in 1894, 15 out of 37 select councilmen sat on the Republican City Committee; in 1899, 19 out of 40; in 1905, 19 out of 42; in 1910, 18 out of 47; and in 1916, 15 out of 48. In 1925 at least 13 of the 20 councilmen (in the new unicameral body organized under the city charter of 1919) sat on the City Committee. These figures are based on the *Manual of Councils* for the respective years and on lists of the Republican City Committee compiled from the *Press,* January 12, 1895; *Public Ledger,* June 18, 1905; *North American,* June 19, 1905; *Record,* June 20, 1905; *Press,* September 3, 1911; and "The Young Republicans," *Respect for Republicans* (Philadelphia: February 1926). For the Organization's control of Common Council, see WLGG, *Facts About Philadelphia,* 53–54, and C of 70, *Recommendations to Voters* (Philadelphia: February 20, 1906).

12. Cox and Meyers, "The Philadelphia Traction Monopoly," 417–18; Davenport, *Power and Glory*, 152–54; Steffens, *Shame of the Cities*, 222–25; Clinton R. Woodruff, "Philadelphia's Street Railway Franchises," *American Journal of Sociology* 7 (1901–2), 216–33.

13. *Press* and *Inquirer*, June 17, 1901; Woodruff, "Philadelphia's Street Railway Franchises," 216–17, 220, 226–28; Municipal League, *Annual Report, 1901–1902*, 5–7.

14. *Plain Talk: Report by Morris Llewellyn Cooke, Director of Public Works to the Mayor* (Philadelphia, 1914), 50. For examples of reform measures sponsored by Blankenburg that were thwarted by the city Councils, see Donald W. Disbrow, "Reform in Philadelphia Under Mayor Blankenburg, 1912–1916," *Pennsylvania History* 27 (October 1960), 386–88.

15. Marcosson, "The Awakening of Philadelphia," 6640.

16. The figures for John Mack's businesses were arrived at by adding together the number of public contracts awarded to John M. Mack, the Mack Paving and Construction Company, the Barber Asphalt Paving Company, the Pennsylvania Asphalt Paving Company, and the Union Paving Company, deduced from the *Mayor's Annual Register of Contracts, 1887–1930*, Department of Records, City Hall, Philadelphia. Arranged numerically, though indexed alphabetically by name of contractor, this annual register contains details (date, nature of work, contractor, bureau and city department, and value of contract) of all authorized contracts for public work in the city carried out by private firms.

Between 1887 (when subsequent to the introduction of the Bullitt City Charter the first register was compiled) and 1930, the City of Philadelphia negotiated almost 70,000 public contracts with private companies. Before 1903, however, the annual register lists only the number of contracts awarded to each firm, not their value. Such information can still be found, though, since individual contracts have been stored and can usually be traced at the Records Center, 410 North Broad Street.

17. *Press*, July 8, 1901, Durham Scrapbook; *Mayor's Annual Register of Contracts, 1887–1902*.

18. Clark, *The Irish in Philadelphia*, 141–42; idem, *The Irish Relations*, 86–96.

19. *Mayor's Annual Register of Contracts, 1903–1911; Press*, September 13, 1911, and *North American*, September 30, 1911, C of 70 Scrapbook.

20. George W. Norris, "Progress and Reaction in Pennsylvania, II: Philadelphia's Strabismus," *Outlook*, December 29, 1915, 1050; *Mayor's Annual Register, 1888–1921, Manual of Councils, 1905–1906*, 150, and *Public Ledger*, August 28, 1905, Durham Scrapbook.

21. *Bulletin*, September 21, 1911, C of 70 Scrapbook; Salter, *The People's Choice*, 66; CMA, *14th Annual Report, 1900*, 110–12.

22. Allinson and Penrose, *City Government*, 65–72; *The Bullitt Bill: What the Reform Charter Is, and Why It Should Become a Law;* Bird, "The Mayor of Philadelphia," 233–36.

23. In 1912, for instance, 204 of the 311 bills passed by the Councils were concerned with paving streets, changing street lines, laying water pipes, locating lights, and so forth. See WLGG, *Facts About Philadelphia*, 51–52.

24. Ibid.

25. Ibid.; *Manual of Councils, 1910–1911*, 25–26, 29; *Press*, September 3, 1911; C of 70, *Recommendations to Voters*, 21–22.

26. *Mayor's Annual Register of Contracts, 1911; Manual of Councils, 1910–1911*, 29; *Press*, September 3, 1911.

27. Kurtzman, "Methods of Controlling Votes," 44–45.

28. *Manual of Councils, 1905–1906*, 78, 95, 126; *1910–1911*, 93, 145; *Record*, June 20, 1905.

29. Cooke, *Business Methods*, 8, 24.

30. *Mayor's Annual Register of Contracts, 1904; Manual of Councils, 1905–1906*, 95, 109; *Record*, June 20, 1905.

31. *Press,* October 13, 1905, Durham Scrapbook.

32. *Public Ledger,* October 30, 1905, Durham Scrapbook.

33. Ibid.

34. Ibid. For further details of the methods that were used to favor McNichol's company in the awarding of contracts for the construction of the Torresdale filtration system, see also the *Press,* July 7, 1901, Durham Scrapbook; *Public Ledger,* July 7, 1906, C of 70 Scrapbook; CMA, *15th Annual Report, 1901,* 44–45; "How Philadelphia Was Bled," *Nation* 81 (August 17, 1905); Blankenburg, "Forty Years in the Wilderness," June 1905, 577–81.

35. *Public Ledger,* October 30, 1905, Durham Scrapbook.

36. "How Philadelphia Was Bled," August 17, 1905.

37. Blankenburg, "Forty Years in the Wilderness," June 1905, 580.

38. *Public Ledger,* November 29, 1910, C of 70 Scrapbook.

39. *North American,* November 28, 1910, C of 70 Scrapbook.

40. Ibid., November 4, 1905, Durham Scrapbook.

41. Ibid., November 28, 1910, C of 70 Scrapbook.

42. Norris, "Philadelphia's Strabismus," 1051.

43. Disbrow, "Reform in Philadelphia," 386–88; L. L. Blankenburg, *The Blankenburgs,* 60–64.

44. Nicholas B. Wainwright, *History of the Philadelphia Electric Company, 1861–1961* (Philadelphia, 1961), 85–86; *The Directory of Directors in the City of Philadelphia, 1905* (Philadelphia, 1905), 84; Bowden, *Boies Penrose,* 117; *Public Ledger,* June 29, 1909.

45. Wainwright, *Philadelphia Electric Company,* 86; *Public Ledger,* June 29, 1909.

46. *Pittsburgh Dispatch,* May 19, 1902, Durham Scrapbook; Blankenburg, "Forty Years in the Wilderness," August 1905, 137; *Public Ledger* and *North American,* June 29, 1909; Marcosson, "The Awakening of Philadelphia," 6648.

47. *Record* and *Public Ledger,* February 6, 1895; *Times,* February 8, 1895; CMA, *9th Annual Report, 1895,* 41–45.

48. CMA, *9th Annual Report, 1895,* 44.

Chapter 6.   Electoral Foundations and Functions of the Republican Machine

1. Banfield and Wilson, *City Politics,* 116.

2. *Manual of Councils,* 1887–1933.

3. Cornwell, "Bosses, Machines, and Ethnic Groups," 22; James C. Scott, "Corruption, Machine Politics, and Political Change," *American Political Science Review* 63 (December 1969), 1150.

4. Scott, *Comparative Political Corruption,* 104–18.

5. Wade, "Urbanization," 187–205; Handlin, *The Uprooted,* 201–26; Whyte, *Street Corner Society;* Merton, *Social Theory and Social Structure,* 71–81.

6. Hofstadter, *The Age of Reform,* 9; Banfield and Wilson, *City Politics,* 40–41, 234–40; Glazer and Moynihan, *Beyond the Melting Pot,* 221–29.

7. Caroline Golab, "The Immigrant and the City: Poles, Italians, and Jews in Philadelphia, 1870–1920," in Davis and Haller (eds.), *The Peoples of Philadelphia,* 203–4.

8. Ibid., 208–9.

9. The mayoral elections of 1899, 1903, and 1916 have been omitted from Table 17 because the equations generated for these elections failed to pass the appropriate F test at the .05 level.

10. The ward returns in the sixteen mayoral elections included in this analysis were taken

from the *Inquirer*, October 11, 1865; October 14, 1868; February 18, 1874; February 21, 1877; February 16, 1887; February 21, 1895; February 20, 1907; November 9, 1911; and the *Manual of Councils, 1881,* 111; *1920,* 274–75; *1927,* 285–86; *1931,* 297–98; as well as the *Eighteenth Annual Report of the Registration Commission* (Philadelphia, 1923), 18–19. The demographic data for the wards was computed from published U.S. Census totals. See U.S. Census Office, *Census of Population, 1870,* 1:460–61; idem, *Census of Population, 1880,* 1:454–65; idem, *Vital Statistics of Boston and Philadelphia Covering a Period of Six Years Ending May 31, 1890* (Washington, D.C., 1894), 118–19; idem, *Census of Population, 1900,* 1:241–42, 677; U.S. Bureau of the Census, *Census of Population, 1910,* 3:605–8; idem, *Census of Population: 1920,* 3:896–99; idem, *Census of Population, 1930,* 3:688–707.

11. The indicator for social class used in this analysis is the number of taxable inhabitants in each ward (expressed as a proportion of the total population of the ward) taken from the yearly statements of real and personal property in the city drawn up by the Board of Revision of Taxes and contained in the annual reports of the mayor. See the *Annual Message of the Mayor of the City of Philadelphia,* 1890–1930.

12. The *t*-statistics of the regression coefficients of the ethnicity variables in these equations test the null hypothesis that the difference in the estimated level of support for the Republican candidate in wards inhabited by the ethnic group in question and those populated by third-generation Americans is not significantly greater than zero.

13. This inference is also consistent with what we would expect given that, in the initial stages of its development, the Republican party had advocated not only an economic program of protectionism (in order to attract the support of both capital and labor) but also nativist policies. See above, Chapter 1 and Clark, *The Irish Philadelphia,* 73, 117–20.

14. The coefficients of the social-class variable would probably have been large, negative, and significant in all five elections if in the two instances (1911 and 1919) where there was no meaningful relationship, the machine's nominees had not been defeated by Independent Republican candidates in the party's primary elections and therefore been unable to stand in the general election. Put another way, the coefficients of the social-class variable generated by multiple regression equations for the Republican party primary elections for 1911 and 1919—that is, $-.44^a$ (.04) and $-.71^c$ (.34), respectively—suggest that if the machine's nominees had stood in the general election, the relationship between social class and Republican party voting would have been consistent in all five elections instead of just three.

15. This quotation is taken from twentieth-ward-leader David Lane's election address to division (precinct) leaders cited in the *Public Ledger,* October 17, 1901. See Salter, "Party Organization in Philadelphia," 620, and Vare, *Forty Years,* 29–30, for details on other party leaders who make the same point.

16. John L. Shover, "Ethnicity and Religion in Philadelphia Politics, 1924–1940," *American Quarterly* 25 (1973), 499–515. The relationship between location and machine voting can be examined in two ways, either by dividing the city's wards into two groups (center and periphery) and estimating separate regression equations for each subset of wards, or by entering dummy variables for "center" and "periphery" in the same regression equations presented in Table 17. In this instance, unfortunately, limitations of data prevented me from generating significant regression equations using either of these two methods—that is, given the small sample size, none of the equations generated passed the appropriate F test at the .05 level.

17. Ibid., 509; John L. Shover, "The Emergence of a Two-Party System in Republican Philadelphia, 1924–1936," *Journal of American History* 60 (1974), 993–94. Philadelphia's urban form at the turn of the century closely resembled Ernest Burgess's model of urban spatial structure in which the socioeconomic status of the population increases with increasing distance from the center of the city. In the zone surrounding the manufacturing and retailing

core—that is, wards 1, 2, 3, 4, and 26—the area in which the machine enjoyed its firmest support, first- and second-generation Jews and Italians made up between two-thirds and four-fifths of the total population in 1910. Put another way, in the early twentieth century, Jews and Italians living in "The Neck" outnumbered their counterparts in suburban areas by 2 to 1. The city's black population was also more heavily congregated in this section of the city, with the largest concentrations in the seventh and thirtieth wards, where they accounted for approximately half of the total population by 1920 (see Figure 7 and sources for Table 14).

18. Golab, "The Immigrant and the City," 206, 210–15, 220–21; Hershberg et al., "A Tale of Three Cities: Blacks, Immigrants, and Opportunity in Philadelphia, 1850–1880, 1930, 1970," in Hershberg (ed.), *Philadelphia: Work, Space, Family, and Group Experience,* 466–68, 473–76.

19. Salter, "Party Organization in Philadelphia," 620. For a good illustration of the "personal service" offered by the Organization, see Salter, "A Philadelphia Magistrate Tells His Story," *National Municipal Review* 22 (October 1933), 514–20; idem, "The Corrupt Lower Courts of Philadelphia," *American Mercury* 33 (October 1934), 236–40; and Spencer Ervin, *The Magistrate Courts of Philadelphia* (Philadelphia, 1931), 104–8—all for details of the dual role magistrates played as both politicians and judges.

20. See note 5 for this chapter.

21. See Introduction.

22. See Introduction, note 15.

23. John F. Bauman, "The Philadelphia Housing Commission and Scientific Efficiency, 1909–1916," in Michael H. Ebner and Eugene M. Tobin (eds.), *The Age of Urban Reform: New Perspectives on the Progressive Era* (Port Washington, N.Y., 1977), 117–30.

24. Ibid.; Zink, *City Bosses,* 225.

25. WLGG, *Facts About Philadelphia,* 14–21.

26. Ibid., 55; Disbrow, "Reform in Philadelphia," 386–88; Norris, "Philadelphia's Strabismus," 1049–52; Blankenburg, *The Blankenburgs,* 60–64; De Schweinitz, "Philadelphia Striking a Balance," 462.

27. For details of the relationship between the Organization and the interests who got rich off the urban poor, see D. C. Gibboney, *Why the "Gang" Seeks to Legislate the Law and Order Society of Philadelphia Out of Existence: The White Slave Traffic, Its Relation to Unscrupulous Officials and Corrupt Politicians* (Philadelphia, 1905), 3–20; Blankenburg, "Forty Years in the Wilderness," August 1905, 130–33; Seaber, "Philadelphia's Machine in Action," 586; Municipal League, *Annual Report, 1902–1903,* 1–2; and *North American,* August 31, 1901; March 5, 1905—all on the police protection of vice and crime and the alliance between the Organization and the white slave and gambling syndicates.

On Philadelphia's horizontal slums and the widespread violations of sanitary and housing laws by slumlords, see WLGG, *Facts About Philadelphia,* 9–27; and John F. Sutherland, "Housing the Poor in the City of Homes: Philadelphia at the Turn of the Century," in Davis and Haller (eds.), *The Peoples of Philadelphia,* 175–202. For the relationship between the state and city "bosses" and the utility financiers, Widener, Elkins, Kemble, and Dolan, see Chapter 7 of this book. And finally, for the aid given to land developers and manufacturers, see Davenport, *Power and Glory,* 132, 184; Klein and Hoogenboom, *A History of Pennsylvania,* 321–23; Warner, *Private City,* 219–21; Dan Rottenberg, "The Rise of Albert M. Greenfield," in Murray Friedman (ed.), *Jewish Life in Philadelphia* (Philadelphia, 1983), 213–34; and above, Chapter 4.

28. Zink, *City Bosses,* 225.

29. See, for instance, Clinton R. Woodruff, "Philadelphia's Water: A Story of Municipal Procrastination," *Forum* 28 (1899–1900), 305–14, in which Woodruff argues that the repeated delay in purifying the city's water supply—which until the construction of the

Torresdale filtration plant (1899–1907) was taken direct from the river—was due to a mixture of "procrastination, corporate greed and official indifference."

30. Zink, *City Bosses*, 228; Warner, *Private City*, 208; Robert E. Drayer, "J. Hampton Moore: An Old Fashioned Republican" (Ph.D. diss., University of Pennsylvania, 1961), 250–54.

31. Edmund Sage, *Masters of the City: A Novel of Today* (Philadelphia, 1909), 94.

32. Warner, *Private City*, ix–x; Bruce Stave, "A Conversation with Sam Bass Warner, Jr.," *Journal of Urban History* 1 (November 1974), 93.

33. Warner, *Private City*, 214, 219–20.

34. Ibid., 215.

35. See Chapters 5 and 7.

36. *North American*, June 29, 1909; Zink, *City Bosses*, 212.

37. *North American*, June 30, 1909.

38. Warner, *Private City*, 217–18.

39. Zink, *City Bosses*, 221–22, 228. See also Vare, *Forty Years*, 21–23, 131, and Salter, *The People's Choice*, 17.

40. Zink, *City Bosses*, 221–22; Warner, *Private City*, 217–18; Salter, "The End of Vare," 215–17.

41. Since the Vare brothers could rely on the collusion of public officials in the awarding and completion of contract work (resulting in "easy specifications, easy performance and high-priced awards," as local reformers put it), it is reasonable to assume that their level of profit would be greater than if there had been fair and open competition among contractors. See above, Chapter 5, and Neva R. Deardorff, "To Unshackle Philadelphia," *Survey*, April 5, 1919, 21. A dramatic illustration of the exorbitant profit the "contractor bosses" enjoyed is provided by the contract work they carried out, extending and developing League Island Park between 1901 and 1909. By using material dredged from the Delaware and Schuylkill rivers as "landfill" for the project, instead of "clean earth" as specified by the contract, City Surveyor John M. Nobre estimated that the Vares made a net profit of as much as $1 million out of the $1,355,462 in contracts awarded by the city for the completion of the scheme. See *Inquirer*, July 29, 1911; *Record*, September 20, 1911; *North American*, September 25, 30, 1911, C of 70 Scrapbook; and "City Contracts" 16829, 17457, 18537, 19840, 22107. For details of the profits that street-cleaning contracts yielded to the Vares, see CMA, *8th Annual Report, 1894*, 45–46; CMA, *10th Annual Report, 1896*, 40; *North American*, November 28, 1910, C of 70 Scrapbook; and Blankenburg, "Forty Years in the Wilderness," July 1905, 21–22.

42. Kehl, *Boss Rule*, 252.

43. Davenport, *Power and Glory*, 105–6.

44. Kehl, *Boss Rule*, chaps. 9, 11, 12; Warner, *Private City*, 219–20.

45. WLGG, *Facts About Philadelphia*, 28.

46. Clinton R. Woodruff, "Progress in Philadelphia," *American Journal of Sociology* 26 (1920), 323–24; Deardorff, "To Unshackle Philadelphia," 19–23.

47. William H. Issel, "Modernization in Philadelphia School Reform, 1882–1905," *PMHB* 94 (July 1970), 381–83; Warner, *Private City*, 218.

48. Issel, "Modernization in Philadelphia School Reform," 365, 370, 380.

49. See above, Chapter 4, note 20, and below, Chapter 8.

50. J. Joseph Huthmacher, "Urban Liberalism and the Age of Urban Reform," *Mississippi Valley Historical Review* 49 (September 1962), 231–41; idem, *Senator Robert F. Wagner and the Rise of Urban Liberalism* (New York, 1968); John D. Buenker, *Urban Liberalism and Progressive Reform* (New York, 1973).

51. Shover, "Ethnicity and Religion in Philadelphia Politics," 512–13.

52. "The Young Republicans," *Respect for Republicans, 1926; Boyd's Co-Partnership and Residence Business Directory of Philadelphia for 1926* (Philadelphia, 1926).

53. This view is also echoed in the childhood recollections of Frank Rizzo. The son of Italian immigrants and controversial mayor of the city in the 1970s, Rizzo (1920–1991) was raised in "Vare-ville," South Philadelphia: Joseph R. Daughen and Peter Binzen, *The Cop Who Would Be King: The Honorable Frank Rizzo* (Boston, 1977), 45–46; Shover, "Ethnicity and Religion in Philadelphia Politics," 512–13.

54. Shover, "Ethnicity and Religion in Philadelphia Politics," 514–15.

55. Because the party organization emerged independent of, and was not subservient to, the business corporation in the late nineteenth century, it follows that the political machine was not the creation of business interests. Put another way, just as the machine did not originate as a response to the "needs" of poor immigrants, so it was not created to satisfy the demands of businessmen, contrary to Merton's claims. Indeed, the party boss, far from serving as the "business community's ambassador," as Merton suggests, was his own master and as such extracted his pound of flesh from every enterprise expecting service from the Republican party organization (Merton, *Social Theory and Social Structure,* 74). See Chapter 7 and note 58 in Chapter 7 for details of the relationship between the party boss and the big businessman. See also *Speeches of Wanamaker on Quayism,* 23, 72–73, 195, 233–35; Blankenburg, "Forty Years in the Wilderness," April 1905, 353–54; Welsh, "The Degradation of Pennsylvania Politics," 1, 6–8, 15–16; "The Growing Impudence of the Bosses," *Century* 52 (1896), 155; Henry Jones Ford, "Municipal Corruption: A Comment on Lincoln Steffens," *Political Science Quarterly* 19 (1904), 678; for examples of business interests being "compelled to stand and deliver" (*Speeches of Wanamaker,* 93) to the party boss and his organization.

56. V. O. Key Jr., "A Theory of Critical Elections," *Journal of Politics* 17 (February 1955), 13; William L. Quay, "Philadelphia Democrats, 1880–1910" (Ph.D. diss., Lehigh University, 1969), 317–18.

57. Quay, "Philadelphia Democrats, 1880–1910," 100.

58. Ibid., 78, 92, 123.

59. Ibid., chap. 8.

60. Democratic City Committee, *A Record of Thirteen Years Perfidy: Judge Gordon and Congressman McAleer Responsible for Democratic Losses in Philadelphia* (Philadelphia: August 12, 1901); *Inquirer,* February 21, 1895.

61. Quay, "Philadelphia Democrats, 1880–1910," 322–23.

62. Ibid., 149; Austin F. MacDonald, "The Democratic Party in Philadelphia: A Study in Political Pathology," *National Municipal Review* 14 (May 1925), 294–96. The elected minority officers included one of the three county commissioners, and one-third of the city's magistrates, while the appointed officers accounted for half of Philadelphia's real estate assessors and two of the five-member Board of Registration Commissioners.

63. Macdonald, "The Democratic Party in Philadelphia," 295.

64. Norris, "Philadelphia's Strabismus," 1050; *Inquirer,* February 21, 1895; *Manual of Councils, 1916,* 301–37.

65. White, "The Philadelphia System," 680. See also Irwin F. Greenberg, "The Democratic Party in Philadelphia, 1911–1934" (Ph.D. diss., Temple University, 1972), 233–80. For further details on the reemergence of a competitive two-party system in the city, see Irwin F. Greenberg, "Philadelphia Democrats Get a New Deal: The Election of 1933," *PMHB* 97 (April 1973), 210–32.

66. MacDonald, "The Democratic Party in Philadelphia," 297–98; Greenberg, "Philadelphia Democrats Get a New Deal," 210–11.

67. J. David Stern, *Memoirs of a Maverick Publisher* (New York, 1962), 228.

68. Durham Scrapbook, 1901.

69. *Inquirer,* July 10, 1901. For other examples of Organization politicians advocating a similar approach, see the *Record,* June 20, 1905, Durham Scrapbook; Blankenburg, "Forty Years in the Wilderness," August 1905, 141; and Abernethy, "Insurgency," 18.

70. See, for example, the reformers' analysis of the 1895 and 1915 mayoral election campaigns in the Municipal League, *Annual Report, 1895–1896,* 15–16; Norris, "Philadelphia's Strabismus," 1051–52; and Steffens, *Shame of the Cities,* 186–89, 212.

71. *Public Ledger,* October 24, 1905, Durham Scrapbook.

72. Salter, *Boss Rule,* 217–18. For details of how the Organization managed to "capture" City Party and Democratic Party nominations in the 1908 and 1910 primary elections, see C of 70, *Report of the Executive Board,* February 28, 1913, 7–8; City Party, *City Party Men of the Ninth Ward Do Not Be Deceived* (Philadelphia, 1908).

73. Woodruff, "Philadelphia's Revolution," 12–13; Seaber, "Philadelphia's Machine in Action," 586–87.

74. Drayer, "J. Hampton Moore," 158–72.

75. Clinton R. Woodruff, "Philadelphia's Election Frauds," *Arena,* October 1900, 401–2; Municipal League, *Annual Report, 1899–1901,* 3–4; MacDonald, "The Democratic Party in Philadelphia," 297; Greenberg, "The Philadelphia Democratic Party, 1911–1934," 254–57; Drayer, "J. Hampton Moore," 272.

76. MacDonald, "The Democratic Party in Philadelphia," 297; Greenberg, "Philadelphia Democrats Get a New Deal," 210–11.

77. Woodruff, "Philadelphia's Revolution," 12.

78. Kurtzman, "Methods of Controlling Votes," 117–20; Maynard C. Kreuger, "Election Frauds in Philadelphia," *National Municipal Review* 18 (May 1929), 299; Woodruff, "Election Methods and Reform in Philadelphia," *Annals of the American Academy of Political and Social Science* 17 (March 1901), 4–5; idem, "Some Permanent Results of the Philadelphia Upheaval of 1905–1906," *American Journal of Sociology* 13 (1907–8), 259–60.

79. Woodruff, "Election Methods," 7; idem, "Permanent Results," 254.

80. Kreuger, "Election Frauds," 295. On why the introduction of a system of personal registration in 1906 failed to seriously impair the Organization's control over voter registration, see Kurtzman, "Methods of Controlling Votes," 117–20.

81. Kreuger, "Election frauds," 296–97. For other instances of ballot-box stuffing, see *Record,* June 20, 1905; Blankenburg, "Forty Years in the Wilderness," May 1905, 467; White, "The Philadelphia System," 681.

82. Kreuger, "Election Frauds," 298.

83. C of 70, *Report of the Executive Board,* March 20, 1912, 7–8.

84. Municipal League, *Annual Report, 1899–1901,* 5–7.

85. Ibid., *1901–1902,* 11.

86. Seaber, "Philadelphia's Machine in Action," 587.

87. Ibid.; Municipal League, *Annual Report, 1899–1901,* 5–7; *1901–1902,* 11.

88. Municipal League, *Annual Report, 1899–1901,* 5–7.

89. Blankenburg, "Forty Years in the Wilderness," January 1905, 1–10; June 1905, 572; Welsh, "The Degradation of Pennsylvania Politics," 1; Steffens, *Shame of the Cities,* 193–229; Theophilus Baker, "Philadelphia: A Study in Political Psychology," *Arena* 30 (1903), 1–14.

90. Blankenburg, "Forty Years in the Wilderness," January 1905, 1, 3.

91. Baker, "Philadelphia: A Study in Political Psychology," 2, 8–9.

92. Blankenburg, "Forty Years in the Wilderness," June 1905, 572.

93. Abernethy, "Insurgency," 3.

94. *Inquirer,* February 20, 1907; November 9, 1911; November 3, 1915; November 13, 1919; *Manual of Councils, 1916,* 301–37; *1920,* 274–75.

95. Abernethy, "Insurgency," 3, 19; *Inquirer,* November 9, 1911; Salter, *The People's Choice,* 19.

96. For an assessment of these reform third parties, see Chapter 8.

97. *Proceedings of the Atlantic City Conference for Good City Government and the Twelfth Annual Meeting of the National Municipal League* (1906), 153–54, quoted in Greenberg, "The Philadelphia Democratic Party, 1911–1934," 12.

98. Quoted in Greenberg, "The Philadelphia Democratic Party, 1911–1934," 13.

99. *Public Ledger,* November 11, 1911.

100. *Evening Ledger,* October 1, 1915.

101. *Record,* October 13, 1915.

102. For a detailed analysis of the electoral behavior of the Independent Republicans in the city's suburban wards in the 1920s, see Greenberg, "The Philadelphia Democratic Party, 1911–1934," 254–63, and Drayer, "J. Hampton Moore," 268–72; Salter, *The People's Choice,* 32–41.

103. Drayer, "J. Hampton Moore," 158–72.

104. *Record,* September 28, 1923.

Chapter 7.   The Utility Monopolists

1. Harold E. Cox and John F. Meyers, "The Philadelphia Traction Monopoly and the Pennsylvania Constitution of 1874: The Prostitution of an Ideal," *Pennsylvania History* 35 (October 1968), 406, 421; Burton J. Hendrick, "Great American Fortunes and Their Making: Street Railway Financiers," *McClure's Magazine* 30 (March 1907), 37; Nicholas B. Wainwright, *History of the Philadelphia Electric Company, 1881–1961* (Philadelphia, 1961), 65–66.

2. Abernethy, "Insurgency," 9; Zink, *City Bosses,* 210; Clinton R. Woodruff, "The Philadelphia Gas Works: A Modern Instance," *American Journal of Sociology* 3 (1897–98), 601–13; Speirs, "The Philadelphia Gas Lease," 718–29.

3. For examples of legislative blackmail (and conversely, the bribery of legislators by businessmen) prior to the establishment of a reliable system of discipline within the state and city Republican party organizations, see Frederic W. Speirs, *The Street Railway System of Philadelphia: Its History and Present Condition* (Philadelphia, 1897), 28; Cox and Meyers, "The Philadelphia Traction Monopoly," 406, 409; Edmund Stirling, "Inside Transit Facts," *Public Ledger,* February 10, 1930; and Klein and Hoogenboom, *A History of Pennsylvania,* 317–18.

4. This type of arrangement was not unusual or unique to Philadelphia. For details of similar alliances between utility financiers and political machines in other American cities, see Frank M. Stewart, *A Half-Century of Municipal Reform: A History of the National Municipal League* (Berkeley, Calif., 1950), 9; Hendrick, "Great American Fortunes," 33; Shefter, "Emergence of the Political Machine," 37–38.

5. Baltzell, *Philadelphia Gentlemen,* 124.

6. Ibid., 126; Hendrick, "Great American Fortunes," 34–36.

7. Baltzell, *Philadelphia Gentlemen,* 124–25; Hendrick, "Great American Fortunes," 34; *Popular Philadelphians,* 171.

8. Hendrick, "Great American Fortunes," 33.

9. Baltzell, *Philadelphia Gentlemen,* 125; Wainwright, *Philadelphia Electric Company,* 10; *The Directory of Directors in the City of Philadelphia, 1905* (Philadelphia, 1905), 132.

10. Hendrick, "Great American Fortunes," 35; Baltzell, *Philadelphia Gentlemen,* 125; Wainwright, *Philadelphia Electric Company,* 10–11; *Popular Philadelphians,* 170.

11. Hendrick, "Great American Fortunes," 36.

12. Ibid., 36–37; Klein and Hoogenboom, *A History of Pennsylvania,* 318.

13. Hendrick, "Great American Fortunes," 37; McClure, *Old Time Notes*, 2:342; Kehl, *Boss Rule*, 7.

14. Cox and Meyers, "The Philadelphia Traction Monopoly," 416; Hendrick, "Great American Fortunes," 37.

15. Baltzell, *Philadelphia Gentlemen*, 96.

16. See Table 6.

17. Baltzell, *Philadelphia Gentlemen*, 96, 125; Wainwright, *Philadelphia Electric Company*, 9; *Popular Philadelphians*, 134; *The Directory of Directors, 1905*, 42.

18. Kehl, *Boss Rule*, 97–98; Wainwright, *Philadelphia Electric Company*, 9; Baltzell, *Philadelphia Gentlemen*, 125.

19. Baltzell, *Philadelphia Gentlemen*, 126. For further details of this "revolution" in turn-of-the-century America, see Kenneth Boulding, *The Organizational Revolution* (New York, 1953).

20. Hendrick, "Great American Fortunes," 33.

21. Baltzell, *An American Business Aristocracy*, 219, chap. 9; Hendrick, "Great American Fortunes," 34–35; George E. Thomas, "Architectural Patronage and Social Stratification in Philadelphia Between 1840 and 1920," in Cutler and Gillette, *The Divided Metropolis*, 87–88.

22. Thomas, "Architectural Patronage," 114–16.

23. Baltzell, *Philadelphia Gentlemen*, 126.

24. For details of a more typical elite response to machine rule—that of opposition—see the biography of physician and reformer George R. Woodward (1863–1952) by David R. Contosta, *A Philadelphia Family: The Houstons and Woodwards of Chestnut Hill* (Philadelphia, 1988).

25. Cox and Meyers, "The Philadelphia Traction Monopoly," 406, 421; Hendrick, "Great American Fortunes," 37.

26. Cox and Meyers, "The Philadelphia Traction Monopoly," 411; Hendrick, "Great American Fortunes," 37; Klein and Hoogenboom, *A History of Pennsylvania*, 264–70; Alfred D. Chandler Jr., *The Visible Hand: The Managerial Revolution in American Business* (Cambridge, Mass., 1977), chap. 4.

27. Cox and Meyers, "The Philadelphia Traction Monopoly," 411; Hendrick, "Great American Fortunes," 37.

28. Cox and Meyers, "The Philadelphia Traction Monopoly," 411.

29. Speirs, *The Street Railway System*, 76–77, 93; Stirling, "Inside Transit Facts," February 11 and 17, 1930.

30. Stirling, "Inside Transit Facts," February 13, 1930.

31. Speirs, *The Street Railway System*, 73–75; Cox and Meyers, "The Philadelphia Traction Monopoly," 409–10.

32. See Speirs, *The Street Railway System of Philadelphia*, 28; Cox and Meyers, "The Philadelphia Traction Monopoly," 406, 409; Stirling, "Inside Transit Facts"; Klein and Hoogenboom, *A History of Pennsylvania*, 317–18.

33. Cox and Meyers, "The Philadelphia Traction Monopoly," 406–7, 410.

34. Albert A. Bird, "Philadelphia Street Railway and the Municipality," *The Citizen*, February 1896, 287.

35. Cox and Meyers, "The Philadelphia Traction Monopoly," 410–11.

36. Ibid., 410.

37. Ibid., 406, 410.

38. Ibid., 411.

39. Ibid., 413, 415.

40. Ibid., 412. See also Stirling, "Inside Transit Facts," February 17, 1930.

41. Ibid., 413; Speirs, *The Street Railway System*, 31.

42. Cox and Meyers, "The Philadelphia Traction Monopoly," 413. See also Speirs, *The*

Street Railway System, 41–42; Bird, "Philadelphia Street Railway," 289–90; Stirling, "Inside Transit Facts," February 19, 1930.

43. Cox and Meyers, "The Philadelphia Traction Monopoly," 414–15.

44. Cox and Meyers, "The Philadelphia Traction Monopoly," 415; Speirs, *The Street Railway System*, 34.

45. Cox and Meyers, "The Philadelphia Traction Monopoly," 415.

46. Ibid., 415–16; Speirs, *The Street Railway System*, 35–36; Stirling, "Inside Transit Facts," February 17, 1930; Bird, "Philadelphia Street Railway," 288.

47. Steffens, *Shame of the Cities*, 3, 5; Moisei Ostrogorski, *Democracy and the Organization of Political Parties* (London, 1902), pt. 4; Matthew Josephson, *The Politicos* (New York, 1963), v; Hofstadter, *The Age of Reform*, 215–71; Merton, *Social Theory and Social Structure*, 74–75; Baltzell, *An American Business Aristocracy*, 57, 444; Banfield and Wilson, *City Politics*, 270–74.

48. This particular incident involving the granting of thirteen franchises to rapid transit companies in Philadelphia for no apparent reason other than political expediency has been extensively reported. In addition to the sources listed below, see also Davenport, *Power and Glory*, 152–54; Morgan, *City of Firsts*, 288; Wainwright, *Philadelphia Electric Company*, 83–85; Stirling, "Inside Transit Facts," February 22, 1930; *Press* and *Inquirer*, June 17, 1901, Durham Scrapbook.

49. Cox and Meyers, "The Philadelphia Traction Monopoly," 416.

50. Ibid., 417; Steffens, *Shame of the Cities*, 222–25; Clinton R. Woodruff, "Philadelphia's Street Railway Franchises," *American Journal of Sociology* 7 (1901–2), 218.

51. Cox and Meyers, "The Philadelphia Traction Monopoly," 417–18.

52. Woodruff, "Philadelphia's Street Railway Franchises," 217, 220, 226.

53. Municipal League, *Annual Report, 1901–1902*, 5–7; Cox and Meyers, "The Philadelphia Traction Monopoly," 418.

54. Quoted in Woodruff, "Philadelphia's Street Railway Franchises," 228.

55. Ibid., 216.

56. Ibid., 224; Steffens, *Shame of the Cities*, 222–25; Cox and Meyers, "The Philadelphia Traction Monopoly," 419.

57. For details of the compromise settlement, which involved the cash payment of $2 million to Mack and the formation of a new company, the Philadelphia Rapid Transit Company, see Cox and Meyers, "The Philadelphia Traction Monopoly," 420.

58. Put another way, it shows that political man was not subject to the control of economic man in turn-of-the-century Philadelphia. The conventional view, which holds the opposite to be the case, is indeed seriously flawed because it fails to take into account that although the political machine and the business corporation both emerged as dominant national institutions in the late nineteenth century, they did so *independent of one another*. Thus, the assumption on which the conventional wisdom rests (that the party boss and his machine were created by business interests) is a false one. For a description of the political dimension of the organizational revolution taking place in late nineteenth-century America, see Jesse Macy, *Party Organization and Machinery* (New York, 1912); and Boulding, *The Organizational Revolution*. For details of how Quay managed to establish a power base that *rivaled* that of industry, and not one that was subservient to it, see Kehl, *Boss Rule*, 26–30, 59–83; *Speeches of Wanamaker on Quayism*, 23, 72–73, 93, 195, 230–35, 325–31; and Welsh, "The Degradation of Pennsylvania Politics," 1, 6–8, 15–16.

59. Speirs, "Philadelphia Gas Lease," 718. On Martin's friendship with Dolan, see Marcosson, "The Awakening of Philadelphia," 6643–45; *Public Ledger*, November 10, 1897, and *Inquirer*, November 9, 1897, Durham Scrapbook.

60. See CMA, *12th Annual Report, 1898*, 28–58 (quote from p. 30); see also *Inquirer*,

October 16, 1897, Durham Scrapbook; Speirs, "Philadelphia Gas Lease," 725, 727; Woodruff, "Philadelphia Gas Works," 602.

61. *Inquirer,* October 12, 1897, Durham Scrapbook; John I. Rogers, "Municipal Gas in Philadelphia," *Municipal Affairs* 4 (1897), 730–33; Speirs, "Philadelphia Gas Lease," 721–24; Woodruff, "Philadelphia Gas Works," 604.

62. CMA, *Communication: Citizens' Municipal Association to the Sub-Committee of the Joint Committee of Finance and Gas of Select and Common Councils of the City of Philadelphia* (Philadelphia, 1897), 11–12.

63. Ibid., 2–3. The Municipal League also expressed a similar viewpoint: *Annual Report, 1897–1898,* 29–35. See also Woodruff, "Municipal League," 344–45.

64. Speirs, "Philadelphia Gas Lease," 725.

65. CMA, *Communication, 1897,* 11–12.

66. *Inquirer,* November 9, 1897; *Public Ledger,* November 10, 1897, Durham Scrapbook; Speirs, "Philadelphia Gas Lease," 727–28; Woodruff, "Philadelphia Gas Works," 602–3.

67. Abernethy, "Insurgency," 9; Marcosson, "The Awakening of Philadelphia," 6649.

68. Abernethy, "Insurgency," 9.

69. Ibid.

70. Vare, *Forty Years,* 89.

71. Abernethy, "Insurgency," 10.

72. Ibid., 14; Marcosson, "The Awakening of Philadelphia," 6639, 6649; Vare, *Forty Years,* 91–93; B. D. Flower, "Philadelphia's Civic Awakening," *Arena* 34 (1905), 197–98.

73. Abernethy, "Insurgency," 14; Vare, *Forty Years,* 93.

74. Abernethy, "Insurgercy," 3.

75. Wainwright, *Philadelphia Electric Company,* 31, 15–19, 23–25, 30–33; CMA, *11th Annual Report, 1897,* 14; *Popular Philadelphians,* 191; E. M. Patterson, *A Financial History of the Philadelphia Electric Company* (an Appendix to the Annual Report of the Director of Public Works, Philadelphia, 1914), 113–19.

76. Wainwright, *Philadelphia Electric Company,* 33.

77. CMA, *9th Annual Report, 1895,* 6.

78. Ibid., 25–27; CMA, *11th Annual Report, 1897,* 14.

79. CMA, *11th Annual Report, 1897,* 14.

80. Municipal League, *Annual Report, 1894–1895,* 23.

81. CMA, *9th Annual Report, 1894–1895,* 23. For further details of how this public electric lighting monopoly operated, see the Municipal League, *Annual Report, 1898–1899,* 9–10; CMA, *7th Annual Report, 1893,* 16–17; CMA, *8th Annual Report, 1894,* 19–20; CMA, *9th Annual Report, 1895,* 6–11; CMA, *11th Annual Report, 1897,* 13–16.

82. Wainwright, *Philadelphia Electric Company,* 49–51.

83. Ibid., 51, 55, 59; Patterson, *A Financial History,* 119.

84. Wainwright, *Philadelphia Electric Company,* 59–66; Patterson, *A Financial History,* 120–41; *Directory of Directors, 1905,* 177.

Chapter 8.   The Nonpartisan Reform Movement

1. Forbidden under its constitution from taking any "part in nominations to public office," the CMA's objectives were "to sustain the constituted authorities in a faithful administration of the public service; to secure a strict fulfilment by public officers, employees and contractors of all their obligations to the city and to the citizen," and, finally, "to promote such legislation as shall be most conducive to the public welfare" (CMA, *Constitution, By-Laws and List of Members* [Philadelphia, 1886], 3).

Although initially involved in organizing the City Party and in directing the wave of reform insurgency that swept the city following Durham's proposal to extend the lease of the gas works to UGI in 1905, the Committee of Seventy quickly abandoned its involvement in the endorsement of candidates for public office and instead concentrated on helping "in securing good government in Philadelphia." More specifically, the committee sought to achieve this goal through the "protection of the ballot" and by "encouraging and aiding faithful officials in the performance of their duties," as well as by "gathering and disseminating reliable information regarding city affairs and candidates" (C of 70, *Report of the Executive Board, 1905,* 8–10.) See also the *Report of the Executive Board,* March 20, 1912, 4–5; Woodruff, "Municipal League," 356–57; and Abernethy, "Insurgency," 6–8—all for details of the Committee's formation and early development.

2. Lloyd M. Abernethy, "Progressivism, 1905–1919," in Weigley (ed.), *Philadelphia: A 300-Year History,* 539–57; Philip S. Benjamin, "Gentlemen Reformers in the Quaker City, 1870–1912," *Political Science Quarterly* 85 (March 1970), 70–79; Bonnie R. Fox, "The Philadelphia Progressives: A Test of the Hofstadter-Hays Theses," *Pennsylvania History* 34 (1967), 376–79.

3. Fox, *Better City Government,* 45, 48–49.

4. Municipal League, *Annual Report, 1896–1897,* 25.

5. Woodruff, "Municipal League," 339.

6. Municipal League, *Annual Report, 1894–1895,* 5–6.

7. Ibid., *1902–1903,* 25.

8. Ibid., *1896–1897,* 25.

9. Woodruff, "Municipal League," 357.

10. Ibid., 339.

11. Municipal League, *Annual Report, 1899–1901,* 3. With regard to membership, the League's roll increased from 3,693 local citizens in 1894–95, to 5,105 by 1895–96. See *Annual Report, 1894–1895,* 5–6; *1895–1896,* 4–6.

12. The League's "vote varied from 5,000 to 58,000" in these local elections, "according to the degree of public interest" (Woodruff, "Municipal League," 337).

13. Municipal League, *Annual Report, 1901–1902,* 13–14; *Press,* October 15, 1901.

14. Woodruff, "Municipal League," 356.

15. C of 70, *Report of the Executive Board, 1905,* 5.

16. Ibid., 6; C of 70, *The Charter,* ix.

17. *Press,* March 24, 1907, C of 70 Scrapbook.

18. C of 70, *Report of the Executive Board, 1905,* 8.

19. Abernethy, "Insurgency," 6–7; Benjamin, "Gentlemen Reformers," 75; C of 70, *Third Report of the Executive Board, 1905,* 7.

20. Woodruff, "Municipal League," 338–39; idem, "Philadelphia's Revolution," 16–17; Abernethy, "Insurgency," 19.

21. Disbrow, "Reform in Philadelphia," 381.

22. C of 70, *Fourth Report of the Executive Board, 1905,* 3–4; Greenberg, "The Philadelphia Democratic Party, 1911–1934," 57–58.

23. Warner, *Private City,* 85–86; Baltzell, *An American Business Aristocracy,* 20, 131; Banfield and Wilson, *City Politics,* 139, 261.

24. Franklin S. Edmonds, "The Significance of the Recent Reform Movement in Philadelphia," *Annals of the American Academy of Political and Social Science* 27 (1906), 188–89. Leading reformers Herbert Welsh, John Wanamaker, and Rudolph Blankenburg also expressed a similar viewpoint. See Welsh, "The Degradation of Pennsylvania," 6; *Speeches of Wanamaker on Quayism,* 283; Blankenburg, "Forty Years in the Wilderness," April 1905, 347–48.

25. C of 70, *Report of the Executive Board, 1905,* 3–4.

26. Ibid., 4.

27. Samuel P. Hays, "The Social Analysis of American Political History, 1880–1920," *Political Science Quarterly* 80 (September 1965), 380.

28. Fox, *Better City Government*.

29. Ibid., xiv, chaps. 2, 3. For details of the role that political scientists played in this process, see Michael H. Frisch, "The Hope of Democracy": Urban Theorists, Urban Reform, and American Political Culture in the Progressive Period," *Political Science Quarterly* 97 (Summer 1982), 295–315.

30. Fox, "The Philadelphia Progressives," 394.

31. Ibid., 382, 386.

32. Ibid., 392–93.

33. The twelve dedicated former Committee members who remained active in local politics and never wavered in their commitment to nonpartisan reform were: Joshua L. Bailey, Rudolph Blankenburg, Robert R. Corson, William Harkness Jr., William H. Jenks, Lewis C. Madeira, Morris Newberger, Francis B. Reeves, Charles Richardson, William Potter, and Walter Wood. See Appendix 2 for details of their individual affiliations.

34. Edmonds, "Significance of the Recent Reform Movement," 188–89.

35. Woodruff, "Municipal League," 345.

36. Ibid., 367.

37. Municipal League, *Annual Report, 1897–1898*, 28.

38. Ibid., *1894–1895*, 3–4.

39. C of 70, *Report of the Executive Board, 1905*, 6.

40. Stewart, *History of the National Municipal League*, 176–77; *Smull's Legislative Hand Book, 1899–1900*, 1184–85.

41. Stewart, *History of the National Municipal League*, 28, 50–53; Frisch, "The Hope of Democracy," 304–6.

42. Schiesl, *The Politics of Efficiency*, 164; Daniel Nelson, "The Making of a Progressive Engineer: Frederick W. Taylor," *PMHB* 103 (October 1979), 448. For an assessment of the role Cooke played in Blankenburg's reform administration, see also Disbrow, "Reform in Philadelphia," 382–84, and Kenneth E. Trombley, *The Life and Times of a Happy Liberal: A Biography of Morris Llewellyn Cooke* (New York, 1954), chap. 2.

43. David J. Pivar, "Theocratic Businessmen and Philadelphia Municipal Reform, 1870–1900," *Pennsylvania History* 33 (July 1966), 300–301.

44. Ibid.; Hays, "Social Analysis of American Political History," 380.

45. For an example of joint cooperative effort in the quest for efficiency, see Bauman, "The Philadelphia Housing Commission," 118–20.

46. Fox, "The Philadelphia Progressives," 394; Benjamin, "Gentlemen Reformers," 78.

47. Wiebe, *The Search for Order, 1877–1920*, 111–32.

48. Schiesl, *The Politics of Efficiency*, 3.

49. For a more detailed breakdown of the goals the various nonpartisan reform groups sought to achieve, see CMA, *Constitution, By-Laws, 1886*, 3–5; Citizens' Committee of Fifty, *First Annual Report* (Philadelphia, 1892), 1–2; Anti-Combine Committee, *For Good Government*, 1895, i; Woodruff, "Municipal League," 337; City Party, *Hand-Book, 1905*, 20–23; C of 70, *Report of the Executive Board, 1905*, 8–10.

50. Bauman, "The Philadelphia Housing Commission," 117–18; Schiesl, *The Politics of Efficiency*, 111–15, 120–22.

51. Bauman, "The Philadelphia Housing Commission," 122.

52. Sage, *Masters of the City*, 31.

53. Woodruff, "Municipal League," 337, 355; Municipal League, *Declaration of Principles and By-Laws* (Philadelphia, 1891), 5.

54. Charles Richardson, *The City of Philadelphia, Its Stockholders and Directors* (Philadelphia: March 1893), 2. Other examples of tracts and addresses published by the Municipal League expressing a similar viewpoint include *Municipal Politics: The Old System and the New,* January 23, 1894; *For the Honor of Philadelphia* (1899); Rev. William I. Nichols, *Duties of Citizens in Reference to Municipal Government,* May 15, 1892; Henry Budd, *The Limits of Party Obligation,* December 15, 1892; Theodore M. Etting, *The Proper Standard of Municipal Affairs,* January 21, 1894.

55. Pivar, "Theocratic Businessmen," 300.

56. Stewart, *History of the National Municipal League,* 156–57; C of 70, *Report of the Executive Board, 1905,* 5.

57. D. C. Gibboney, *The White Slave Traffic,* 4–9; Blankenburg, "Forty Years in the Wilderness," August 1905, 133.

58. Blankenburg, "Forty Years in the Wilderness," 130, 132–33; Seaber, "Philadelphia's Machine in Action," 586; *North American,* August 31, 1901, and March 5, 1905.

59. *North American,* March 5, 1905; Abernethy, "Progressivism," 544.

60. Greenberg, "The Philadelphia Democratic Party, 1911–1934," 57–58; Disbrow, "Reform in Philadelphia," 380–81.

61. Benjamin, "Gentlemen Reformers," 77; Abernethy, "Insurgency," 11. Paul Boyer, *Urban Masses and Moral Order in America, 1820–1920* (Cambridge, Mass., 1978), provides a detailed study of the convergence of moral and political reform nationwide.

62. See above, Chapter 6.

63. Abernethy, "Insurgency," 9.

64. Ibid., 19.

65. *Public Ledger,* October 2, 1911; *Inquirer,* November 9, 1911.

66. *Public Ledger,* October 2, 1911; Vare, *Forty Years,* 116; Disbrow, "Reform in Philadelphia," 381.

67. William Vare subsequently claimed that he and his brothers were loyal to the Republican ticket in 1911, though both his biographer and Penrose's biographer—as well as my analysis—suggest that the Vares did help Blankenburg defeat Earle in the mayoral election. See Vare, *Forty Years,* 118; Salter, *The People's Choice,* 19; Davenport, *Power and Glory,* 189.

68. *Public Ledger,* October 2, 1911; *Inquirer,* November 9, 1911.

69. See Table 18.

70. Ibid.

71. Woodruff, "Permanent Results," 252.

72. Ibid., 252–71; Woodruff, "Philadelphia's Revolution," 18–20; Abernethy, "Progressivism," 543.

73. Woodruff, "Philadelphia's Revolution," 8; George Woodward, "A Triumph of the People: The Story of the Downfall of the Political Oligarchy in Philadelphia," *Outlook,* December 2, 1905, 811–15.

74. Woodruff, "Election Methods," 4–5.

75. Woodruff, "Permanent Results," 259–60; Kurtzman, "Methods of Controlling Votes," 117.

76. Woodruff, "Philadelphia's Revolution," 19–20. See above, Chapter 4, and Chapter 4, notes 50–52.

77. WLGG, *Facts About Philadelphia,* 62. The WLGG's recommendation was incorporated into the new city charter introduced in 1919, but because councilmen (like the mayor) invariably remained loyal to the Organization, this reform initiative also failed to loosen the machine's grip on the control of public appointments. See Kurtzman, "Methods of Controlling Votes," 55–56.

78. WLGG, *Facts About Philadelphia,* 60–61; Deardorff, "To Unshackle Philadelphia," 22.

79. C of 70, *Report of the Executive Board,* March 20, 1912, 8–10, 25–28; Harry, "Philadelphia's Political Redemption," 126–27.

80. *The Political Assessment of Officeholders,* 4.

81. Cooke, *Business Methods,* 26–27. See also De Schweinitz, "Philadelphia Striking a Balance," 460; C of 70, *Report of the Executive Board,* February 28, 1913, 15–16; *Plain Talk,* 28–30, for details on public employees who were disciplined for taking an active part in local elections.

82. Kurtzman, "Methods of Controlling Votes," 94–96; "Philadelphia Reformed and Discontented," *Literary Digest,* October 11, 1924, 14–15. The most spectacular example of the resumption of political activity by officeholders is provided by the murder of a police officer on primary election day in September 1917. For details of the notorious "Bloody Fifth" (ward) incident, see William A. McGarry, "Government by Murder," *Independent,* October 27, 1917, 178–80; Abernethy, "Progressivism," 561–62.

83. Blankenburg, *The Blankenburgs,* xx; "Address of Rudolph Blankenburg," September 27, 1917, 2–3; WLGG, *Facts About Philadelphia,* 36; Deardorff, "To Unshackle Philadelphia," 21–22; Kurtzman, "Methods of Controlling Votes," 74–76.

84. Abernethy, "Progressivism," 543.

85. Woodruff, "Permanent Results," 270–71.

86. Abernethy, "Progressivism," 544; Benjamin, "Gentlemen Reformers," 75–76.

87. *Charles E. Carpenter, Chairman of the City Party Campaign Committee When It Won the Election of Nov. 1905, Supports Reyburn and Black: Why?* (Philadelphia, 1907).

88. Those contemporary observers who believed that Blankenburg's administration constituted a reform triumph included T. E. Harry, 'Philadelphia's Political Redemption," 125–28; De Schweinitz, "Philadelphia Striking a Balance," 458–62; Owen Wister, "The Case of the Quaker City," *Outlook,* May 25, 1912, 163–73; and Civic Club of Philadelphia, *Non-Partisanship and Business Efficiency* (Philadelphia, 1913).

89. "Reform in Philadelphia," *New Republic,* November 27, 1915, 93.

90. Disbrow, "Reform in Philadelphia," 382.

91. *Plain Talk,* 28–30.

92. Cooke, *Business Methods,* 15. See also Charles F. Jenkins, "The Blankenburg Administration in Philadelphia: A Symposium," *National Municipal Review* 5 (April 1916), 213.

93. *Plain Talk,* 4–6.

94. Disbrow, "Reform in Philadelphia," 383–84.

95. Ibid., 384–86; Harry, "Philadelphia's Political Redemption," 127.

96. Jenkins, "The Blankenburg Administration," 211; Blankenburg, *The Blankenburgs,* 65–66.

97. Disbrow, "Reform in Philadelphia," 382–86; Jenkins, "The Blankenburg Administration," 211–17.

98. "Reform in Philadelphia," *New Republic,* November 27, 1915, 93; De Schweinitz, "Philadelphia Striking a Balance," 459; Jenkins, "The Blankenburg Administration," 223; Disbrow, "Reform in Philadelphia," 388.

99. Disbrow, "Reform in Philadelphia," 389.

100. Jenkins, "The Blankenburg Administration," 219; Wister, "Case of the Quaker City," 122–23; De Schweinitz, "Philadelphia Striking a Balance," 459; Blankenburg, *The Blankenburgs,* 77–78; Norris, "Philadelphia's Strabismus," 1051–52.

101. Jenkins, "The Blankenburg Administration," 219; "Reform in Philadelphia," *New Republic,* November 27, 1915, 94; Disbrow, "Reform in Philadelphia," 386–88; Norris, "Philadelphia's Strabismus," 1051; *Plain Talk,* 50; WLGG, *Facts About Philadelphia,* 55.

102. Deardorff, "To Unshackle Philadelphia," 19; WLGG, *Facts About Philadelphia,* 55; Bauman, "Philadelphia Housing Commission," 129.

103. Disbrow, "Reform in Philadelphia," 386; Jenkins, "The Blankenburg Administration," 214–15.

104. Disbrow, "Reform in Philadelphia," 388; Louis F. Post, "Taxation in Philadelphia," *National Municipal Review* 2 (1913), 57–67.

105. Disbrow, "Reform in Philadelphia," 387–88; Jenkins, "The Blankenburg Administration," 219.

106. Jenkins, "The Blankenburg Administration," 213.

107. Disbrow, "Reform in Philadelphia," 391, 394–95.

108. See above, Chapter 6.

109. Woodruff, "Progress in Philadelphia," 323. Before 1919, the city legislature provided unequal representation; central city and river front wards (that is, the Vares' stronghold) were overrepresented in Councils, and large residential wards in Germantown and West Philadelphia were underrepresented. By replacing the unwieldy bicameral, 146-member City Council with a smaller (21-member) unicameral body, and by providing that councilmen be elected from the eight state senatorial districts, the 1919 charter sought to make the new local legislature more representative than the one it replaced.

110. Ibid., 318. See also "How Philadelphia Got Its Charter," *Outlook,* July 16, 1919.

111. C of 70, *The Charter,* 3.

112. Salter, "The End of Vare," 214.

113. Fox, *Better City Government,* 126–27.

114. Ibid., 127. See also Chapter 6.

115. See Chapter 6.

116. *Times,* January 10, 1895; *Public Ledger,* January 7, 1895; *Press,* January 11, 1895, Durham Scrapbook; Letters from Joshua L. Bailey (October 31, 1891) and William H. Rhawn (October 22, 1891) to Herbert Welsh, Welsh Papers, Anti-Combine Committee Box, HSP.

117. Those reformers who organized "The Business Men's Republican Association" are listed on an election circular of February 1895, Welsh Papers, Anti-Combine Committee Box.

118. Edmonds, "Significance of Recent Reform Movement," 185; *Charles E. Carpenter . . . Supports Reyburn and Black: Why?; "The Cats Came Back": A Political History of Philadelphia from May 1905 to April 1907, by the Cat That Stayed Home* (Philadelphia, 1907).

119. Republican Nomination League, *Advantage of the Primary Act* (Philadelphia, 1911).

120. *Public Ledger,* October 24, 1905, Durham Scrapbook.

121. See Chapter 6.

122. Blankenburg, "Forty Years in the Wilderness," June 1905, 572.

123. *Record,* September 28, 1923.

124. Steffens, *Shame of the Cities,* 193.

Conclusion

1. On this point, and for a trenchant critique of Samuel Hays's contribution to the study of American political history, see Terrence J. McDonald, "Putting Politics Back into the History of the City," *American Quarterly* 34 (1982), 200–209; idem, "The Problem of the Political in Recent American Urban History," 338–43.

2. See the Introduction, above.

3. See Jon C. Teaford, "New Life for an Old Subject: Investigating the Structure of Urban Rule," *American Quarterly* 37 (1985), 346–56; Robert J. Kolesar, "The Politics of Development," *Journal of Urban History* 16 (November 1989), 21–23.

4. David P. Thelen, "Urban Politics: Beyond Bosses and Reformers," *Reviews in American History* 7 (September 1979), 412.

BIBLIOGRAPHY

Primary Sources

Unless otherwise noted, primary sources are listed in chronological order, within sections.

MANUSCRIPTS

Personal Papers

Rudolph Blankenburg Papers, Historical Society of Pennsylvania.
Henry C. Lea Papers, Van Pelt Library, University of Pennsylvania.
Herbert Welsh Papers, Historical Society of Pennsylvania.

Scrapbooks

Committee of Seventy, 1896–1910 (microfilm). Collected by Secretary Thomas Raeburn White, Urban Archives Center, Temple University, Philadelphia.
Israel W. Durham, 1891–1911. 21 vols. Historical Society of Pennsylvania.

PHILADELPHIA NEWSPAPERS AND NEWSPAPER ARTICLES

North American
The Philadelphia Inquirer
The Press
Public Ledger
The Record
The Times
Leach, Frank Willing. "Twenty Years with Quay." *North American,* July 31, 1904–June 25, 1905.
Stirling, Edmund. "Inside Transit Facts." *Public Ledger,* February 10–March 13, 1930.

PUBLIC DOCUMENTS

United States

U.S. Census Office. *Census of Population.* Washington, D.C., 1860, 1870, 1880, 1900, 1910, 1920, 1930.
U.S. Census Office. *Vital Statistics of Boston and Philadelphia Covering a Period of Six Years Ending May 31, 1890.* Washington, D.C., 1894.

Pennsylvania

Smull, John A. *Smull's Legislative Hand Book*. Harrisburg, Pa.

Philadelphia: Department of Records, City Hall, Philadelphia

Annual Message of the Mayor of the City of Philadelphia.
Annual Reports of the Board of Health.
Annual Reports of the Board of Revision of Taxes.
Annual Reports of the Bureau of Street Cleaning.
Annual Reports of the City Controller.
Water Department. Patronage Appointment Book. 1875, 1876, 1879.
City Contracts, 1887–1930 (Nos. 1–70,000). Records Center, 410 North Broad Street, City of Philadelphia.
Manual of the City Councils of Philadelphia.
Mayor's Annual Register of Contracts, 1887–1930.
Report of the Joint Special Committee Appointed Under Resolution Adopted in Common Council on May 18 and November 16, 1882 (Common Council Appendixes Nos. 66 and 67) with an Act Entitled "An Act to Provide for the Better Government of Cities of the First Class in This Commonwealth." Philadelphia, 1882.
Report of Sub-Committee of the Finance Committee of Councils of Philadelphia upon the Investigation of the City's Deposits in the Keystone National and Other Banks, and the Transactions of John Bardsley, Late City Treasurer in the Management of Public Funds. Philadelphia, March 31, 1892.
The Political Assessment of Officeholders: A Report on the System as Practiced by the Republican Organization in the City of Philadelphia, 1888–1913. Department of Public Works, Philadelphia, 1913.
Business Methods in Municipal Works: An Informal Record of the Operations of the Department of Public Works, of the City of Philadelphia, under the Administration of Mayor Blankenburg. Philadelphia, 1913.
Plain Talk: Report by Morris L. Cooke, Director of Public Works to the Mayor. Philadelphia, 1914.
Patterson, E. M. *A Financial History of the Philadelphia Electric Company*. Appendix to the Annual Report of the Director of Public Works. Philadelphia, 1914.

PAMPHLETS

All the pamphlets listed are held by the Historical Society of Pennsylvania and published in Philadelphia, unless otherwise stated.

Citizens' Municipal Association (CMA)

Constitution, By-Laws, and List of Members. 1886, 1891, 1895.
Letter of Presentation of Report on Asphalts. May 25, 1894.
Report of the Committee on Municipal Contracts to the Executive Committee of the Citizens' Municipal Association of Philadelphia, Concerning the Queen Lane Reservoir. December 24, 1894.
Communication: To the Sub-Committee of the Joint Committee of Finance and Gas of Select and Common Councils of the City of Philadelphia. October 1, 1897.
Proposed Ordinance of Philadelphia Rapid Transit Company. 1907.

Citizens' Municipal Reform Association (CMRA)

Committee and Membership. 1871.

Address. September 20, 1871.

The Citizens' Reform Ticket. October 1871.

Fifty Reasons for Supporting the Citizens' Reform Ticket. October 1871.

Address of the Executive Committee. October 26, 1871.

Reform Tracts No. 1, Municipal Taxation. December 1871.

Reports of the Executive Committee and of the Committee on the Treasury Defalcation. December 13, 1871.

Reform Tracts No. 2, The Registry and Election Laws. C. 1872.

Address of the Executive Committee. March 18, 1872.

Address. May 1872.

Memorial to the Constitutional Convention of Pennsylvania. January 13, 1873.

Some Facts Relating to the Pardon of James Brown. January 20, 1873.

Memorial to the Constitutional Convention. February 3, 1873.

To Taxpayers. March 31, 1873.

To Taxpayers. April 15, 1873.

Address. September 1873.

Facts for the People. October 1873.

Facts for the People. March 4, 1874.

The Gas Trust. April 20, 1874.

Second Report on the Philadelphia Gas Trust. May 18, 1874.

Third Report on the Philadelphia Gas Trust. June 15, 1874.

City Party

Hand-Book. 1905.

To the Voter! 1905.

Campaign Committee. October 2, 1905.

Vote for the Entire City Party Ticket, November 5th, and Against the $10 Million Loan Bill. 1905.

Report of the Women's Committee for the City Party. November 1905, February 1906, February 1907.

Report of Expenditures Made by the City Party. November 1905, November 1906.

Speech of D. Clarence Gibboney Accepting the City Party Nomination for District Attorney. October 10, 1906.

Your Candidates for the Legislature. 1906.

The Councilmanic Situation in the 22nd Ward: Shall the People or Bosses Rule? 1907.

City Party Men of the 9th Ward Do Not Be Deceived. 1908.

Committee of Seventy

Report of the Executive Board. 1905.

Argument of the Committee of Seventy—In Support of the Protest Against the Bills Giving to Councils in Cities of the First Class the Power of Appointment and Removal of the Heads of the Departments of Public Safety, Public Works, Public Health, and Supplies. April 26, 1905.

Third Report of the Executive Board. May 29, 1905.

Fourth Report of the Executive Board. September 27, 1905.

Necessary Legislation Affecting the City of Philadelphia. January 18, 1906.

Proceedings of the Town Meeting Held in the Academy of Music. January 18, 1906.

Recommendations to Voters. February 20, 1906.

Sixth Report of the Executive Board. May 8, 1906.
Legislation Affecting Philadelphia Enacted by the Special Session of the General Assembly of Pennsylvania. 1906.
Recommendations to Voters. February 19, 1907.
The Police Outrage at the Polling Place in the 2nd Division of the 7th Ward, at the November Election. 1909.
A Synopsis of Bills Prepared by the Committee on Revision of the Philadelphia Charter, Also a Synopsis of Bills Prepared by the Committee of Seventy and the Civil Service Reform Association. March 1, 1917.
To the Citizens of Philadelphia. September 22, 1917.
The Long Arm of Public Opinion. 1927.

Municipal League

Nichols, Rev. William I. *Duties of Citizens in Reference to Municipal Government.* May 15, 1892.
Budd, Henry. *The Limits of Party Obligation.* December 15, 1892.
Richardson, Charles. *The City of Philadelphia, Its Stockholders and Directors.* March 1893.
Etting, Theodore M. *The Proper Standard of Municipal Affairs.* January 21, 1894.
Municipal Politics: The Old System and the New. January 23, 1894.
    For the Honor of Philadelphia. 1899.
Woodruff, Clinton R. *Report of the Chairman of the Campaign Committee of the Municipal League.* December 11, 1901.

Reform Club

Constitution and By-Laws. 1875.
In the Court of Common Pleas No. 1 for the County of Philadelphia Sitting in Equity, Between J. V. Ingham, Plaintiff, and the Reform Club of Philadelphia. December, 1876.
To the Members of the Reform Club. 1876.
To the Members of the Reform Club. July 10, 1877.

Republican Party

The Republican Manual Containing Information in Relation to the Government of the Republican Party in the City of Philadelphia. 1857.
Rules of the Union Republican Party of Philadelphia. 1868, 1871, 1877, 1888, 1895.
Union Republican City Executive Committee, 1869–1870. 1869.
Minutes Book. Nineteenth Ward Union Republican Executive Committee, 1875–1880. Department of Records, City Hall, Philadelphia.
Republican Campaign Committee. *Cause for Civic Pride.* 1905.
Official Proceedings of the Republican National Conventions. Library of the Union League of Philadelphia. 1884–1912.
"The Young Republicans." *Respect for Republicans.* February 1926.

Miscellaneous (Alphabetical Order)

Anti-Combine Committee for the Election of Robert E. Pattison as Mayor of Philadelphia. *For Good Government.* 1895.
———. *The Key to Good Government in Philadelphia.* 1895.
———. *To Secure a Business Administration of City Affairs.* 1895.
Blankenburg Campaign Committee. *For Mayor Rudolph Blankenburg: The Candidate of the People.* 1907.

————. *The Man of the Hour—Our Next Mayor.* 1907.

————. *Our Next Mayor.* 1907.

Bullitt, John C. *A Paper Read Before the Social Science Association and the Civil Service Reform Association on the Form of Municipal Government of the City of Philadelphia.* January 18, 1882.

The Bullitt Bill: What the Reform Charter Is, and Why It Should Become a Law. C. 1885.

The Bullitt Bill: Who Favor and Who Oppose Its Enactment. C. 1885.

Bureau of Municipal Research. *Municipal Street Cleaning in Philadelphia.* June 1924.

Business Men's Committee for the Election of John E. Reyburn. February 14, 1907.

"The Cats Came Back": A Political History of Philadelphia from May 1905 to April 1907, by the Cat That Stayed Home. 1907.

Charles E. Carpenter, Chairman of the City Party Campaign Committee When It Won the Election of November 1905, Supports Reyburn and Black. Why? February 5, 1907.

The Civic Club of Philadelphia. *Non-Partisanship and Business Efficiency.* June 1913.

Civil Service Reform Association of Pennsylvania. *Draft of an Act to Regulate and Improve the Civil Service of Pennsylvania and Its Municipalities, with Summary and Argument.* 1894.

Committee of One Hundred. *Independent Citizens' Ticket.*

Committee of One Hundred. C. 1882.

Connell, George. *The Delinquent Tax Bill: Its History, Passage, and Provisions.* Harrisburg, Pa., April 17, 1870.

Daguerrotype Sketches of the Members of the First Common Council After Consolidation for 1854 and 1855. 1855.

Democratic City Committee. *A Record of Thirteen Years Perfidy: Judge Gordon and Congressman McAleer Responsible for Democratic Losses in Philadelphia.* August 12, 1901.

Dougherty, Daniel. *"The Cameron Dynasty": Earnest Protest Against Its Continuance.* Lancaster, Pa., October 21, 1878.

Evans, Thomas. *What Price Boss Rule.* December 1945.

Garrett, Philip C. *Party Politics in Great Cities.* March 16, 1882.

Gibboney, D. C. *Why the "Gang" Seeks to Legislate the Law and Order Society Out of Existence: The White Slave Traffic, Its Relation to Unscrupulous Officials and Corrupt Politicians.* April 1905.

Hart, Edwin K. *The Duty of the Hour: An Open Letter to Chairman Creasy of the Democratic State Committee.* August 12, 1901.

Hicks, Thomas L. *Address to a Mass Meeting of Citizens in the 34th Ward.* October 29, 1901.

The History of a Crime. 1895.

Jenkins, Charles F. *Address Delivered Before the Germantown Club.* December 13, 1915.

Keystone Party. *City Committee.* October 24, 1912.

Lea, Henry C. *Constitutional Reforms.* October 31, 1872.

————. *Justices' Courts in Philadelphia.* September 1, 1873.

McClure, Alexander K. *Address.* January 31, 1874.

————. *Constitutional Reform.* November 12, 1873.

————. *Restraints upon the Sovereign Power.* December 1873.

The Man of the Hour: Hon. John E. Reyburn. 1907.

Page, S. Davis. *Philadelphia Finances!* October 14, 1879.

Philadelphia Board of Trade. *Municipal Taxation and Expenditures.* December 16, 1878.

The Platform of the Town Meeting Party. October 16, 1917.

The Report of a Committee of One on the Official Life and Administration of the Hon. William S. Stokley, Mayor of Philadelphia. 1880.

Report of the Sub-Committee of the Committee of One Hundred on the Bullitt Bill. April 2, 1885.

Republican Nomination League. *Advantage of the Primary Act.* 1911.

————. *A Square Deal for Mayor Hon. Dimner Beeber.* September 1911.

Richardson, Charles. *The Philadelphia Situation.* 1883.

————. *Taxes on Working Men.* 1902.

Ring Rule: What Has the Republican Party Done for Philadelphia? Report of a Committee of 80,000.
    1881.

Speakman, Thomas H. *The People v. the Politicians: Where and How the People's Money Goes, and
    How Political Morals Are Corrupted.* February 1878.

————. *Political Parties, Their Uses and Abuses: Evils of Drawing Party Lines in Local Affairs.*
    September 1873.

Stewart, R. A. *Philadelphia Reform: Cartooned Music Poems.* 1913.

Ten Years Work of the Law and Order Society of Philadelphia. January 29, 1892.

The True Cause of This "Reform." 1905.

The True John Weaver. 1905.

Women's League for Good Government. *Facts About Philadelphia.* 1919.

————. *Fusion Alphabet.* October 30, 1913.

————. *Fusion and Victory.* 1913.

Workingmen's Club of Philadelphia. *Tract No. One.* 1875.

ANNUAL REPORTS

Citizens' Municipal Reform Association. 1872–73.

Civil Service Reform Association of Philadelphia. 1882–88.

Citizens' Municipal Association. 1887–1906.

Municipal League of Philadelphia. 1891–1903.

Citizens' Committee of Fifty for a New Philadelphia. 1892.

Committee of Seventy. 1905, 1912–13.

Women's League for Good Government. 1914–15.

DIRECTORIES

Boyd's Co-Partnership and Residence Business Directory of Philadelphia. 1881–1906.

The Directory of Directors in the City of Philadelphia, 1905. Philadelphia, 1905.

Gopsill's Philadelphia City Directory. 1870–1911.

Hudson, Sam. *Pennsylvania and Its Public Men.* Philadelphia, 1909.

"North American." *Philadelphia and Popular Philadelphians.* Philadelphia, 1891.

CONTEMPORARY MAGAZINE AND PERIODICAL ARTICLES (ALPHABETICAL
ORDER)

"Annals of Quayism." *Civil Service Chronicle,* May 1891.

Bailey, George S. "Mellonism Takes Court." *Nation* (December 2, 1931), 594–95.

Baker, Theophilus. "Philadelphia: A Study in Political Psychology." *Arena* 30 (1903), 1–14.

Blankenburg, Rudolph. "Quay." *Independent* 53 (1901), 209–11.

————. "Forty Years in the Wilderness; or, Masters and Rulers of 'The Freemen' of Pennsylva-
    nia." *Arena* 33 (January 1905), 1–10; (February 1905), 113–27; (March 1905), 225–
    39; (April 1905), 345–60; (May 1905), 457–74; (June 1905), 569–83; 34 (July
    1905), 15–30; (August 1905), 128–42.

Branson, Walter J. "The Philadelphia Nominating System." *Annals of the American Academy of Political and Social Science* 14 (1899), 18–37.

Budenz, Louis F. "Vare's Last Triumph?" *Nation,* October 2, 1929, 349–50.

"The Campaign in Philadelphia." *Outlook,* September 16, 1911, 97–98.

"Career and Character of Quay." *Current Literature* 37 (1904), 13–14.

Carson, Saul. "Don't Overlook Philadelphia!" *Nation* (September 28, 1932), 279.

Cooper, Charles P. "Progress and Reaction in Pennsylvania, 1:Harrisburg's Vision, a Personal Interview with Governor Brumbaugh." *Outlook,* December 29, 1915, 1045–49.

"Costly Bosses." *Nation* 66 (1898), 455–56.

Deardorff, Neva R. "To Unshackle Philadelphia." *Survey,* April 5, 1919, 19–23.

De Schweinitz, Karl. "Philadelphia Striking a Balance Between Boss and Business Rule." *Survey,* January 17, 1914, 458–62.

Eaton, Dorman B. "Political Assessments." *North American Review* 135 (September 1882), 214–15.

Edmonds, Franklin S. "The Significance of the Recent Reform Movement in Philadelphia." *Annals of the American Academy of Political and Social Science* 27 (1906), 180–90.

Flower, B. D. "Philadelphia's Civic Awakening." *Arena* 34 (1905), 196–99.

Fuller, Edward. "The Redemption of Philadelphia." *Review* 1 (September 27, 1919), 435.

"The Growing Impudence of the Bosses." *Century Magazine* 52 (1896), 155.

Gruenberg, Frederick P. "Philadelphia's Charter Victory." *Survey,* August 9, 1919, 700–701.

Harry, T. Everett. "Philadelphia's Political Redemption." *International,* November 1912, 125–28.

Hendrick, Burton J. "Great American Fortunes and Their Making: Street Railway Financiers." *McClure's Magazine* 30 (March 1907), 33–48.

"How Philadelphia Got Its Charter." *Outlook,* July 16, 1919, 421.

"How Philadelphia Was Bled." *Nation* 81 (1905).

"The Ills of Pennsylvania." *Atlantic Monthly* 88 (1901), 558–66.

Jenkins, Charles F. "The Blankenburg Administration in Philadelphia: A Symposium." *National Municipal Review* 5 (April 1916), 211–25.

Kendrick, Alexander. "The End of Boss Vare." *Nation* 137 (November 29, 1933), 621–22.

"King George: King Matthew." *Nation* 66 (1898), 218–19.

Kreuger, Maynard C. "Election Frauds in Philadelphia." *National Municipal Review* 18 (May 1929), 294–99.

"The Latest Exposure of Quay." *Nation* 67 (1898), 271–72.

Lea, Henry C. "A Letter to the People of Philadelphia." *Forum* 2 (January 1887), 532–38.

MacDonald, Austin F. "The Democratic Party in Philadelphia: A Study in Political Pathology." *National Municipal Review* 14 (May 1925), 293–99.

———. "Philadelphia's Political Machine in Action." *National Municipal Review* 15 (January 1926), 28–35.

McGarry, William A. "Government by Murder." *Independent* 92 (October 27, 1917), 178–80.

Mapes, George E. "An Uncompromising Fighter." *Outlook* 83 (May 26, 1906), 220–23.

Marcosson, Isaac F. "The Awakening of Philadelphia." *World's Work* 11 (1905), 6639–51.

———. "The Fall of the House of Quay." *World's Work* 11 (1906), 7119–24.

"M. Quay, Reformer." *Nation* 76 (1903), 165–66.

Myers, Gustavus. "The Most Corrupt City in the World." *The Living Age* 22 (1904), 449.

"A New Charter for Philadelphia." *Outlook,* July 16, 1919, 420–21.

Norris, George W. "Progress and Reaction in Pennsylvania, II: Philadelphia's Strabismus." *Outlook,* December 29, 1915, 1049–52.

Oakley, Imogen B. "Two Dictatorships." *Outlook,* December 22, 1926, 527–28.

"Pennsylvania Again." *Nation* 64 (1897), 376–77.

"The Pennsylvania Campaign." *Nation* 66 (1898), 437–38.
"Pennsylvania Republicans." *Nation* 45 (1887), 148–49.
"Philadelphia Reformed and Discontented." *Literary Digest,* October 11, 1924, 14–15.
"Philadelphia's Epoch-Making Charter." *American City* 21 (September 1919), 202.
Post, Louis F. "Taxation in Philadelphia." *National Municipal Review* 2 (1913), 57–67.
Quay, Matthew S. "The Man or the Platform." *North American Review* 154 (1892), 513–15.
"Quayism in Pennsylvania." *Nation* 53 (1891), 250.
Quicksall, Harold P. "Government by Murder: The Unhappy Plight of Philadelphia." *Outlook,*
    October 17, 1917, 283–84.
Quicksall, Harold P., and McGarry, William A. "Political Crime in Philadelphia." *New
    Republic,* September 29, 1917, 247–48.
"Reform in Philadelphia." *Nation* 70 (1900), 159–60.
"Reform in Philadelphia." *New Republic,* November 27, 1915, 93–94.
"The Republican Independent in Pennsylvania." *Nation* 34 (1882), 456–57.
"Republican Tactics in Pennsylvania." *Nation* 53 (1891), 154–55.
Rogers, John I. "Municipal Gas in Philadelphia." *Municipal Affairs* 4 (1897), 730–45.
Rogers, Sherman. "A New Golden Age in Philadelphia." *Outlook* 130 (April 12, 1922),
    542–45.
Salter, John A. "The Corrupt Lower Courts of Philadelphia." *American Mercury* 33 (October
    1934), 236–40.
———. "Party Organization in Philadelphia: The Ward Committeeman." *American Political
    Science Review* 27 (August 1933), 618–27.
———. "A Philadelphia Magistrate Tells His Story." *National Municipal Review* 22 (October
    1933), 514–20.
Seaber, Louis. "Philadelphia's Machine in Action." *Independent* 58 (1905), 584–87.
"Senator Quay and the Republican Machine." *Outlook* 62 (1899), 13–16.
Smalley, E. V. "The Philadelphia Committee of One Hundred." *Century Magazine* 4 (1883),
    395–99.
Spiers, Frederic W. "The Philadelphia Gas Lease." *Municipal Affairs* 4 (1897), 718–29.
Stewart, William R. "The Real John Weaver." *October Cosmopolitan* (1905), 1–30.
Welsh, Herbert. "The Degradation of Pennsylvania Politics." *Forum,* November 1891, 1–16.
White, Thomas R. "The Philadelphia System." *Forum* 77 (1927), 678–88.
Williams, Talcott. "After Penrose, What?" *Century Magazine* 151 (1921), 49–55.
Williams, Thomas E. "Will Pennsylvania Go Democratic?" *Nation* 135 (November 9, 1932),
    451–52.
Wister, Owen. "The Case of the Quaker City." *Outlook* (May 25, 1912), 163–73.
———. "The Keystone Crime: Pennsylvania's Graft-Cankered Capital." *Everybody's Magazine*
    17 (1907), 435–40.
Woodruff, Clinton R. "Election Methods and Reform in Philadelphia." *Annals of the American
    Academy of Political and Social Science* 17 (March 1901), 1–24.
———. "The Municipal League of Philadelphia." *American Journal of Sociology* 11 (1905–6),
    336–58.
———. "Municipal Review." *American Journal of Sociology* 15 (1909–10), 502–35.
———. "The Philadelphia Gas Works: A Modern Instance." *American Journal of Sociology* 3
    (1897–98), 601–13.
———. "Philadelphia's Election Frauds." *Arena* 24 (October 1900), 397–404.
———. "Philadelphia's Revolution." *Yale Review* 30 (May 1906), 8–23.
———. "Philadelphia's Street Railway Franchises." *American Journal of Sociology* 7 (1901–2),
    216–33.

———. "Philadelphia's Water: A Story of Municipal Procrastination." *Forum* 28 (1899–1900), 305–14.

———. "Progress in Philadelphia." *American Journal of Sociology* 26 (1920), 315–32.

———. "Some Permanent Results of the Philadelphia Upheaval of 1905–6." *American Journal of Sociology* 13 (1907–8), 252–71.

Woodward, George. "A Triumph of the People: The Story of the Downfall of the Political Oligarchy in Philadelphia." *Outlook,* December 2, 1905, pp. 811–15.

AUTOBIOGRAPHIES, DIARIES, AND SPEECHES (ALPHABETICAL ORDER)

McClure, Alexander. *Old Time Notes of Pennsylvania.* 2 vols. Philadelphia, 1905.

Morley, Christopher. *Travels in Philadelphia.* Philadelphia, 1920.

Pennypacker, Samuel W. *The Autobiography of a Pennsylvanian.* Philadelphia, 1918.

Shannon, David A. (ed.). *Beatrice Webb's Diary, 1898.* Madison, Wis., 1963.

The Speeches of Hon. John Wanamaker on Quayism and Boss Domination in Pennsylvania Politics. Philadelphia, c. 1898.

Stackpole, Edward J. *Behind the Scenes with a Newspaperman: Fifty Years in the Life of an Editor.* Philadelphia, 1927.

Steffens, Lincoln. *The Autobiography of Lincoln Steffens.* New York, 1931.

Stern, J. David. *Memoirs of a Maverick Publisher.* New York, 1962.

Vare, William S. *My Forty Years in Politics.* Philadelphia, 1933.

Wainwright, Nicholas B. (ed.). *A Philadelphia Perspective: The Diary of Sidney George Fisher Covering the Years 1834–1871.* Philadelphia, 1967.

NOVELS

Biddle, Francis. *The Llanfear Pattern.* New York, 1927.

Sage, Edmund. *Masters of the City: A Novel of Today.* Philadelphia, 1909.

Shapley, Rufus E. *Solid for Mulhooly.* Philadelphia, 1881.

Secondary Sources

BIOGRAPHIES

Blankenburg, Lucretia L. *The Blankenburgs of Philadelphia.* Philadelphia, 1929.

Bowden, Robert D. *Boies Penrose, Symbol of an Era.* New York, 1937.

Bradley, Edward S. *Henry Charles Lea: A Biography.* Philadelphia, 1931.

Contosta, David R. *A Philadelphia Family: The Houstons and Woodwards of Chestnut Hill.* Philadelphia, 1988.

Davenport, Walter. *Power and Glory: The Life of Boies Penrose.* New York, 1931.

Gibbons, Herbert A. *John Wanamaker.* 2 vols. New York, 1926.

Kehl, James A. *Boss Rule in the Gilded Age: Matt Quay of Pennsylvania.* Pittsburgh, 1981.

Salter, John T. *The People's Choice: Philadelphia's William S. Vare.* New York, 1971.

Silcox, Harry C. *Philadelphia Politics from the Bottom Up: The Life of Irishman William McMullen, 1824–1901.* Philadelphia, 1989.

Trombley, Kenneth E. *The Life and Times of a Happy Liberal: A Biography of Morris Llewellyn Cooke*. New York, 1954.

ARTICLES RELATING TO PHILADELPHIA

Abernethy, Lloyd M. "Insurgency in Philadelphia, 1905." *Pennsylvania Magazine of History and Biography* (hereafter *PMHB*) 87 (January 1963), 3–20.

Astorino, Samuel J. "The Contested Senate Election of William Scott Vare." *Pennsylvania History* 28 (April 1961), 187–201.

Baldwin, Frederick D. "Smedley D. Butler and Prohibition Enforcement in Philadelphia, 1924–1925." *PMHB* 134 (July 1960), 352–68.

Baltzell, E. Digby. "The Protestant Establishment Revisited." *The American Scholar* 45 (Autumn 1976), 499–518.

Benjamin, Philip S. "Gentlemen Reformers in the Quaker City, 1870–1912." *Political Science Quarterly* 85 (March 1970), 61–79.

Bloom, Robert L. "Edwin A. Van Valkenburg and the Philadelphia *North American*, 1899–1924." *Pennsylvania History* 21 (April 1954), 109–19.

———. "Morton McMichael's North American." *PMHB* 77 (April 1953), 164–77.

Butterfield, Roger. "The Cats on City Hall." *PMHB* 77 (October 1953), 439–48.

Carson, Hampton L. "The Life and Services of Samuel Whitaker Pennypacker." *PMHB* 41 (1917), 1–125.

Collins, Bruce. "The Democrats' Loss of Pennsylvania in 1858." *PMHB* 109 (October 1985), 499–536.

Contosta, David R. "George Woodward, Philadelphia Progressive." *PMHB* 111 (July 1987), 341–70.

Cox, Harold E., and Meyers, John F. "The Philadelphia Traction Monopoly and the Pennsylvania Constitution of 1874: The Prostitution of an Ideal." *Pennsylvania History* 35 (October 1968), 406–23.

Disbrow, Donald W. "Herbert Welsh, Editor of *City and State*, 1895–1904." *PMHB* 94 (1970), 62–73.

———. "Reform in Philadelphia Under Mayor Blankenburg, 1912–1916." *Pennsylvania History* 27 (October 1960), 379–96.

Dudden, Arthur P. "Lincoln Steffens's Philadelphia." *Pennsylvania History* 31 (October 1964), 449–58.

Fishbane, Richard B. "The Shallow Boast of Cheapness: Public School Teaching as a Profession in Philadelphia, 1865–1890." *PMHB* 103 (1979), 66–84.

Fox, Bonnie R. "The Philadelphia Progressives: A Test of the Hofstadter-Hays Theses." *Pennsylvania History* 34 (1967), 372–94.

Gerrity, Frank. "The Disruption of the Philadelphia Whigocracy: Joseph R. Chandler, Anti-Catholicism, and the Congressional Election of 1854." *PMHB* 111 (April 1987), 161–94.

Gienapp, William E. "Nebraska, Nativism, and Rum: The Failure of Fusion in Pennsylvania." *PMHB* 109 (October 1985), 425–71.

Gillette, Howard F. "Philadelphia's City Hall: Monument to a New Political Machine." *PMHB* 97 (April 1973), 233–49.

Greenberg, Irwin F. "Philadelphia Democrats Get a New Deal: The Election of 1933." *PMHB* 97 (April 1973), 210–32.

Hoogenboom, Ari. "Pennsylvania in the Civil Service Reform Movement." *Pennsylvania History* 28 (1961), 268–79.

Huston, James L. "The Demise of the Pennsylvania American Party, 1854–1858." *PMHB* 109 (October 1985), 473–97.

Issel, William H. "Modernization in Philadelphia School Reform, 1882–1905." *PMHB* 94 (July 1970), 358–83.

———. "The Politics of Public School Reform in Pennsylvania, 1880–1911." *PMHB* 102 (1978), 59–92.

Kelley, Brooks M. "Simon Cameron and the Senatorial Nomination of 1867." *PMHB* 87 (1963), 375–92.

Laurie, Bruce. "Nothing on Compulsion: Life Styles of Philadelphia Artisans, 1820–1850." *Labor History* 15 (Summer 1974), 350–66.

McCarthy, Michael P. "The Philadelphia Consolidation of 1854: A Reappraisal." *PMHB* 110 (October 1986), 531–48.

McGeary, M. Nelson. "Gifford Pinchot's 1914 Campaign." *PMHB* 81 (July 1957), 303–18.

———. "Gifford Pinchot's Years of Frustration, 1917–1920." *PMHB* 83 (July 1959), 327–42.

Mackey, Phillip E. "Law and Order 1877: Philadelphia's Response to the Railroad Riots." *PMHB* 96 (April 1972), 183–202.

Montgomery, David. "Radical Republicanism in Pennsylvania, 1866–1873." *PMHB* 85 (1961), 439–57.

Nelson, Daniel. "The Making of a Progressive Engineer: Frederick W. Taylor." *PMHB* 103 (October 1979), 446–66.

Pivar, David J. "Theocratic Businessmen and Philadelphia Municipal Reform, 1870–1900." *Pennsylvania History* 33 (July 1966), 289–302.

Robinson, Elwyn P. "The *Public Ledger:* An Independent Newspaper." *PMHB* 64 (January 1940), 43–55.

Salter, John T. "The End of Vare." *Political Science Quarterly* 50 (June 1935), 214–34.

Shover, John L. "The Emergence of a Two-Party System in Republican Philadelphia, 1924–1936." *Journal of American History* 60 (March 1974), 985–1002.

———. "Ethnicity and Religion in Philadelphia Politics, 1924–1940." *American Quarterly* 25 (December 1973), 499–515.

Stewart, John D. "The Deal for Philadelphia: Simon Cameron and the Genesis of a Political Machine, 1867–1872." *Journal of the Lancaster County Historical Society* 77 (1973), 41–52.

Wilcox, Harry C. "William McMullen: Nineteenth-Century Political Boss." *PMHB* 110 (July 1986), 389–412.

BOOKS RELATING TO PHILADELPHIA

Allinson, Edward P., and Penrose, Boies. *The City Government of Philadelphia.* Baltimore, 1887.

Baltzell, E. Digby. *An American Business Aristocracy.* New York, 1958.

———. *Philadelphia Gentlemen: The Making of a National Upper Class.* Glencoe, Ill., 1958.

———. *The Protestant Establishment.* New York, 1964.

———. *Puritan Boston and Quaker Philadelphia.* New York, 1979.

Bradley, Erwin S. *The Triumph of Militant Republicanism: A Study of Pennsylvania and Presidential Politics, 1860–1872.* Philadelphia, 1964.

Burt, Nathaniel. *The Perennial Philadelphians: The Anatomy of an American Aristocracy.* Boston, 1963.

Clark, Dennis. *The Irish in Philadelphia.* Philadelphia, 1973.

————. *The Irish Relations: Trials of an Immigrant Tradition*. Philadelphia, 1982.

The Committee of Seventy. *The Charter: A History*. Philadelphia, 1980.

Cornog, William H. *School of the Republic, 1893–1943: A Half Century of the Central High School of Philadelphia*. Philadelphia, 1952.

Crumlish, Joseph D. *A City Finds Itself: The Philadelphia Home Rule Charter Movement*. Detroit, 1959.

Cutler, William, and Gillette, Howard F. *The Divided Metropolis: Social and Spatial Dimensions of Philadelphia, 1800–1975*. Westport, Conn., 1980.

Daly, John, and Weinberg, Allen. *Genealogy of Philadelphia County Sub-Divisions*. 2nd ed. Philadelphia, 1966.

Daughen, Joseph R., and Binzen, Peter. *The Cop Who Would Be King: The Honorable Frank Rizzo*. Boston, 1977.

Davis, Allen F., and Haller, Mark H. (eds.). *The Peoples of Philadelphia: A History of Ethnic Groups and Lower Class Life, 1790–1940*. Philadelphia, 1973.

Du Bois, W.E.B. *The Philadelphia Negro*. Philadelphia, 1899.

Dusinberre, William. *Civil War Issues in Philadelphia, 1856–1865*. Philadelphia, 1965.

Ervin, Spencer. *The Magistrate Courts of Philadelphia*. Philadelphia, 1931.

Evans, Frank B. *Pennsylvania Politics, 1872–1877: A Study in Political Leadership*. Harrisburg, 1966.

Feldberg, Michael. *The Philadelphia Riots of 1844: A Study of Ethnic Conflict*. Westport, Conn., 1975.

Friedman, Murray (ed.). *Jewish Life in Philadelphia, 1830–1940*. Philadelphia, 1983.

Golab, Caroline. *Immigrant Destinations*. Philadelphia, 1977.

Hershberg, Theodore. *Philadelphia: Work, Space, Family, and Group Experience in the Nineteenth Century*. New York, 1981.

Klein, Philip S., and Hoogenboom, Ari. *A History of Pennsylvania*. New York, 1973.

Laurie, Bruce. *Working People of Philadelphia, 1800–1850*. Philadelphia, 1980.

Morgan, George. *The City of Firsts: A Complete History of the City of Philadelphia*. Philadelphia, 1926.

Oberholtzer, Ellis P. *Philadelphia: A History of the City and Its People*. 4 vols. Philadelphia, 1912.

Price, Eli K. *The History of the Consolidation of the City of Philadelphia*. Philadelphia, 1873.

Salter, John T. *Boss Rule: Portraits in City Politics*. New York, 1935.

Scharf, John T., and Westcott, Thompson. *History of Philadelphia, 1609–1884*. 3 vols. Philadelphia, 1884.

Scranton, Philip. *Proprietary Capitalism: The Textile Manufacture at Philadelphia, 1800–1885*. Cambridge, 1983.

Speirs, Frederic W. *The Street Railway System of Philadelphia: Its History and Present Condition*. Philadelphia, 1897.

Sprogle, Howard Oscar. *The Philadelphia Police: Past and Present*. Philadelphia, 1887.

Steffens, Lincoln. *The Shame of the Cities*. New York, 1904.

Vickers, George. *The Fall of Bossism: A History of the Committee of One Hundred and the Reform Movement in Philadelphia and Pennsylvania*. Philadelphia, 1883.

Wainwright, Nicholas B. *History of the Philadelphia Electric Company, 1881–1961*. Philadelphia, 1961.

Warner, Sam B. Jr. *The Private City: Philadelphia in Three Periods of Its Growth*. Philadelphia, 1968.

Weigley, Russell F. (ed.). *Philadelphia: A 300-Year History*. New York, 1982.

Whiteman, Maxwell. *Gentlemen in Crisis: The First Century of the Union League of Philadelphia*. Philadelphia, 1975.

GENERAL ARTICLES

Banfield, Edward C., and Wilson, James Q. "Political Ethos Revisited." *American Political Science Review* 65 (December 1971), 1048–62.

Boulay, Harvey, and DiGaetano, Alan. "Why Did Political Machines Disappear?" *Journal of Urban History* 12 (November 1985), 25–49.

Brown, M. Craig, and Halaby, Charles N. "Machine Politics in America, 1870–1945." *Journal of Interdisciplinary History* 17 (Winter 1987), 587–612.

Cornwell, Elmer Jr. "Bosses, Machines, and Ethnic Groups." *Annals of the American Academy of Political and Social Sciences* 353 (May 1964), 27–39.

Ebner, Michael H. "Urban History: Retrospect and Prospect." *Journal of American History* 68 (June 1981), 69–84.

Ford, Henry Jones. "Municipal Corruption: A Comment on Lincoln Steffens." *Political Science Quarterly* 19 (1904), 673–86.

Formisano, Ronald P. "Deferential-Participant Politics: The Early Republic's Political Culture, 1789–1840." *American Political Science Review* 68 (1974), 473–87.

Frisch, Michael H. "The Hope of Democracy: Urban Theorists, Urban Reform, and American Political Culture in the Progressive Period." *Political Science Quarterly* 97 (Summer 1982), 295–315.

———. "Oyez, Oyez, Oyez: The Recurring Case of Plunkett v. Steffens." *Journal of Urban History* 7 (February 1981), 205–18.

Greenstein, Fred. "The Changing Pattern of Urban Party Politics." *Annals of the American Academy of Political and Social Sciences* 353 (1964), 1–13.

Guterbock, T. M. "Community Attachment and Machine Politics: Voting Patterns in Chicago Wards." *Social Science Quarterly* 60 (Summer 1979), 185–202.

Hammack, David C. "Elite Perceptions of Power in the Cities of the United States, 1800–1900: The Evidence of James Bryce, Moisei Ostrogorski, and Their American Informants." *Journal of Urban History* 4 (August 1978), 363–96.

———. "Problems in the Historical Study of Power in the Cities and Towns of the United States, 1800–1960." *American Historical Review* 83 (1978), 323–49.

Hays, Samuel P. "The Changing Political Structure of the City in Industrial America." *Journal of Urban History* 1 (November 1974), 6–38.

———. "The Politics of Reform in Municipal Government in the Progressive Era." *Pacific NorthWest Quarterly* 55 (October 1964), 157–69.

———. "The Social Analysis of American Political History, 1880–1920." *Political Science Quarterly* 80 (September 1965), 373–94.

Huthmacher, J. Joseph. "Urban Liberalism and the Age of Reform." *Mississippi Valley Historical Review* 49 (September 1962), 231–41.

Issel, William. "Business Power and Political Culture in San Francisco, 1900–1940." *Journal of Urban History* 16 (November 1989), 52–77.

Kolesar, Robert J. "The Politics of Development: Worcester, Massachusetts, in the Late Nineteenth Century." *Journal of Urban History* 16 (November 1989), 3–28.

Lowi, Theodore J. "Machine Politics—Old and New." *The Public Interest* 9 (Fall 1967), 83–92.

McDonald, Terrence J. "The Burdens of Urban History: The Theory of the State in Recent American Social History." *Studies in American Political Development* 3 (1989), 3–29.

———. "The Problem of the Political in Recent American Urban History: Liberal Pluralism and the Rise of Functionalism." *Social History* 10 (October 1985), 323–45.

———. "Putting Politics Back into the History of the American City." *American Quarterly* 34 (1982), 200–209.

McKitrick, Eric L. "The Study of Corruption." *Political Science Quarterly* 72 (December 1957), 502–14.

Nelli, Humbert S. "John Powers and the Italians: Politics in a Chicago Ward." *Journal of American History* 57 (June 1970), 67–84.

Rundquist, B. S. "Corrupt Politicians and Their Electoral Support: Some Experimental Observations." *American Political Science Review* 71 (Summer 1977), 954–63.

Scott, James C. "Corruption, Machine Politics, and Political Change." *American Political Science Review* 63 (December 1969), 1142–58.

Stave, Bruce. "A Conversation with Sam Bass Warner, Jr." *Journal of Urban History* 1 (November 1974), 89–97.

Stave, Bruce, et al. "A Reassessment of the Urban Political Boss: An Exchange of Views." *The History Teacher* 21 (May 1988), 293–312.

Teaford, Jon C. "Finis for Tweed and Steffens: Rewriting the History of Urban Rule." *Reviews in American History* 10 (December 1982), 133–49.

———. "New Life for an Old Subject: Investigating the Structure of Urban Rule." *American Quarterly* 37 (1985), 346–56.

Thelen, David P. "Social Tensions and the Origins of Progressivism." *Journal of American History* 56 (September 1969), 323–41.

———. "Urban Politics: Beyond Bosses and Reformers." *Reviews in American History* 7 (September 1979), 406–12.

Vecoli, Rudolph. "Contadini in Chicago: A Critique of *The Uprooted.*" *Journal of American History* 51 (December 1964), 404–17.

Wald, Kenneth D. "The Electoral Base of Political Machines: A Deviant Case Analysis." *Urban Affairs Quarterly* 16 (Summer 1980), 2–29.

GENERAL WORKS

Allswang, John M. *Bosses, Machines, and Urban Voters: An American Symbiosis.* Port Washington, N.Y., 1977.

Banfield, Edward C. *The Moral Basis of a Backward Society.* New York, 1958.

———. *Political Influence.* New York, 1961.

Banfield, Edward C. (ed.). *Urban Government: A Reader in Administration and Politics.* New York, 1969.

Banfield, Edward C., and Wilson, James Q. *City Politics.* Cambridge, Mass., 1963.

Benson, George C. S. *Political Corruption in America.* Lexington, Ky. 1978.

Boulding, Kenneth E. *The Organizational Revolution: A Study in the Ethics of Economic Organization.* New York, 1953.

Boyer, Paul. *Urban Masses and Moral Order in America, 1880–1920.* Cambridge, Mass., 1978.

Bridges, Amy. *A City in the Republic: Antebellum New York and the Origins of Machine Politics.* New York, 1984.

Brooks, Robert C. *Corruption in American Politics and Life.* New York, 1910.

Brownwell, Blaine A., and Stickel, Warren E. *Bosses and Reformers: Urban Politics in America, 1880–1920.* New York, 1973.

Bryce, James. *The American Commonwealth.* 2 vols. New York, 1914.

Buenker, John D. *Urban Liberalism and Progressive Reform.* New York, 1973.

Callow, Alexander B. *The City Boss in America: An Interpretive Reader.* New York, 1976.

———. *The Tweed Ring.* New York, 1966.

Chambers, William, and Burnham, Walter Dean. *The American Party Systems.* New York, 1967.

Chandler, Alfred D. Jr. *The Visible Hand: The Managerial Revolution in American Business.* Cambridge, Mass., 1977.

Dahl, Robert A. *Who Governs? Democracy and Power in an American City*. New Haven, 1961.
DeMarco, William M. *Ethnics and Enclaves: Boston's Italian North End*. Cambridge, Mass., 1981.
Dorsett, Lyle. *The Pendergast Machine*. New York, 1968.
Dykstra, Robert R. *The Cattle Towns*. New York, 1971.
Ebner, Michael H., and Tobin, Eugene M. (eds.). *The Age of Urban Reform: New Perspectives on the Progressive Era*. New York, 1977.
Erie, Steven P. *Rainbow's End: Irish-Americans and the Dilemmas of Urban Machine Politics, 1840–1985*. Berkeley, Calif., 1988.
Formisano, Ronald P., and Burns, Constance K. (eds.). *Boston 1700–1980: The Evolution of Urban Politics*. Westport, Conn., 1984.
Fox, Kenneth. *Better City Government: Innovation in American Urban Politics, 1850–1937*. Philadelphia, 1977.
Frisch, Michael H. *Town into City: Springfield, Massachusetts, and the Meaning of Community, 1840–1880*. Cambridge, Mass., 1972.
Fuchs, Lawrence. *The Political Behavior of American Jews*. Glencoe, Ill., 1956.
Gerth, H. H., and Mills, C. Wright. *From Max Weber: Essays in Sociology*. New York, 1946.
Hammack, David C. *Power and Society: Greater New York at the Turn of the Century*. New York, 1982.
Harris, Carl V. *Political Power in Birmingham, 1871–1921*. Knoxville, Tenn., 1977.
Heidenheimer, Arnold J. *Political Corruption: Readings in Comparative Analysis*. New York, 1970.
Hershkowitz, Leo. *Tweed's New York: Another Look*. Garden City, N.Y., 1977.
Hofstadter, Richard. *The Age of Reform: From Bryan to F.D.R.* New York, 1955.
Holli, Melvin G. *Reform in Detroit: Hazen S. Pingree and Urban Politics*. New York, 1969.
Hoogenboom, Ari. *Outlawing the Spoils: A History of the Civil Service Reform Movement, 1865–1883*. Urbana, Ill., 1961.
Howe, Frederic C. *The City: The Hope of Democracy*. New York, 1906.
Hutchinson, Edward P. *Immigrants and Their Children*. New York, 1956.
Huthmacher, J. Joseph. *Senator Robert Wagner and the Rise of Urban Liberalism*. New York, 1963.
Issel, William, and Cherny, Robert C. *San Francisco, 1865–1932: Politics, Power, and Urban Development*. Berkeley, Calif., 1986.
Josephson, Matthew. *The Politicos, 1865–1896*. New York, 1938.
Katznelson, Ira. *City Trenches: Urban Politics and the Patterning of Class in the United States*. Chicago, 1981.
Kent, Frank R. *The Great Game of Politics*. New York, 1923.
Kleppner, Paul, et al. *The Evolution of American Electoral Systems*. Westport, Conn., 1981.
Kolko, Gabriel. *The Triumph of Conservatism: A Reinterpretation of American History, 1900–1916*. Princeton, N.J., 1963.
Lasch, Christopher. *The New Radicalism in America, 1889–1963: The Intellectual as a Social Type*. New York, 1965.
Lowi, Theodore J. *At the Pleasure of the Mayor: Patronage and Power in New York City, 1898–1958*. New York, 1964.
McCormick, Richard L. *From Realignment to Reform: Political Change in New York State, 1893–1910*. Ithaca, N.Y., 1981.
———. *The Party Period and Public Policy: American Politics from the Age of Jackson to the Progressive Era*. New York, 1986.
McCormick, Richard L. (ed.). *Political Parties and the Modern State*. New Brunswick, N.J., 1984.

McDonald, Terrence J. *The Parameters of Urban Fiscal Policy: Socioeconomic Change and Political Culture in San Francisco, 1860–1906.* Berkeley, Calif., 1986.

McDonald, Terrence J., and Ward, Sally K. (eds.). *The Politics of Urban Fiscal Policy.* Beverly Hills, Calif., 1984.

Macy, Jesse. *Party Organization and Machinery.* New York, 1902.

Mandelbaum, Seymour J. *Boss Tweed's New York.* New York, 1965.

Marcus, Robert. *Grand Old Party: Political Structure in the Gilded Age, 1880–1896.* New York, 1971.

Mayhew, David R. *Placing Parties in American Politics: Organisation, Electoral Settings, and Government Activity in the Twentieth Century.* Princeton, N.J., 1986.

Merton, Robert K. *Social Theory and Social Structure.* Glencoe, Ill., 1949.

Miller, Zane L. *Boss Cox's Cincinnati: A Study in Urbanization and Politics, 1880–1914.* New York, 1968.

Monkkonen, Eric H. *America Becomes Urban: The Development of U.S. Cities and Towns, 1780–1980.* Berkeley, Calif., 1988.

Morison, Samuel E., et al. *The Growth of the American Republic.* 2 vols. 7th ed. New York, 1980.

Myers, Gustavus. *History of the Great American Fortunes.* New York, 1936.

Orth, Samuel P. *The Boss and the Machine.* New Haven, 1919.

Ostrogorski, Moisei. *Democracy and the Organization of Political Parties.* 2 vols. New York, 1902.

Patton, Clifford W. *The Battle for Municipal Reform.* Washington, D.C., 1940.

Riordan, William L. *Plunkitt of Tammany Hall.* New York, 1905.

Rothman, David J. *Politics and Power: The United States Senate, 1869–1909.* Cambridge, Mass., 1966.

Schiesl, Martin J. *The Politics of Efficiency: Municipal Administration and Reform in America, 1880–1920.* Berkeley, Calif., 1977.

Scott, James C. *Comparative Political Corruption.* Englewood Cliffs, N.J., 1972.

Silbey, Joel, et al. (eds.). *The History of American Electoral Behavior.* Princeton, N.J., 1978.

Stave, Bruce M. *Urban Bosses, Machines, and Progressive Reformers.* Lexington, Mass., 1972.

Stewart, Frank M. *A Half-Century of Municipal Reform: History of the National Municipal League.* Berkeley, Calif., 1950.

Teaford, Jon C. *The Unheralded Triumph: City Government in America, 1870–1900.* Baltimore, 1984.

Weinstein, James. *The Corporate Ideal in the Liberal State, 1900–1918.* Boston, 1968.

Weiss, Nancy J. *Charles Francis Murphy, 1858–1924: Respectability and Responsibility in Tammany Politics.* Northampton, Mass., 1968.

Whyte, William F. *Street Corner Society.* Chicago, 1943.

Wiebe, Robert H. *The Search for Order, 1877–1920.* New York, 1968.

Wolfinger, Raymond. *The Politics of Progress.* Englewood Cliffs, N.J., 1974.

Woodward, C. Vann (ed.). *The Comparative Approach to American History.* New York, 1968.

Yearley, Clifton K. *The Money Machines: The Breakdown and Reform of Governmental and Party Finance in the North, 1860–1920.* Albany, N.Y., 1970.

Zink, Harold. *City Bosses in the United States: A Study of Twenty Municipal Bosses.* Durham, N.C., 1930.

DOCTORAL DISSERTATIONS

Astorino, Samuel J. "The Decline of the Republican Dynasty in Pennsylvania, 1929–1934." University of Pittsburgh, 1962.

Drayer, Robert Edward. "J. Hampton Moore: An Old Fashioned Republican." University of Pennsylvania, 1961.

Gillette, Howard F. "Corrupt and Contented: Philadelphia's Political Machine, 1865–1887." Yale University, 1970.

Greenberg, Irwin F. "The Democratic Party in Philadelphia, 1911–1934." Temple University, 1972.

Kelley, Brooks M. "A Machine Is Born: Simon Cameron and Pennsylvania, 1862–1873." University of Chicago, 1961.

Kurtzman, David H. "Methods of Controlling Voters in Philadelphia." University of Pennsylvania, 1935.

Neilly, Andrew H. "The Violent Volunteers: A History of the Volunteer Fire Department of Philadelphia, 1736–1871." University of Pennsylvania, 1960.

Quay, William L. "Philadelphia Democrats, 1880–1910." Lehigh University, 1969.

INDEX